Warfare
in the
Middle Ages

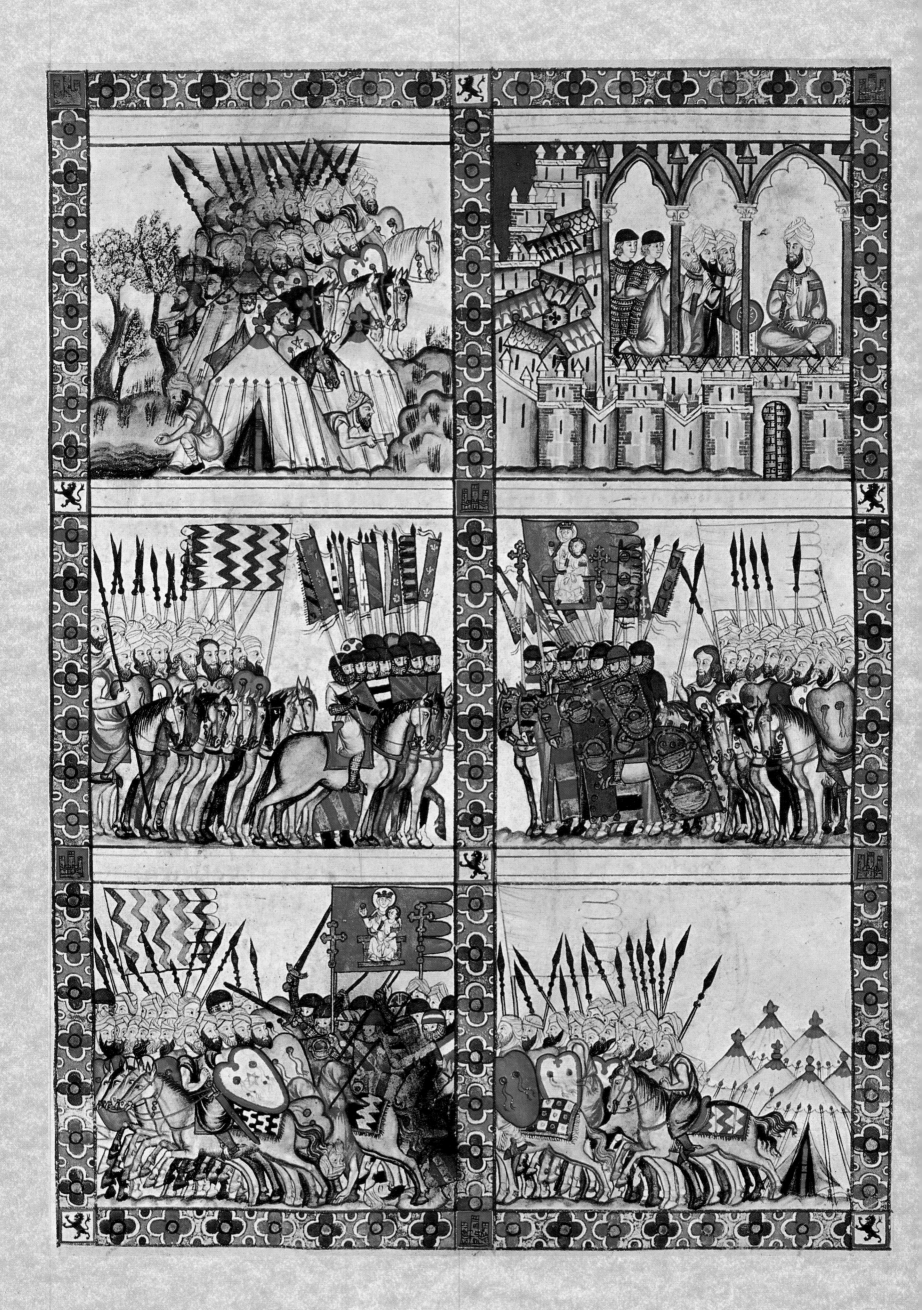

Warfare
in the
Middle Ages

Richard Humble

MALLARD
PRESS

Page 1: A fifteenth century illuminated manuscript depicting,
somewhat fancifully, an encounter between Romans and Gauls.

Page 2: A scene from the *Chronicle of Alfonso X of Castile*
showing Christians and Arabs in battle.

Page 4: English troops under Sir Walter de Manny attempt to
storm the main gate of Calais, an episode from the Hundred Years
War.

Contents

Introduction

Apologies are due for the necessary limitation of this volume's coverage to Europe, the Mediterranean, and western Asia. The inclusion of India, South-East Asia, China, and Japan would have required either a book of double the size, or a historical period of half the breadth. It would also have helped considerably if the Middle Ages had been somewhat less eventful.

What did the 'Middle' Ages separate? The most appropriate answer, as convenient as it is vague, is 'the period between the fall of Rome and the Renaissance.' Including as it does the so-called 'Dark Ages' (which, apart from being a gross misnomer, is a term of even vaguer definition), this provides a 'middle' period between the collapse of the Western Roman Empire in the early fifth century AD, and the rise of imperial power under the Hapsburg Emperor Charles V in the early sixteenth century. If arbitrary terminal dates are required, we can say that the Middle Ages separated the fall of Rome to Alaric's Visigoths in AD 410 from the fall of Rome to the imperial troops of Charles V in 1527.

During these eleven centuries what we know today as Europe, the Mediterranean, and the Middle East underwent a complete transformation. The last vestige of an Eastern Roman Empire was swept away when the Ottoman Turks took Constantinople in 1453. A new 'eastern empire' towered up in the form of militant Islam: the Moslem world, whose orbit stretched from the central Mediterranean to the China Sea. In 1527, as it had done for the past 800 years, the Moslem world confronted the newer, fiercely disparate Christian nation states which had evolved from the wrecked provinces of the old Western Roman Empire. Among the latter, the only common tie was the Christian faith and spiritual allegiance to Rome. At best a tenuous bond, this had never prevented vicious and exhausting wars between the Christian countries and was soon to be shattered by the Protestant Reformation, potent catalyst of even more bitter strife.

Nothing is more inappropriate than the modern tendency to use 'medieval' or 'Middle Ages' as pejorative terms, signifying just about

Left: A carved detail from the sledge found within the Oseberg ship burial. Such complexity of design and execution is an indication that not every 'barbarian' society was solely preoccupied with pillage.

Right: Another view of the sledge carving from Oseberg. This ninth century Norwegian ship burial contained many such examples of Viking craftsmanship.

Below: This Northumbrian carved whalebone casket, made in the eighth century, is decorated with a savage battle scene; the other side of life in the period.

every negative value from general ignorance, stupidity, and stagnation to rank barbarism. The Middle Ages were a period of restless energy and enquiry. They ended with Europe, frustrated by the Moslem strangle-hold on oriental trade, taking to the world's oceans in efforts to find a way round. In a very real sense, therefore, the Middle Ages were the crucible of the modern world order. Their study is a fascinating one from any viewpoint, but the warfare of the Middle Ages presents an unusually varied panorama. No other millennium in world history shows the established power balance so repeatedly shaken by the onslaught of successive military supremacies, each of which, in its heyday, carried all before it.

Left: A sixth century Swedish gold collar of the finest quality.

Right: Detailed carvings such as these on Trajan's Column in Rome tell us much about the Roman army of the second century AD.

Below: Elements of Norse mythology, combined with the trappings of war, on a carved panel from Oseberg.

Our story opens with the first of these phenomena: the westward surge of the Huns, driving before them the Goths and Vandals to bring down the Western Roman Empire. The second was the eruption of the Arabs and the outward march of Islam, engulfing the eastern, southern, and western shores of the Mediterranean, reducing the Eastern Empire to a beleaguered and ever-shrinking enclave, and breaking into southern France before being halted. The third phenomenon broke from the north: the Vikings of Scandinavia, masters of the sea, and terror of the Christian world. Following hard on the Viking onslaught came the Magyars from the middle Danube. No less formidable than the Vikings, the Magyars spread flame and fear west to the Rhineland, Alsace, and France during their brief ascendancy in the early tenth century.

The eleventh century brought no respite, for Scandinavian settlement in northern France produced the Normans. These iron professionals of war not only ended five centuries of English independence from continental rule: they became the leading military power in the western Mediterranean and spearheaded the First Crusade against the Moslems in the east. And the long struggle between Cross and Crescent was still unresolved when, in the early thirteenth century, the Mongols fell upon both Islam and Christian Europe. Surpassing even the ancient Assyrians in their ferocity and mastery of mobile war the Mongols, in their skyrocket rise and fall, must still be counted the most amazing military phenomenon of the Middle Ages.

Here, then, is the basis for this review of *Warfare in the Middle Ages* which begins, as G. K. Chesterton puts it in *The Ballad of the White Horse:*

. . .When the ends of the world waxed free,
When Rome was sunk in a waste of slaves,
And the sun drowned in the sea. . .

When the ends of the earth came marching in
To torch and cresset gleam,
And the roads of the world that lead to Rome
Were filled with faces that moved like foam,
Like faces in a dream.

Rome's Destroyers

In the opening paragraph of his great history, Gibbon calls the decline and fall of the Roman Empire 'a revolution which will ever be remembered, and is still felt by the nations of the world.' Gibbon was writing in the days when the word 'revolution' was still used in its literal sense of an overturning or decisive spin of fortune's wheel. To modern ears 'revolution' has very different overtones, implying the overthrow of a political regime by internal sedition and a decisive act of insurgency. We do not regard revolutions as the impartial workings of providence but believe that they are self-created. A nation which undergoes the trauma of a full-blooded political revolution does so as the result of self-created weaknesses and pressures. Despite the fact that this modern interpretation of 'revolution' is radically different to that used by Gibbon, it nevertheless has considerable relevance to the process which destroyed the Western Roman Empire between the middle third and middle fifth centuries AD.

Established as a workable entity by Augustus after the last of the Republican civil wars, the Roman Empire was never free, in shadow or substance, from that crudest form of revolution – military usurpation. The security of the imperial frontiers depended on the Roman army, and the army did a magnificent job as the Empire's sword – but even the short stabbing-sword of the Roman legions had two edges. What finally brought the Empire down was the fatal blend of external military pressure with internal military weakness: the danger, real or imagined, of yet another bid for the imperial title by an ambitious general. The Empire's most insidious foe was the open secret that the successful general of today might become the emperor of tomorrow. The Empire's purely external

problem, that of keeping the barbarians outside the frontiers, was never insoluble in itself. The trouble was that external military pressure could so seldom be dealt with in isolation.

This was abundantly proved by the events of the third century AD. Down to the death of Marcus Aurelius in 180, successive emperors had tried to create an outer bastion of provinces beyond the Rhine and Danube Rivers proclaimed by Augustus as the Empire's 'natural frontiers' in the north. Trajan (98-117) had protected the lower Danube with his new province of Dacia; Aurelius died at Vienna while still campaigning against the German tribal confederacies menacing the upper Danube and Rhine frontiers. If Aurelius had managed to do for Germany what Julius Caesar had done for Gaul and Trajan had done for Dacia, there is no calculating how many centuries of military security the Empire might have enjoyed behind its new Elbe frontier. After Aurelius, however, the great imperial plan was never resumed in the north, and successive emperors resumed and retained the 'passive defensive' prescribed for the Empire by Augustus. The expansionism of the second century gave place to purely defensive strategy in the third.

Aurelius was the sixteenth emperor to succeed Augustus, and five of those 16 emperors had been usurpers or the puppets of mutinous troops. But between the deaths of Aurelius and Constantine the Great (180-337) there were 22 emperors – a somewhat arbitrary figure, excluding candidates eliminated by their first defeats. In the nine-year reign of Gallienus (259-68) the Empire was infested with so many military pretenders that the period has been called the age of the 'Thirty Tyrants.' Of the latter 22 emperors from Aurelius to Constantine, only five had not

been usurpers or the victors of civil wars. Yet during those 16 strife-torn decades, no less than 12 invasions were repelled by the imperial troops and the integrity of the frontiers restored.

The Empire was preserved, but at a heavy price. The third century had opened with a severe population crisis due to the plague epidemic which had devastated the provinces in the reign of Marcus Aurelius. A depleted population inevitably made it harder to keep the army up to strength, and this was no short-term problem. (In the European countries most heavily depopulated by the Black Death of the fourteenth century – a comparable scourge – it took 200 years or more before the population levels returned to pre-plague levels.) In the third century the Empire was forced to tighten its territorial belt, resulting in the abandonment of the Dacian bastion north of the Danube by Aurelian (270-5). This significant contraction of the northern frontier, coming as it did within a

Above: A coin of the Emperor Gallienus (AD 259-268).

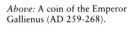

Left: Trajan's Column depicts the Roman military machine destined to be swept aside by the barbarian hordes.

Right: The Emperor Augustus (27 BC-AD 14); a Roman statue from Prima Porta.

SECVRITATAVG
SACRVM

25

AUGUSTO DI PRIMA PORTA

century of the death of Marcus Aurelius, served formal notice that the expansionism of the second century was over for good. Aurelian put the best possible face on the withdrawal by carving out a new 'Dacia' south of the Danube. But the unseen surge of nomad population movements out in the southern Eurasian steppe, hundreds of kilometers to the northeast of the lower Danube, meant that the reduction of pressure on the Empire's vulnerable northern frontier was only temporary.

Aurelian was the second of six capable emperors from the Danubian provinces of Illyria – Claudius Gothicus, Aurelian, Claudius Tacitus, Probus, Carus and Diocletian – who repelled a highly dangerous sequence of barbarian invasions in the second half of the third century. These invasions occurred when the welter of provincial revolts and usurpations threatened the total dismemberment of the Empire. In the east Zenobia, Queen of Palmyra in Syria, defied Rome at the head of an independent state (262-73). In the west Gaul fell prey to a succession of usurpers between 259 and 274. It was during this chaotic interlude that the Empire was a victim of full-blooded invasions by the Goths, driven southwest by the expansion of the Huns from Mongolia and Turkestan.

The Gothic Invasions

The Goths emerged as the Empire's deadliest foes in the third and fourth centuries. They were an east Germanic people who had migrated south across the Baltic from Scandinavia, settling briefly in Pomerania and Prussia around the end of the first century AD before moving southeast up the Vistula and down the Dnieper to reach the coast of the Black Sea. The Goths were the latest demonstration of circumstances which had recurred several times in the ancient world. As long as a warrior nomad race kept on the move without settling down to fixed town and country life, it tended to remain a deadly threat to its more sedentary neighbors. For example, in about 1678 BC the invading nomads known as

Above: A third century bas-relief depicting Romans fighting and subduing barbarians; an increasing preoccupation of Roman society and thought.

Left: The Roman Emperor Decius ruled for only two years before he and his army were massacred by the Goths at Forum Terebronii in AD 251.

Right: The Ludovisi Sarcophagus which shows the Emperor Marcus Aurelius (AD 161-180) in triumph over barbarians.

emerged as the administrative capital of the Western Empire some 20 years before. Honorius got clear and headed for southern Gaul in flight. Alaric pursued, and Stilicho intercepted Alaric at Pollentia in the first week of April. The ensuing battle was remarkable because Stilicho used Christian religious practice to achieve surprise, attacking the Christian Visigoths while they were preparing to observe Easter Sunday. Alaric's troops, however, resisted fiercely and broke Stilicho's Alan cavalry assault, and only a well-judged infantry advance on the Visigothic camp saved the day. Stilicho then negotiated a treaty providing for Alaric's unmolested retreat from Italy, which Alaric violated by besieging Verona in order to save face before his chieftains; but Stilicho had kept in close touch with the Visigothic retreat and swept in on the flanks and rear of Alaric's army outside Verona. After this second defeat Alaric accepted Stilicho's terms and pulled east into Illyria. Though Italy had been temporarily saved, the result of the crisis of 402-3 was the moving of the imperial capital from Milan to the coastal refuge city of Ravenna on the Adriatic.

Within a year, however, Italy was invaded again, this time by Radagaisus and his composite host, which included a powerful force of Ostrogoths and probably numbered about 150,000 warriors all told. This was no mere military invasion but a full-blooded race migration, with women and children in train. Scouring every province of the Western Empire yielded Stilicho no more than 40,000 troops of doubtful quality, including slaves encouraged to enlist by a bounty of gold. As in his previous campaign, Stilicho depended on his Huns and Alans, but since Verona he had been joined by Sarus, a Visigothic renegade, and a useful force of Visigothic deserters from Alaric's army. Stilicho repeated his Verona tactics in 405 – letting the enemy commit himself to a siege (in this case Florence) before

Above right: Some modern reconstructions of second century Roman military equipment: in the foreground stands a trumpeter, while behind him is a legionary soldier wearing *lorica segmentata* armor.

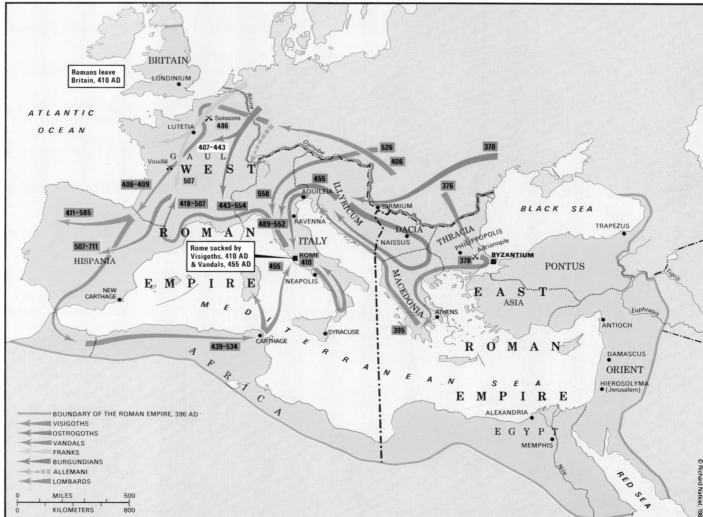

Left: Panel from an ivory diptych (about AD 400) depicting the Vandal chieftain Stilicho, 'Master-General' of the Roman army.

Right: The barbarian migrations and invasions of Europe during the last years of the old Roman Empire.

BOUNDARY OF THE ROMAN EMPIRE, 396 AD
VISIGOTHS
OSTROGOTHS
VANDALS
FRANKS
BURGUNDIANS
ALLEMANI
LOMBARDS

27

launching a countermove. On the approach of Stilicho's army Radagaisus abandoned his clumsy attempts to take Florence, moving his womenfolk and children up to the heights of Faesulae (Fiesole) and ringing them with his fighting men. Stilicho thereupon surrounded Faesulae and proceeded to starve out Radagaisus, whose failure to shatter the feeble ring surrounding him remains one of the major mysteries of the campaign. Two-thirds of the trapped host did break out, but the siege ended in August 405 with the surrender of Radagaisus (who was beheaded) and the enslavement of the emaciated survivors who had stayed with him.

Stilicho was content to shepherd the surviving warriors out of Italy rather than enlist or destroy them. This was a fatal mistake, for they joined forces with Godegisl's Vandals and prepared for an assault on Gaul. This was launched on 31 December 406, a mass march across the ice of the frozen Rhine at Mainz. Godegisl fell in battle with the Frankish *federati*, who failed to stop the Vandals from breaking out into central Gaul. The ease with which the walled cities of Gaul fell throughout 407 may be partially explained by the early loss of Trier (Augusta Treverorum), mentioned in the *Notitia Dignitatum* as one of the major centers for the manufacture of siege engines. Alaric, who was invariably unsuccessful against walled cities, never enjoyed such a bonus.

Only a prompt and generous alliance with Alaric on the part of Stilicho and the imperial government could have reversed the disaster in

Left: In contrast to the heavily armored second century legionary soldier shown below, this fourth century Roman auxiliary is more lightly clad in a mail shirt. The frontiers of the Roman Empire were increasingly defended by such troops.

Below left: Note the weapons of the Roman legionary: a short stabbing sword (*gladius*), a large curved rectangular shield and a throwing spear (*pilum*), the iron head of which was designed to bend on impact.

Gaul, but this was dismissed out of hand by the minions of Honorius at Ravenna. Those parts of Gaul left untouched by the Vandal irruption, feeling utterly betrayed by the imperial government, took a desperate but hardly unprecedented step. They declared for Constantine, the commander in Britain, who crossed the Channel with the mobile troops of the Saxon Shore defenses. Stilicho could not be blamed for having failed to keep the barbarians out of Gaul, but he was blamed, and viciously, for his refusal to tackle Constantine. All Stilicho's attention remained fixed on Alaric, who had followed the Vandals west, occupied Noricum, and demanded a vast retainer of 8000 pounds in gold from Ravenna.

The hostility to Stilicho rose to a climax when the Eastern emperor Arcadius died in the spring of 408. Stilicho then announced his intention of leaving Constantine and Gaul to Alaric while he himself went to Constantinople to establish Honorius as regent of the East. There was no doubt that Stilicho would be the real regent. It was the last straw not only for the imperial government but for the Roman remnants of the Western army who, together with Sarus and his Visigoths, broke out in mutiny. To his credit, Stilicho refused to try and save himself by resorting to civil war, but was left totally exposed when Sarus contrived a massacre of his Hunnish bodyguard. Stilicho claimed sanctuary, only to be treacherously lured out and executed by order of Honorius on 23 August 408.

Stilicho's fall deprived Honorius of his greatest general and left Alaric without an effective rival, but the treacherous circumstances of Stilicho's execution had a deadly effect. They were a public demonstration of how contemptible the so-called rulers of Rome had become in the eyes of all *federati*, actual and potential; the emperor and his officials were revealed as back-stabbing

Right: Two Roman legionaries with their officer. By definition, a legionary was always a citizen of Rome; the auxiliary was not, but (at least initially) could aspire to such privilege through service.

cowards, not great lords whose patronage could be solicited and respected. Here, in a truly Wagnerian sense, was the *leitmotif* signaling the final doom of the Roman West; but it was also to prove one of the most enduring realities of the succeeding 'Middle Ages'. For the next 1100 years, military supremacy would lie with kings and warlords whose trustworthiness *as* lords – leaders whom fighting men would follow with confidence – was not in question. After the liquidation of Stilicho, hitherto loyal *federati* deserted *en masse* to Alaric, who now had Italy at his mercy.

Thus it was the despised barbarians, not the inheritors of the imperial Roman tradition, who accepted that the world had changed and tried to reach a workable solution. Alaric spent two years in trying to pressure Ravenna into making a reasonable treaty with the Visigoths, repeatedly holding the city of Rome to ransom but get-

ting nothing but repeated treachery for his pains. Finally he decided to loot Italy bare, Rome included, and ship his host across to Africa, the granary of what was left of the Roman West. Rome fell to Alaric (appropriately, by treachery and not by assault) two years to the day after the legal murder of Stilicho on 23 August 410.

Apart from its tremendous psychological impact on world history, the fall of Rome in 410 provides an interesting commentary on barbarian discipline. Even when allowances are made for the fact that the Visigoths did not have to storm Rome and entered the city without having been worked up to fighting frenzy, Alaric certainly seems to have kept his warriors well in hand. Though heartily plundered of portable loot, Rome was not destroyed as a living city – church buildings and property were particularly respected – and speedily recovered after the Visigoths moved on into southern Italy. Alaric,

having already abandoned the idea of embarking for Africa, died before the year was out. Though never a general in the same mold as his predecessors Kniwa and Fritigern, and completely outclassed by his great rival Stilicho, Alaric deserves recognition for raising the fighting capacity of his people by his intelligent use of the Roman armories which fell into his hands.

Alaric's successor Arthaulf finally came to the decision to invade southern Gaul, and the removal from Italy of the Visigothic host in 412 kept the Western Empire in tenuous being. It produced a successor to Stilicho in the Illyrian general Constantius, an inspiring leader of troops and mercenaries who took the field against the usurper Constantine. The latter's grandiose bid to conquer Gaul, Spain and Italy had already failed and by 411 he was besieged in Arelatum (Arles) by his own rebel forces. Constantine surrendered to Constantius and was

Left: Two Roman siege engines, the onager and the ballista.

Right: The invasion of Europe by the Huns.

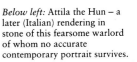

Below left: Attila the Hun – a later (Italian) rendering in stone of this fearsome warlord of whom no accurate contemporary portrait survives.

Below right: Theodoric, King of the Ostrogoths, pursuing a stag into Hell, a twelfth century sculpture in Verona, Italy.

executed by Honorius. For ten years Constantius successfully emulated and even surpassed Stilicho's technique, preserving a shrunken Western Empire at the price of accepting the Vandals in Spain, the Visigoths in Aquitaine and the Burgundians in Alsace as *federati*. But in 422, within a year of being raised as co-emperor of the West with Honorius, Constantius died, followed in 423 by Honorius himself.

Valentinian III, son of Constantius, was finally installed two years later as emperor of the West by Theodosius II, the Eastern emperor. Valentinian was in every way a faithful copy of Honorius. He became emperor at the age of six in 425 and grew into a weak and treacherous monarch, resenting the inevitable domination of his most successful general. This was a Roman patrician by the name of Aëtius, son of a cavalry general, reared as a hostage among the Huns from boyhood. Like Stilicho, Aëtius recruited lavishly from the Huns in his efforts to save the hard core of Gaul from the encroachments of the Visigoths, Burgundians and Franks; but he could do nothing to save Spain from the Vandals and Alans under their formidable King Gunderic. The latter advanced to the southern Spanish coast, seized the main ports and shipping and finally (429) acted where Alaric had hesitated back in 410, invading Roman Africa. The Vandal successes in Spain and Roman Africa confirmed the dissolution of the Western Empire, but the energy and ability of Aëtius preserved a precarious balance in Gaul until, in 451, Attila the Hun launched his great assault on the West.

Attila the Hun

Attila resembled Alaric the Goth only in that he was the first war-leader to give the Hunnish tribesmen unity. His brutal reign dated from the murder of his brother Bleda in 445 and was based on a huge encampment north of the Danube on the River Theiss. The unity which Attila forced on the Huns, combined with their natural ferocity and numbers (at its peak Attila's host may have approached a strength of 150-200,000) gave the Huns inevitable superiority over the rival Germanic tribes and kingdoms – Gepids, Ostrogoths, Herulians, Burgundians and Rhineland Franks. But plunder on the grand scale was Attila's only real objective. Unlike Alaric, he not only lacked any kind of permanent strategic goal, he was a positively stupid tactician. Hunnish mounted archers were the most elusive and hardest-hitting mobile troops between the ancient Assyrians in the seventh century BC and the Magyars in the ninth century AD. With his mounted archers, Attila had the perfect medium from which to mold an unbeatable army. Instead, he became mesmerized by the imperial and *federati* models on which he preyed, but proved unable to adapt with intelligence as Alaric had done. Attila's clumsy aping of the way in which the imperial generals fought led him to form cumbersome heavy cavalry and infantry formations which cramped the style of the horsed archers by depriving them of their maneuverability. In the Battle of Campus Mauriacus near Châlons (also known as the Battle of the Catalaunian Fields) in 451, the limitations of Attila both as strategist and tactician were amply revealed.

As had been the case ever since Hadrianopolis over 70 years before, the strategy behind this invasion of imperial territory depended on which side could command the most effective array of allies. Attila hoped that his sudden invasion of Gaul would detach the Visigoths from their imperial alliance and terrorize the smaller fry – Alans, Bretons and Salian Franks – into submission. But Aëtius won the crucial diplomatic battle at the outset, retaining the allegiance not only of King Theodoric's Visigoths but that of the Bretons, Salian Franks and Burgundians settled in southeast Gaul (Savoy).

Attila's invasion of Gaul in 451 proceeded at the same runaway pace as that of the Vandal surge across the frozen Rhine in 406-7; the days were long gone since the cities of Gaul had been manned by effective garrisons. But Orléans, commanding the crossing of the Loire, was an exception. Aëtius had left Orléans well-garrisoned and with its fortifications repaired. Both sides needed Orléans as a symbol. Aëtius to retain and Attila to attract the allegiance of the Alans settled in the Loire valley. Attila's host besieged Orléans, forced a breach with battering-rams and were on the point of overrunning the city when Aëtius and Theodoric advanced briskly to the rescue. With great confidence and precision they forced a street battle on the Huns – of all imaginable forms of combat the least to the liking or experience of the warriors of the steppe. Attila withdrew from Orléans in some disorder, heading for the open country of Champagne where he must have hoped to annihilate his enemies on terrain more suited to his horsemen. But Aëtius reacted by taking up a defensive position where, if Attila wanted to fight a decisive battle, the Huns would have to attack on terms least favorable to themselves.

At Campus Mauriacus Aëtius followed the drill-book for generals faced with grossly superior numbers, by choosing a position where the enemy had to attack on a front no wider than his own. The allied army backed into a bend of the River Marne with its left flank anchored on the river and its front screened by a hill occupied by a strong Visigothic force. Behind this hill, Aëtius stationed the most dubious element in the allied host – the Alan contingent. The allied right was

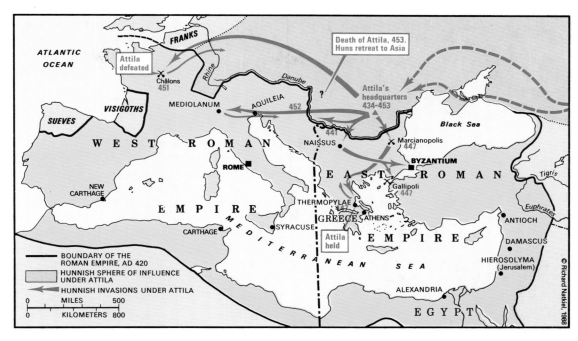

The fall of the Western Empire

After the death of Aëtius it was only a matter of time before the barbarian kingdoms and mercenaries of the West wearied of maintaining their comic-opera allegiance to the ignominious imperial figure-heads at Ravenna. In Africa, the now-powerful Vandal kingdom had never abased itself by accepting this allegiance. Showing all the early versatility of the Goths back in the 260s, the Vandals had taken to the sea and become the biggest naval threat to Italy since the heyday of Carthage (now the Vandal capital) over 700 years before. The Balearics, Sicily and Corsica fell to the Vandal fleets, and in June 455 the Vandal King Gaiseric succeeded where Carthage had failed. He landed in Italy and sacked Rome with immense plunder (including the spoils of the temple in Jerusalem taken in the first century AD).

Thanks to the unique benefits of the sea power which he had acquired, Gaiseric remained the virtual overlord of the western Mediterranean until his death in 477. His reign amounted to the first chapter in the history of medieval naval warfare, when Vandal corsair fleets became an annual scourge along the Italian coastline. In 468, the Eastern emperor Leo I launched a combined sea and land offensive against the Vandal kingdom: a seaborne army to strike direct at Carthage while a land army from Egypt advanced westward along the North African coast. Gaiseric reacted to this deadly threat by using fireships to burn half the Roman fleet off Cape Bon, after which disaster the Eastern Roman land army retreated precipitately. No further attempts were made to curb the power of the Vandals, which continued unchecked until Gaiseric's death.

Gaiseric was still alive when, in September 476, an event took place which signified the formal end of the Western Roman Empire. Last of the Western emperors to be recognized by the Senate of Rome, the young Romulus Augustulus was captured and deposed in Ravenna by Odovacar, ruler of the German mercenaries in northern Italy and the first barbarian warlord to rule the Roman heartland as a king. After 476 all attempts to control events in the former provinces of the Western Empire were made by barbarian kingdoms, with or without reference to the emperors of the East.

The decline of the Roman military machine

The late imperial Roman army, recast with new emphasis on the cavalry arm, reached its zenith in the middle fourth century AD. Under the most capable of the single military emperors it not only proved able to defend the Empire's overloaded northern frontier, but also (under Julian) of waging an offensive campaign against Persia.

Persistent usurpations and the repeated partition of the Empire into East and West reduced the permanent cadre of the imperial army in civil wars until the Empire was no longer able to defend itself with its own resources. After this point had been reached (with the Hadrianopolis disaster of 378) the defense of the Western Empire depended on long-term accommodation with the most effective barbarian *federati*.

Unfortunately the last emperor worthy of the name to rule in both West and East, Theodosius the Great, died in 395. His contemptible successors in the West not only proved incapable of inspiring long-term loyalty from the *federati*, the very weakness of their characters and political

formed by the Visigoths, who faced their old enemies, the Ostrogoths in Attila's service.

Accounts of the action were confused and tinged by obvious poetic licence, but they reveal a sufficiently clear basic framework. The allied troops held their ground and let the Huns come to them. Attila could easily have retained the initiative by declining battle and continuing his rampage through Gaul until Aëtius was forced to fight; but Attila's determination to fight over this particular terrain deprived his horsed archers of free maneuver except on the Visigoths' flank. Not that Attila used them there. The main Hunnish assault came in the center, against the Alans, who broke. The Visigoths also wavered when King Theodoric was unhorsed by an Ostrogothic javelin, but they rallied when the force on the hilltop, commanded by Theodoric's son Thorismund, attacked in support of their countrymen. Aëtius then ordered a general advance to bring on close-quarter fighting along the entire front, thus depriving the Huns of their superiority in archery.

After a gory and demoralizing bout of close-quarter combat it was Attila's host which gave ground, retiring to its wagon laager in the rear. Quite possibly with thoughts of Hadrianopolis in mind, Aëtius did not pursue. Nor did he resume the action the next day, being more than content with Attila's subsequent withdrawal from Gaul and re-crossing of the Rhine. After

Campus Mauriacus Aëtius' most urgent concern was to see Thorismund confirmed as king of the Visigoths, temporarily extending the alliance which had met the crisis so capably and preserved the *status quo* in Gaul. Aëtius was quite unable to prevent Attila from invading Italy in 452, but this turned out to be a passing threat. Famine and plague had been rife in northern Italy for the past 18 months and the invaders suffered badly. Attila turned back to his Hungarian base, daunted, it was said, by an embassy from Rome led by Pope Leo I, whose warnings against sacrilege probably did help demoralize Attila's Ostrogothic confederates. In 453 Attila died of a stroke. Once deprived of his personal domination, the Hunnish union broke up, together with its hold over the Germanic people.

Campus Mauriacus can only be regarded as a decisive battle in world history in that it fulfilled Aëtius' strategy of defending Gaul by means of the Visigothic alliance. It did nothing to eliminate Attila as a menace to what was left of the Western Empire, and the subsequent Hunnish invasion of Italy was turned against Aëtius by the general's enemies at court in Ravenna. These factors nerved Valentinian to take the remarkable step of stabbing Aëtius with his own hand in September 454. Six months later, Valentinian was assassinated in revenge by two of Aëtius' officers, and the Western Empire entered its last 20 years of nominal existence.

Left: The ruins of Carthage, one of the richest, most strategically important city-ports on the North African coast.

Right: Roman daggers of the third century AD, excavated in Germany; these had fallen into barbarian hands.

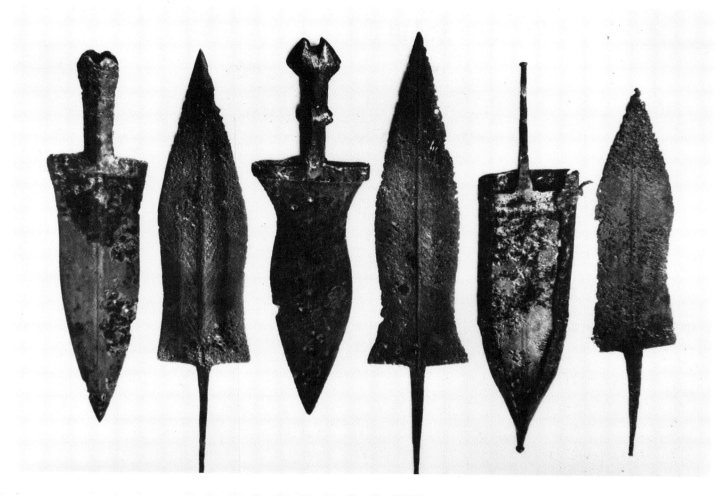

Below: Fifth century iron *spangenhelms* were made in Roman arsenals which were later overrun by the barbarian armies.

power inspired them to hatred and distrust of their most capable generals. Stilicho and Aëtius were both liquidated at the height of their careers by such imperial distrust, the real origin of which dated from the first military usurpations in the first century AD.

Apart from a myriad internal ills (low manpower, the rigidity of the imperial regime and social caste system, the increasing breakdown of order, and spread of banditry in the provinces) the later Empire was notably hamstrung by the decay of Roman sea power. Once the Mediterranean world had been brought under centralized imperial rule and piracy eliminated as a maritime threat (long before the end of the first century AD), maintaining a permanent fleet became an expensive luxury. In the late fourth and fifth centuries, however, effective use of the Mediterranean sea lanes to switch troops to the greatest danger spots could have done much to stave off the ruin of the West.

The barbarian nations which adapted most readily – and effectively – to Roman military techniques in the late fourth and fifth centuries were the Visigoths under Alaric and the Vandals under Gaiseric. Not surprisingly, the barbarian nations produced nothing new in the way of weaponry or tactics, but their sheer numbers were always formidable. Not all barbarian attempts to adopt Roman techniques were felicitous, and those of Attila in particular proved positively disastrous to the Huns' mounted archers.

In general, the passing of the Western Empire's numerous arsenals and weapons factories to barbarian control by the middle fifth century kept alive many skills in armor and weapon manufacture. The dissolution of the later Roman army by the end of the fourth century was not followed by a decline to masses of unarmored infantry. Two of the biggest casualties in the barbarian conquests were the skills of masonry fortification and the construction of spring-gun artillery, with a resultant period of eclipse in the art of siege warfare.

The Eastern Empire

In the opening decade of the fifth century AD the prospects of the Eastern Empire were hardly brighter than those of the embattled West. Like his brother Honorius in Ravenna, the Eastern emperor Arcadius was a powerless nonentity; in the East as in the West, the indigenous Roman army had been eroded practically to vanishing point; Asia Minor in particular teemed with brigands and the immense residual wealth of the East remained a standing temptation for barbarian warlords bent on extortion and plunder. When Rome fell to Alaric in 410 there was certainly no reason for contemporary thinkers to predict with any confidence that Constantinople would survive Rome by as much as 100 years, let alone 1000.

The natural defenses of the Eastern Empire

Yet the Eastern Empire did possess enduring advantages over the West, and those advantages enabled the Eastern Empire to stagger through the crisis-ridden decades of the fifth century. In the early years the East could boast few, if any, advantages which were primarily military. They

were mostly geographical, or at least caused by the flow of events beyond the control of Constantinople. But they amounted to an impressive strategic potential which could be, and was, drawn upon with profit during the reigns of the most capable Eastern emperors.

Geography certainly played a major part in the Eastern Empire's survival. Even before Diocletian first partitioned the Roman Empire into East and West, the East had had far less vulnerable frontiers to worry about than the West. In Africa the Eastern Empire held no more than Libya and Egypt. Like Palestine and southern Syria, these provinces were screened by deserts from anything more serious than nomad raids. Egypt had a bigger problem in the form of the Kushite Blemye of the Sudan, a remarkable civilization only recently brought to light which developed a highly efficient armored cavalry in imitation of the late Roman model; but the Blemye raiders never came near to ousting the Romans from Egypt, which remained under Byzantine control until the Persian and Arab conquests in the early seventh century.

The eastern or Euphrates front had been re-

peatedly disputed with the Parthians and Sassanid Persians for over 400 years; but it was a narrow front, studded with frontier defenses and forts making any sudden collapse (such as happened to Gaul in 406-7) virtually impossible. From the upper Euphrates and the Armenian frontier it reached less than 400 kilometers south to Palmyra on the fringe of the Arabian desert – nearly five times shorter than the West's Rhine and upper Danube frontier.

Asia Minor, territorial heartland of the Eastern Empire, had been terrorized in the third century by the coastal raids of the Goths; but the Goths' efficient early experiments with combined operations were not repeated in the fourth and fifth centuries. Nor were the Huns ever remotely tempted to take to the sea as the Goths had once done. This left the long northern coastline of Asia Minor as protected by sea as the southeast sector of the Eastern Empire was protected by desert.

The Bosphorus was commanded by the imperial capital of Constantinople, and Constantinople was the best protected city in the world bar none. The already formidable Wall of Constan-

Left: The mausoleum of the Emperor Theodoric was built in AD 526 (Ravenna, Italy).

Right: Sixth century mosaic of the Emperor Justinian and his court, in the Basilica of St Vitale (Ravenna).

tine was enclosed in 413 by the positively awesome Wall of Theodosius, generally regarded as one of the wonders of the world throughout the Middle Ages, which stood unbreached until the battering of the giant Turkish siege guns 1040 years later. In the fifth century the strength of Constantinople's walls meant that land investment was a waste of time. In any event it could be no more than partial, for Constantinople's maritime approaches (the Sea of Marmara on one side, Golden Horn and Bosphorus on the other two) meant that the city could bring in constant supplies and reinforcements by sea.

But Constantinople was not merely an impregnable imperial capital: it was the ultimate citadel for Roman-controlled Greece and the lower Danube provinces. The lower Danube might be overrun; barbarian hordes might rampage all over the Balkans; but once they had reached the walls of Constantinople, they had to stop – until the time came for an imperial counteroffensive. In the fifth century the rapidly expanding sea power of the Eastern Empire (which made possible the expedition against the Vandal kingdom in Africa of 468) included a powerful flotilla on the lower Danube, which proved a highly effective deterrent to barbarian break-ins. By 500 AD the East's hold on Greece, the northern Balkans and the lower Danube was as secure and extensive as it had been under Diocletian, 200 years before.

Geography also explains why Roman sea power was retained and expanded in the East and not in the West. As long as Greece and the Aegean were dominated by Constantinople, it was impossible for a barbarian sea people to copy the Vandals' achievement in the western Mediterranean basin. Together with the Balkan peninsula, Asia Minor, Syria-Palestine and Egypt-Libya formed a natural enclosure. The Eastern Empire was held together by a web of internal sea lanes half as long as those of the West.

One final geographical advantage of the East over the West was the absence of a territorial incubus like Britain – part of the empire yet geographically isolated on the extreme periphery, hard to hold yet constantly demanding support. Britain was not only the biggest nonessential drain on the Western Empire's military resources; the island province's detachment from mainland Gaul encouraged separatism and tempted successive military governors to launch attempts on the imperial title. The civil war against the British usurper Maximus was one of the untimely blows from which the West never fully recovered – and Maximus was followed by the usurper Constantine in 407-11, when Gaul had been overrun from across the Rhine and the West already had more enemies than it could handle.

Such were the unchanging geographical benefits enjoyed by the Eastern Empire in the fifth century AD. Sheltered from the mainstream of westward barbarian pressure by the Persian Empire in the east and the Black Sea in the north, these advantages of the Eastern Empire were speedily revealed in the flow of events which ruined the Roman West. The execution of Stilicho in 408 soon proved disastrous for the West; but it was a positive blessing for the East, because of the subsequent westward surge of the Visigoths out of Illyria into Italy and Gaul. In the same period, Constantinople's relations with Persia on the eastern front were particularly good. The young Theodosius II (408-50), son of Arcadius, was actually reared under the benevolent guardianship of the Persian emperor Yazdagird I (399-421). Persian attempts later in the century to reopen the old feud with the Eastern Roman Empire were inhibited by repeated attacks on eastern Persia by the White Huns of the steppe – geography once again coming to Constantinople's aid, with the Hunnish attacks soaked up by Persia.

The Ostrogoths replaced the Visigoths as the biggest menace to the Balkans and the land approaches to Constantinople. As the Visigoths had done under Alaric, the Ostrogoths greatly improved their fighting capacity at the expense of the dying West. The charge of the Ostrogothic armored lancers was particularly feared. Like the Visigoths, the Ostrogoths were accorded the fragile status of *federati* in Illyria; also like the Visigoths, the Ostrogoths finally turned west, not east. It was with the nominal approval of the Eastern emperor Zeno that Theodoric led the Ostrogoths into Italy (488) to break the power of Odovacar. With Theodoric's conquest of Italy and western Illyria, comparative stability returned to the East Roman Balkans.

The most dramatic result of this strategic pampering was that the Eastern Empire never degenerated into total reliance on barbarian *federati* and mercenaries, but retained an indigenous Roman army. By the second half of the century this army's commanders were providing the Empire with capable rulers, the first of which was Marcian (450-57). The fifth century ended under the reign of Athanasius (491-518), an officer of the imperial bodyguard who married the late emperor Zeno's widow. His successor Justin I (518-27) was an Illyrian guard officer who entrusted the succession to his own nephew Justinian (527-65). This military leavening of the imperial line of succession was naturally good for the Empire, balancing as it did the effete dynasticism of the early fifth century. It also reflected the resurgence and enhanced status of the imperial Roman army, which reached and indeed surpassed the degree of excellence last seen under Julian in the middle fourth century.

The development of weaponry

The military trumps of the Eastern Roman army (or Byzantine, to use the conventional if illogical adjective) were cavalry mobility with missile

tine cavalry took to stirrups, it was the commonsense adoption of a fundamental aid to steadiness and confidence on horseback, long overdue in the Roman service. It is easy to put the blame for the delay on the age-old reluctance of cavalry purists to adopt change. Traditional Roman horsemanship, with the rider sitting on his horse without stirrups, thighs correctly parallel to the ground, had never inhibited the training of horsed lancers, javelinmen or swordsmen. Throughout the third and fourth centuries Roman cavalry tradition had continued to scorn the stirrup as fit only for inept barbarians. But by the end of the fifth century even the most die-hard military conservative could no longer regard barbarian cavalry – Hunnish or Ostrogothic – as inept. Their formidable horsed archers (Hunnish) and lancers (Ostrogothic) used stirrups; they were worth copying. Stirrups made the training of regular cavalry quicker and easier. And in a *mêlée* the average cavalry trooper fought all the better for having his feet braced in stirrups; it gave him a wider repertoire of cuts and slashes, while making him harder to unhorse.

Serving mainly on the Persian front, the Byzantines deployed 'super-heavy', Persian-style *clibanarii* – shock troopers with the head protected by helmet and mail hood, the forearms by overlapping splint armor, riding horses carrying head, neck and chest armor. All in all, by the reign of Justinian the Byzantine cavalry was a marvelously flexible arm – heavy, medium and light and horsed archer – of a quality unsurpassed since the art of cavalry tactics had first been devised by the ancient Assyrians.

Covered by well-trained, well-armed cavalry, the foot archers and spearmen of the Byzantine infantry went into action with a new confidence. The foot archer carried a useful light axe and small shield or target with which to defend himself at close quarters. The Byzantine heavy spearman blended the best features of the ancient

power, the latter being extended to both horse and foot. The Byzantine army of the late fifth and early sixth century had learned much from barbarian practice. Though Hunnish horsed archers continued to serve with the imperial army and mercenary and allied troops, the Eastern Empire recruited its own horsed archers. The latter rode, like the ancient Assyrians and Persians, with a combined bowcase and quiver. Bows and arrows were bigger and heavier than those in normal Asiatic barbarian use – rate of fire sacrificed for the sake of superior range and hitting power. Byzantine light and heavy cavalry did not carry the bow, but neither was deprived of missile power to supplement the long lance

(*kontos*) and sword. Heavy armored *kataphraktoi* and unarmored light cavalry both carried supplies of the weighted darts (*martiobarbuli* in Latin, *marzobaboula* in Greek) first adopted by the imperial Roman army in the late third century.

By the reign of Justinian all elements of the Byzantine cavalry rode with stirrups, an improvement which needs to be kept firmly in proportion. Though its importance in military history has been wildly exaggerated – the stirrup did not revolutionize warfare – it made life easier for the soldier on horseback, and especially for heavy-armored troopers required to make repeated charges with the lance. When the Byzan-

Left: Part of the city walls of Constantinople, built by the Emperor Theodosius II in the mid-fifth century.

Right: A *spangenhelm* of about AD 500, the descendant of late Roman types carried east and west by the barbarian hordes who overran Roman arsenals.

however, the Empire went over from defense to attack – or rather counterattack, as Justinian believed that his mission was to re-establish the old Roman Empire by conquering the barbarian kingdoms of the West. No soldier himself, and a most indifferent economist, Justinian was too vain to see that reconquering the West was a task beyond the resources of the East. It came down to manpower and finance. The army was well able to win victories – some of those won by Justinian's excellent generals Belisarius and Narses remain classics of the military art – but it was far too small to garrison and hold the conquered territories.

The career of Belisarius

Justinian's great general Belisarius began his career as a guards' officer and promising tactician of the new cavalry during the reign of Justin. In the biography written by his secretary Procopius, Belisarius emerges as a general whom Justinian hated and distrusted (unjustly) as a potential usurper, yet with whom the emperor could not afford to dispense. Apart from his string of victories Belisarius, like the Duke of Marlborough, relied considerably on feminine influence at court through the friendship of his wife Antonia with Justinian's forceful empress, Theodora. As for the basic nature of Belisarius' military genius, this has been summed up by Robert Graves as:

. . . the familiar table-problem of the poor country innkeeper who is forced to provide a banquet at short notice for a number of hungry guests: namely, how to make a little go a long way. . .like the innkeeper, too, he solved his problem by a carefully laid table and a brave smile and by putting the best food and wine foremost, keeping the coarser food and the worse wine in reserve. The coarser food and the worse wine were his infantry, half of whom were recent recruits . . . the better food and wine. . .were his cavalry.

Justinian inherited his first war from his predecessors Anastasius and Justin. It was a largely unnecessary frontier wrangle with Kobad I of Persia (501-31) over a new Roman fortress recently built at Daras, which the Persians considered provocatively close to their own frontier fortress at Nisibis. A timely exchange of gifts, courtesies and mutual concessions between the two monarchs would have sufficed to resolve the matter; but Justinian shrank from losing face in the first international confrontation of his reign, and Kobad was well aware that he could field more troops than the Byzantines. The result (530) left Belisarius to hold Daras with 25,000 men against 50,000 Persians.

Belisarius showed his quality, and his confidence in Byzantine firepower, by choosing to fight a battle of attrition. He deployed his outnumbered force outside the walls of Daras as bait. The front of his foot archers was covered by a deeply indented line of trenches, spanned by bridges defended by spearmen in phalanx. Heavy cavalry formations guarded the ends of the trench line from attempts at encirclement. Two formations of Hunnish horsed archers were stationed inside the welcoming recess of the trench line to inflict crossfire on massed Persian formations making a frontal assault. A third formation of Huns was sent out to the left flank to lie in ambush, hidden by a low hill. The latter ploy shows the enduring impression left on Roman military thinking by the Battles of Naissus and Hadrianopolis against the Goths, each battle having been decided by a surprise cavalry

Greek hoplite, Macedonian phalangite and early imperial Roman legionary. He was protected with helmet, mail cuirass and a large oval or circular shield. His thrusting spear, though not as lengthy as the classic Macedonian *sarissa*, lent itself well to forming bristling phalanxes for attack or defense. Missile power was provided by a clutch of *marzobaboula* darts, while a long sword (*securis*) was the hand-to-hand combat weapon.

With all the virtues listed above, the Byzantine army of the early sixth century was economic on manpower and admirably suited to the defense of the Empire on all fronts. Under Justinian,

Left: The land walls of Constantinople, capital of the Eastern Roman Empire. They stretched seven kilometers from the Sea of Marmara to the Golden Horn.

Right: A page from an eleventh century Byzantine military treatise explaining the 'Hippic Phalanx' formation; knowledge of military strategy was an important part of the education of any potential ruler.

attack. Belisarius' deployment before Daras was a calculated risk in that the Persians could have used half their army to pin down the Byzantines in front while the other half by-passed Daras and cut the Byzantine communications. But Belisarius was counting on the age-old Persian confidence in superior numbers on which the Asian victories of Alexander the Great had been based, and disposed his troops so artfully that their line looked irresistibly weak to any enemy not actually on top of it.

The ensuing battle fulfilled Belisarius' hopes. The trench line prevented the Byzantine foot archers from being ridden down and exterminated, but the sheer weight of the Persian attack broke through on the right. The battle was won by the tight control Belisarius retained over his Greek and Hunnish cavalry and horsed archers, kept in hand for charge after charge. The final Hunnish charge broke clean through the Persian reserve heavy cavalry advancing in column to complete the apparent engulfment of the Byzantine center. After this disaster in their rear, the spearmen of the Persian center threw down their shields and fled.

Belisarius was well content with having saved Daras and repelled the Persians with heavy loss to themselves (approaching 9000). He made no attempt to follow up the victory, being aware that negotiations for a formal peace were pending and that excessively heavy Persian losses might only prolong the war. Kobad, however, surprised the Byzantines in 531 by making a final effort to recoup the humiliation at Daras. This was to be a surprise blow at the eastern capital of Antioch, launched up the line of the Euphrates and west across the Syrian desert – well to the south of the conventional battle zone. But Belisarius had deployed patrols and set up warning beacons on the desert sector and the ample intelligence yielded by this 'early-warning system'

enabled him to intercept the approaching Persian force of 15,000 halfway across the desert between the Euphrates and Antioch.

With all surprise lost and with Belisarius reinforced by 5000 Arab allies, the Persians were outnumbered by 6000 and immediately retreated without risking battle. Belisarius advanced as the Persians fell back, and by Easter Week 531 both armies, still in contact, were on the Euphrates. Vigilance and prompt countermoves had won this second eastern campaign without the need for battle; but Belisarius was now obliged to yield to widespread pressure, from the ranks and from his officers, to force an action.

At Callinicum on Easter Sunday 531 Belisarius experienced one of the few defeats of his career, for he came up against a cavalry tactician as good as himself. The Persian commander launched a shattering cavalry attack against the Arab horsemen holding the Byzantine right flank, then swung in and broke the cavalry forming the Byzantine center. Total disaster was only staved off by superior Byzantine archery, which inflicted casualties at the ratio of two to one, and by the heroic resistance of the Byzantine spearmen infantry, whom Belisarius rallied in an arc with their backs to the Euphrates. Though only 3000 strong, they formed a shield-wall bristling with spears which repelled repeated cavalry attacks until nightfall, when the Persians withdrew to camp. The Persians claimed a victory, but it was a Pyrrhic one: Belisarius had lost 6000 men, the Persians 7000. In any event, Callinicum ended the campaign, and the war. By the end of the year King Kobad had died, and his successor Chosroes I signed the 'Perpetual Peace' with Justinian. It lasted eight years.

In 533 Justinian launched his invasion of Vandal Africa, commanded by Belisarius. It is hard to judge whether this gamble was the result of in-

sane overconfidence or excellent intelligence. Certainly the Vandals were nothing like the threat they had been under Gaiseric. Sicily and Sardinia had revolted against Vandal rule and there was good reason to hope that the Africans would do the same. The *casus belli* was the deposition of 530 of the pro-Byzantine King Hilderic by his cousin Gelimer – a boastful, foolish, emotionally unstable man and, as events soon proved, an execrable war leader. But odds against Byzantine success were great. The last Byzantine expedition against Vandal Africa had been a disaster; the memory of the Vandals' prowess at sea under Gaiseric was still vivid. It was known that Gelimer could raise at least 80,000 fighting men, and if the Vandal fleet managed to get the upper hand on the Byzantine sea communications with Sicily and Greece the expeditionary force would be hopelessly isolated. It consisted of a mere 16,000 men – 10,000 infantry, 5000 Byzantine cavalry and 1000 Huns, carried by a fleet of 500 transports and light warships. Such confidence as Belisarius had in a successful outcome lay in the knowledge that the Vandals' cavalry, like that of the Goths', relied on the lance rather than on missile power; and that the Vandals' strength was dispersed, a powerful expedition having been sent from Carthage by Gelimer to put down the Sardinian rebels.

Belisarius landed 240 kilometers down the Tunisian coast from Carthage and began a cautious march on the Vandal capital, supported by the accompanying fleet. As the Byzantine advance proceeded at barely 19 kilometers a day, Gelimer and his brother had plenty of time in which to assemble at least 50,000 men. Gelimer tried to trap the Byzantines at Decimum, 16 kilometers from Carthage, by means of a lamentably executed pincer movement. The key to the position was a defile through which the Byzantine advance cavalry passed but failed to secure. On

Left: The Castle of St Angelo in Rome was extensively altered throughout the Middle Ages and again during the Renaissance, but much of the original ground plan and masonry at the lowest level can still be seen.

Above right: The extent of the Eastern Roman Empire under the Emperor Justinian (sixth century AD).

the far side the advance guard met and routed the Vandal cavalry of Ammatas, who was killed, while Gelimer's main body drove back Belisarius' leading cavalry outposts and occupied the defile. Though the Huns managed to scatter a third Vandal column advancing to cut off the Byzantines' inland line of retreat, Belisarius' forces were now apparently fatally separated by the Vandal main body in the defile. At this point Gelimer heard the news of his brother's death and collapsed in torrents of grief, incapable of giving further orders. Belisarius seized the initiative, dividing his cavalry to inflict archery crossfire and repeated charges on the Vandals in the defile. Gelimer and his men scattered and fled, leaving the Byzantines to march triumphantly into Carthage and fortify it.

The defeat of the Vandals was sealed in December at Tricamaron, 32 kilometers from Carthage. Gelimer had re-formed his army, reinforced by the return of the Sardinian expedition, but his furtive negotiations had failed to detach the Huns and Romanized Goths in Carthage from their loyalty to Belisarius. The latter now sought battle, with the confidence of having a fortified sea port at his back in the event of another setback like Callinicum; but once again Vandal ineptitude handed Belisarius victory on a plate. Gelimer ordered his army to stand on the defensive and refuse all but hand-to-hand combat with the sword, thus offering his cavalry as an immobile target for the Byzantine charges. The Vandal army broke and fled to its camp after less than an hour, its demoralization being completed by the flight of Gelimer on horseback. He ended up besieged on a hilltop near Hippo Regius, finally surrendering to Belisarius in the following year.

Apart from the success of the African expedition, the military highlight of Justinian's reign was the reconquest of Italy from the Ostrogoths. Here the Byzantines were greatly helped by the fact that the Ostrogoths, like the Vandals, lacked effective leadership with no great warlords of the stature of Gaiseric or Theodoric. Nor had they developed any proficiency in siege warfare, either in defense or attack, which enabled Belisarius to take and hold Naples and Rome. A third advantage was the Ostrogoths' lack of a fleet which could have halted the reinforcements sent overseas from Constantinople and stopped the Romans from exploiting coastal footholds such as Ostia (the port of Rome), Ravenna and Rimini.

Even so, the reconquest of Italy was a desperate business and its centerpiece was the epic year-long defense of Rome by Belisarius (537-8). King Witiges failed to achieve a total investment of the city, enabling Belisarius not only to evacuate his 'useless mouths' (women and children), but also to run in supplies and even to pay for his troops. The Ostrogoths cut the aqueducts supplying the city but could do nothing about the Tiber, which flowed through the city inside the Wall of Aurelian. Their attempts at escalade with scaling ladders and siege towers were broken up by archery and catapult fire from the walls, not to mention chunks of statuary ripped from the drum-shaped mass of Hadrian's mausoleum, the Castel Sant'Angelo. Belisarius used repeated cavalry sorties to keep the besiegers on the *qui vive* and ended by catching them between the garrison of Rome and the Byzantine relief force marching up from Naples.

The premature recall of Belisarius led to a temporary Ostrogothic recovery under a new king,

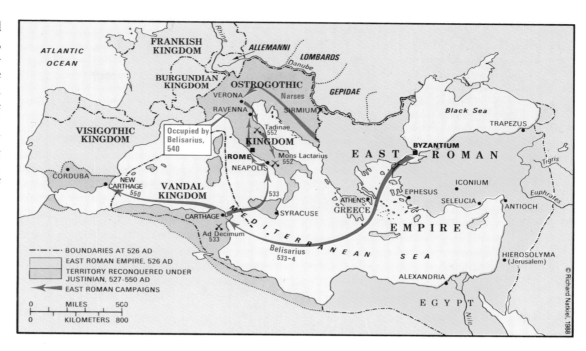

Totila; but in the early 550s Byzantine rule was re-established in Italy by a new expedition under Narses, who was given the biggest army ever fielded under Justinian (maybe 35,000 men). Unlike Belisarius, Narses was Justinian's confidant and former chamberlain, a civilian turned soldier in old age. He nevertheless displayed a flair for the unorthodox solution worthy of Belisarius himself. Narses' great victory over Totila was won at Taginae in the Apennines (552). Narses' deployment put dismounted lancers in the center to bring on a Gothic cavalry assault, with archers on the flanks to provide a crossfire and a concealed cavalry strike force out on the left. The Goths duly charged the lancers, shrank under the archers' crossfire and recoiled when the concealed cavalry broke in on their flank and rear. Narses then unleashed his cavalry reserve from behind the infantry center and shattered the Goths, with Totila dying in the rout.

But these imperial successes in the West were paid for at a heavy price – the price of waging wars of conquest with an army best suited to defensive strategy. In 540 war flared out again on the eastern front, with Chosroes I succeeding where his predecessor had failed. He launched a massive raid through Syria and plundered Antioch, second city of the Empire, withdrawing with immense riches in plunder and tribute money; in 541 he struck northwest through the Caucasus foothills to reach the Black Sea and menace the Byzantine fortress of Petra. Even the belated dispatch of Belisarius to the Persian front failed to inflict a decisive defeat on Chosroes, and a wearing pattern of raid and counterraid dragged on until another peace was agreed between the Byzantines and Persians in 561.

The Byzantine Empire never produced another general like Belisarius, who died in March 565 (eight months before Justinian). Belisarius was a nonpareil, the supreme all-rounder, master of all-arms field and siege campaigning. Because of the tiny forces he was given to command he perfected his talents as an intuitive improviser, seizing on the enemy's mistakes like lightning and extracting everything he could even in defeat. When Belisarius' achievements were set beside those of Alexander the Great or Julius Caesar, it is immediately obvious that neither of the latter had to cope with the orders of a capricious and frequently distrustful lord. Belisarius baffled his contemporaries by his refusal to defy Justinian and accept the royal dignity which the peoples he conquered were happy to offer him, as so many successful Roman

generals before him had done. His personal choice not to break faith with his lord was in startling accord with the medieval romantic ideal of the true Christian knight. The story of Belisarius has twice been brilliantly presented by his contemporary Procopius and, in the twentieth century, by Robert Graves, who summed up the relationship of early medieval myth and reality as follows:

How these two ages overlapped will be seen in this story of Count Belisarius. Here is a Roman general whose victories are not less Roman, nor his strategical principles less classical, than Julius Caesar's. Yet the army has by now changed beyond recognition, the old infantry legion having at last disappeared, and Belisarius (one of the last Romans to be awarded the dignity of the Consulship and the last to be awarded a triumph) is a Christian commander of mail-clad Household knights, nearly all of barbarian birth, whose individual feats rival those of King Arthur's heroes.

In short Belisarius, imbued with Roman military tradition yet quite at home with the tiny conglomerate armies which went to war after the world empire shrunk to a parcel of kingdoms, stands with one foot in the Roman world and the other in the Middle Ages.

The reasons for survival

Though the Eastern Roman Empire owed much of its survival to geographical and other advantages, its biggest military asset was the preservation of professional armored cavalry. In the late fifth and early sixth centuries the Byzantines achieved a unique blend of horsed archer and armored lancer – shock and missile power combined – in whose formations barbarian allied troops served with devastating effect under Belisarius and Narses. This professionalism enabled the Empire to field armies less than half as big as those of the old Roman Empire at its zenith. It was a long step toward the shrinkage of armies to a level characteristic of the Middle Ages.

Under the much-lauded reign of Justinian the Great, however, the inequitable flow of lavish imperial spending was never regulated to provide a regular budget for the upkeep and training of the armed forces. Justinian's imperial ambitions weakened the Empire to a dangerous extent and were already being paid for by the time of his death. Under his successors the Empire lost irreplaceable recruiting areas before much-needed reforms in the following century kept the army, and the shrunken Empire, in being.

The Arab Phenomenon

About five years after the deaths of Belisarius and Justinian in 565, the Prophet Muhummad was born in Arabia. By the time he died (7 June 632) Muhummad had made himself the overlord of the Arab tribesmen of the Hedjaz, the region of Arabia adjoining the Red Sea, and had begun to attack the borders of Byzantine Palestine. Over the following 100 years Muhummad's successors, the Caliphs or 'representatives of the Prophet,' stamped the last and most dynamic of the world religions – Islam – across the face of Asia, North Africa and southwest Europe, from the River Indus to the Pyrenees.

The Arab story is without parallel in world history. Over 1300 years have elapsed since the Arab conquests began, yet nearly all the territory reduced by the Caliphs remains loyal to Islam. Even in the nuclear age, Arab nationalism and the faith of the Prophet continue to overturn empires and dominate the counsels of the strongest military nations on the planet. Only the conquests of Alexander the Great and Jenghiz Khan bear the remotest comparison with the Arab achievement, but they had none of the permanence of the Arab conquests. They are, however, far easier to understand, for Alexander and Jenghiz Khan each had at his disposal a unique military machine which none of their victims could resist. In the early seventh century the Arabs possessed absolutely nothing out of the ordinary in the way of military organization, strategy or weaponry to guarantee them victory. What the Arabs did have were sufficient numbers, a rapid succession of ferociously able leaders, an amazing capacity for learning their enemies' techniques – and above all the supreme opportunity presented by the mutual exhaustion of the Byzantine and Sassanid Persian Empires.

The pressures on the Byzantine Empire

The 50 years after Justinian's death saw the Byzantine-Persian wars reach their greatest intensity, while at the same time both empires had to cope with parallel wars on other fronts, internal disaffection and revolt. The Byzantines, on balance, came off worst. They had to fight not on two but on three fronts – Persia, the Balkans and Italy – a strategic overload ominously reminiscent of the old Roman Empire's progressive exhaustion in the third and fourth centuries.

In the Balkans the old menace of horsed nomad invasions took on a new guise in the form of the Avars. They were formidable horsed archers who rode, unlike the Huns, armored and wielding long lances. The Avars had come surging west in the last years of Justinian's reign and had speedily crushed and replaced the Gepids north of the middle Danube. They proved naturally amenable to Persian diplomacy and in 619, assaulting Constantinople in harmony with the Persians, brought the Empire within an inch of destruction. In Italy the Lombards emerged as an equally durable foe. Driving south across the upper Danube, the Lombards had caught the beaten Ostrogoths between hammer and anvil during the Byzantine re-conquest of Italy under Justinian. Under their ferocious King Alboin, said to have made a drinking cup from the skull of the Gepid King Cunimund, the Lombards were nudged into Italy by Avar pressure from the

east. In 568 the Lombard horsed lancer-swordsmen poured into Italy and speedily reduced the Byzantine exarchate to enclaves around Ravenna, Rome and the southernmost promontories. As with Alaric's Visigoths the Lombards, once ensconced in Italy, greatly increased the armored element in the cavalry and none of the sporadic Byzantine attempts to oust them met with any success.

It was not until the reigns of Tiberius II (578-82) and Maurice (582-602) that Byzantine rulers began to develop a policy of mingled opportunism and economy best suited to survival with profit. At the core of the policy was the realization that the East must come first, with Italy and the Balkans being left to their own devices if necessary. Opportunism was required because the Persians were finding the long wars no less strenuous than the Byzantines, and in 590 Ormuzd IV was assassinated in a palace coup. His son Chosroes II fled into exile and appealed to Maurice for aid. Maurice had the choice between ignoring the appeal and seizing the chance to inflict a shattering but probably temporary blow on the Persian Empire, or supporting Chosroes at the price of a prolonged peace on the Persian front in order to tackle the Avars. He chose the latter alternative, sending an expedition to defeat the Persian usurper Bahram, restoring Chosroes and obtaining in return the cession of the lion's share of Christian Armenia.

This diplomatic breakthrough gave Maurice the chance to switch his armies to the Balkan-Danube front, while at the same time commencing internal reforms. The ten-year Avar war (592-602) ended splendidly thanks to Priscus, the Byzantine general who found the secret of beating the Avars in the field. In the five-week Viminiacum campaign of 601, fought 32 kilometers east and north of modern-day Belgrade, Priscus finally got the upper hand over the ageing Bayan, Great Khan (Khagan) of the Avars and their subject Gepids and Slavs. Priscus favored a three-division deployment in 'hedgehog' formation to frustrate the Avar tactic of launching swarming attacks from all directions. Where possible, he deployed on high ground to take the sting out of the Avar charges and facilitate counterattack. After fighting three defensive battles in as many weeks and inflicting increasing losses each time (4000, 9000 and 15,000) Priscus took the offensive and hustled the battered Avar host west to the River Theiss, ending up well inside Avar territory. He clinched the campaign with two more victories, the final number of Avar and subject troops killed or captured being 17,200. But all the Byzantine victories were thrown away by the aftermath. Maurice had been an inspiring commander of troops in his younger days, but since his accession he had followed the tradition (dating back to Arcadius) that the emperor must not leave Constantinople. This inevitably resulted in losing touch with the feelings of the troops and their officers. In 602 Maurice sent out the order that Priscus' army must remain north of the Danube for the winter of 602-3, instead of returning home in triumph. The strain of the campaign erupted in mutiny.

Led by a roughneck centurion, Phocas, the

army of the Danube marched vengefully on Constantinople. Maurice, after a 20-year program of high taxation and low public expenditure, found no popular support in the capital. He fled with his sons when the mob riotously hailed Phocas as emperor, all the royal fugitives being caught and killed. Under Phocas, the Empire slumped into eight appalling years of anarchy, civil war and foreign invasions, throughout which Phocas was only kept in power by the bond of the barrack-room and the loyalty of the troops.

This chaos in the Byzantine Empire gave Chosroes II of Persia a free hand and a clear conscience, for as Maurice and all his sons were dead Chosroes could not be accused of treachery against the family of his former benefactor. He did not enquire too deeply into the credentials of an adventurer who turned up at the Persian court claiming to be Theodosius, son of Maurice, and used the pretender as a *casus belli*. In 606 Chosroes launched the first of a devastating series of attacks on the Byzantine Empire, overrunning Roman Mesopotamia and the whole of Syria by the end of 607. Over the next two years the Persian attacks were directed to the northwest, throwing the Byzantines out of Armenia and raiding the entire length of Asia Minor, finally appearing on the eastern shore of the Sea of Marmara at Chalcedon.

The Empire was saved by Justinian's African conquests, which now proved their true worth after decades of expensive maintenance. In 610 Heraclius, Exarch of Africa, sent a land expedition under Nicetas to invade Egypt, take Alexandria and cut off the corn supply to Constantinople. Heraclius himself led a naval expedition to the Aegean, taking Thessalonika as his base. Inside Constantinople he had a fellow conspirator in Priscus, former victor over the Avars, who had saved his neck after the 602 mutiny by marrying Phocas' daughter. In October 610 the fleet of Heraclius anchored under the walls of Constantinople, and another mob dragged Phocas before Heraclius in chains. His long-overdue execution was followed by the elevation of Heraclius (son of the liberator) to the rank of emperor.

Heraclius reigned from 610 to February 641, and few governments in any age have begun with such a calamitous 12 years. The run of the Persian triumphs continued, the Balkans were once again relentlessly preyed upon by Avars and Slavs out for revenge after their humiliation in Maurice's time and Heraclius was also threatened for a while by the scheming of Priscus, bitter that he had not been made emperor after the overthrow of Phocas. (Heraclius eliminated Priscus in 612 by the typically Byzantine ploy of sentencing the man to become a monk.) Heraclius could hardly have survived without genuine popular loyalty, stoutly maintained and preserved by the Patriarch of Constantinople, Sergius. With its treasury empty and its tiny, extemporized field armies lurching from defeat to defeat, the Empire seemed to be approaching its final dissolution. Chosroes completed the conquest of Syria by taking Damascus in 613, then assaulted Palestine in 614. He subsequently took the city of Jerusalem and carried off the most venerated relic in Christendom: the True Cross.

Right: This battle formation (a massed infantry phalanx in the center with cavalry and archers on the flanks), so effective in the late Roman period, continued to be employed throughout the Middle Ages – as shown here in a fifteenth century Flemish manuscript illustration of Cyrus of Persia and his troops.

A disaster was narrowly avoided in 617 when the Avars again reached the walls of Constantinople, and Heraclius had to ride for his life after venturing out for a parley with the Khagan, who treacherously attacked. But the supreme crisis was reached when Egypt fell to the Persian general Shahrbaraz (617-19) and the African corn supply was cut off. With the Byzantine fleet as the last card in his hand, Heraclius considered the desperate expedient of shifting the imperial capital to Carthage, but Sergius persuaded him to drop the idea. Money and hostages were found to buy a temporary peace from the Avars, and Heraclius resumed the strategy of Tiberius and Maurice, making every effort against the Persians.

The defeat of Persia

The result was the 'Byzantine Crusade' of 622-6. This was a supreme effort by the Empire to re-gain the initiative by raising a new army paid for by the vast treasures of the Church, then launching it against the Persian lines of communication. In such an endeavor Heraclius managed to persuade his advisers that nothing less than the personal command of the emperor would do. He must leave Constantinople to rely on its own defenses and take the field at the head of his troops. This was not merely intended to boost morale. Heraclius had devised a grand strategy of pure maneuver intended to make the Persian armies dance to his tune – a strategy often attempted by other commanders in later years, but hardly pursued with great success until the

campaigns of Wellington in the Peninsular War, and Robert E Lee in the American Civil War. Such a strategy demanded that the army be kept in being, avoiding untimely or unnecessary battles. Over the past 20 years there had been too many of both.

Leaving Constantinople in April 622, Heraclius got astride the Persian communications by shipping the army round the coast of Asia Minor and landing at Issus. He then struck northeast into Armenia and for the next three years campaigned with perfect success in Persian Armenia and Azerbaidjan, retiring westward for the winter months before launching the next year's foray. Chosroes riposted by concluding a new alliance with the Avars and launching yet another overland drive against Constantinople in 625-6, which forced Heraclius to pull back into northern Asia Minor. In July 626 Constantinople was furiously assaulted by the Avars, with the Persians only two kilometers away across the strait. After a 17-day siege the Theodosian Wall was still holding out, the Avars' flotilla of small craft had been scattered, and the Khagan raised the siege and retreated. Meanwhile Heraclius had not only managed to ship reinforcements into the city, his brother Theodore had also beaten an ill-assorted Persian relief army hurled into Asia Minor by Chosroes.

The way was clear for Heraclius to resume the offensive, this time for good, in 627. Leaving the Persian army of Shahrbaraz isolated in Asia Minor, Heraclius struck south through Azerbaidjan into Assyria, desperately pursued by a

Persian army commanded by the general Rahzadh. The Persian commander foolishly sought battle before all his reinforcements had come in, compounding his folly by challenging Heraclius to personal combat. In killing Rahzadh under the exultant gaze of his troops, Heraclius gained immortal glory as far as antique Roman military tradition was concerned. In the 1380 years since the founding of Rome, only two Roman commanders before Heraclius had won the 'Supreme Spoil' by killing their opposite numbers in personal combat. In the ensuing Battle of Nineveh (12 December 627) the despondent Persians were defeated and the way to Ctesiphon, the Persian capital, was open. Prudent to the last, Heraclius decided that Ctesiphon's defenses were too strong and went into winter quarters – but the campaign was already over. After coming so close to victory over the Byzantine Empire, Chosroes II met the same fate as his former benefactor, Maurice. His troops mutinied rather than continue the fruitless war. Chosroes was murdered, and the new king Kobad II hastened to make peace with Heraclius.

Thoroughly humiliated, Persia gave back not only the True Cross but all of Chosroes II's conquests in Armenia, Syria, Palestine and Egypt. The two empires ended the war in an equally shattered and exhausted condition, however. The Byzantines at least had Heraclius, who settled down to repair his Empire with a program of strict economy and provincial reforms aimed at long-term imperial security. He laid down a new framework of military administration, reorganizing the provinces into *themata*, with each *theme* governed by a *strategos* (general) and divided into free landholdings for the troops – on condition that each landholding must continue to supply recruits for the army. This system, which took decades to establish, came too late to save Syria, Palestine or Egypt from Arab assault, but at least it helped preserve the bulk of Asia Minor. There was no such will toward postwar retrenchment and reform in Persia. After the humiliation of 628 the Persians suffered the fate endured by the Byzantines under Phocas: anarchy and civil war, with ten kings in four years – one of them, briefly, the general Shahrbaraz, whom Heraclius politely repatriated from Asia Minor with his army and who wasted little time in making his bid for the Persian throne. Finally, in 632, Yezdegird III was installed as the aristocracy's figurehead on the throne. With an almost pathetic fidelity, his feckless reign was to the downfall of Sassanid Persia what the reign of Honorius had been to the fall of the Roman West.

Arab expansion into the weakened Byzantine and Persian Empires

So it was that the two empires which for centuries had resisted Arab raids with comparative ease and enlisted Arab tribes as allies for their desert campaigns, were in the worst possible case to stand up to the flood-surge which came out of Arabia after the death of the Prophet Muhammad in 632. Certainly the impact of that flood would have been far less formidable if the Byzantine and Persian Empires had kept the Arab tribes on the fringe of the 'Fertile Crescent' content as fully paid-up allies. The cutting-off of imperial subsidies, encouraging raids to make up the border tribesmen's losses, must be counted as a compelling material motive for the Arabs who spearheaded the first expeditions.

The abstract motive was, of course, the religious inspiration of Islam (which, lest we forget, means 'surrender'). 'Arabs could be swung on an idea as on a cord; for the unpledged allegiance of their minds made them obedient servants,' remarks T E Lawrence in *Seven Pillars of Wisdom*. 'They were a people of starts, for whom the abstract was the strongest motive, the process of infinite courage and variety, and the end nothing. They were as unstable as water, and like water would perhaps finally prevail.' Even before Muhammad received the submission of the holy city of Mecca in 630, he had revealed that his mission as the Prophet of God was not limited to Arabia. It was worldwide. It was certainly not to be diverted by initial setbacks such as the repulse of the 3000 tribesmen whom Muhammad sent against Byzantine Palestine in 629. The expeditionary force assembled for a second attack on Palestine by the time of the Prophet's death was the instrument which enabled Abu Bakr to make good his supremacy as Muhammad's 'successor,' or Caliph. And it was under Abu Bakr that the implementation of the Prophet's will outside Arabia was commenced in 633-4.

The very nature of Islam was one of the Arabs' greatest assets. It was not an alien, implacable creed. Muhammad had preached respect for both Jew and Christian, holding that Moses and Jesus had been his predecessors. This approach was particularly bad news for the Byzantine Empire in which the Jews and dissident Christian churches had long been subject to religious persecution by 'orthodox' Constan-

Left: This sixth-seventh century Persian silver dish depicts a Sassanid king using the re-curved bow typical of Eastern archery. This weapon was to gain a fearsome reputation throughout the Middle Ages.

Right: Moslem pilgrims on their way to Mecca. The fact that the two major religions of Europe shared the same geographical birthplace was to turn the Middle East into a battleground for the next 1000 years or more.

Left: The general form of armor depicted in this early fifteenth century miniature from Shiraz is similar to that worn in the Middle East centuries earlier, with only relatively minor modifications.

tinople. Islam became the natural religion of subject peoples; and as the success of the 'Black Moslem' movement in the United States has proved, it still is. This made the faith a unique asset to rapid expansion. The Arabs did not set about the extermination of the peoples whose armies they defeated. Usual Arab terms were for the defeated to be invited to accept conversion to Islam, or pay tribute after an interval had been allowed for military and civilian evacuation.

Seventh-century Arab weaponry was of the crudest. The basic hand-to-hand weapon was the sword – not the lightweight scimitar of popular image, which was a Turkish innovation centuries after the initial conquests, but the straight sword or *saif*. The bow had been a traditional Arab weapon long before Muhammad who, we are told, was known to lean on a bow when

وَكَادَ يَنْزِعُ الْجِمَالَ الشَّمَّرُ وَأَنْشَدُ

مَا لِلْحَجِّ سَيْرُكَ تَأْوِيبًا وَإِدْلَاجَا وَلَا لِعِيَامِكَ أَحْمَالًا وَأَحْدَاجَا

الْحَجُّ أَنْ تَقْصِدَ الْبَيْتَ الْحَرَامَ عَلَى تَحْرِيلٍ لَا الْحَجُّ لَا يَبْغِي بِهِ حَاجَا

وَتَنْطُوِي كَأَهْلِ الْإِنْصَافِ مُنْتَدِرًا رَدْعَ الْهَوَى هَادِيًا وَالْحَقَّ مِنْهَاجَا

teaching – but it was the straightforward stave or self-bow, not the long-range composite bow carried by the steppe nomads. This meant that Arab archers could be outranged, but the advantage of the self-bow was that it could be used in all weathers, whereas the glued layers of the composite bow deteriorated rapidly in contact with moisture. Archery missile power was supplemented by slingers. As well as the *saif*, infantry carried thrusting spears, cavalry carried lances, and both favored a modest-sized circular shield. Helmets and mail armor were adopted later – after the conquest of Syria and Persia. Here again, as with Alaric's Visigoths and Gaiseric's Vandals, it was a case of 'have-not' victors profiting from the superior technology of the peoples they conquered. The same applied to the rapid adoption of sea power in the Mediterranean, Red Sea, Persian Gulf and Indian Ocean.

The Arabs' biggest tactical assets were speed of movement and horsemanship, relying on the superior maneuverability of the lightweight horseman over more heavily armored opponents. As relying on walking speed in the Arabian desert was suicide, the Arabs had learned to transport even their infantry on mules or camels. In the 630s and 640s, neither the Byzantines nor the Sassanid Persians had ever tackled enemies who could move so rapidly. With the Arabs as with the ancient Assyrians, horses and mules were a prized spoil of war. When the Arabs beat the Spanish Visigoths on the River Lakka in 711, they captured so many horses that they were able to mount nearly all their Berber infantry and overrun Spain before the year was out. With this technique, one victory led rapidly to the next.

Speed and maneuverability were exploited to the full in Arab tactics. Arabs were masters of the feigned flight, attack from all quarters and bypassing enemy positions to strike at key objectives in the rear. They were noted for surprise attacks, too – ambushes, night attacks, dawn attacks, attacks in the hottest (or coldest) hours of the day and attacks in sandstorms. This versatility cloaked their unfitness for fighting pitched battles. Arab armies were particularly allergic to well-drilled enemy infantry able to fend off cavalry attacks and bring the indifferent Arab infantry to close quarters. But the instances when well-drilled enemy infantry was supplemented by superior enemy cavalry were rare. The Arab tendency to discouragement after an initial repulse was offset by the growing knowledge that the best infantry in the world, once deprived of cavalry cover and support, could not hold out for ever. When its ammunition and provisions ran out it must either accept piecemeal destruction or surrender.

As with Scandinavia on the eve of the Viking era, one of the biggest mysteries is the actual size of the Arab population when Muhammad died. Though it must have reached or been approaching a peak for so much manpower to have been unleashed, Arab armies during the conquest never relied on numbers alone, and were often outnumbered. The average Arab army consisted of between 20,000 and 50,000 men, often comparable to but never dwarfing the enemy strength. At Nihawand, the Arabs' 'victory of victories' over the Persians in 642, the Arab army was about 30,000 strong and was outnumbered by at least four to one. But as many of the Persian infantry levies had been chained together to stop them from running away, this disparity in numbers did not embarrass the Arabs unduly.

Left: A seventh century Frankish *spangenhelm* made of iron segments within a bronze frame. This composite construction also occurred in many contemporary eastern variants of helmet.

Right: The Guarrazar treasure, found near Toledo in 1859, consists of Visigothic (Christian) gold and jewels perhaps hidden during the Arab conquest.

The brief reign of Abu Bakr (632-4) cracked the fragile Byzantine-Persian frontier enclosing Arabia and exposed the rich possibilities that lay beyond. In 633 Abu Bakr directed the main Arab attack against southern Palestine, routing the skimpy Byzantine forces there. Meanwhile the 'Sword of God,' Khalid, accepted the invitation of the Bakr and Banu Shaiban tribesmen, and led 500 picked men north to help in attacks on Persian Babylonia (Iraq). After extorting a ransom from the Persian frontier town of Hira, Khalid's men stormed west across the desert and joined the main Arab army near Damascus. Their united forces beat the Byzantine army sent against them under Theodore, brother of Heraclius, at Ajnadain in July 634.

When Omar succeeded Abu Bakr as Caliph in 634 he was determined to maintain his predecessor's simultaneous attacks on the Byzantine and Persian Empires. In 635 Khalid kept up the pressure in the west, defeating the Byzantine general Baanes at Marj-as-Suffar and pushing north to take Damascus and Emesa from the apathetic provincials. Also in 635, the Persian general Rustam was beaten by a small Arab force under Muthanna at Buwaib. Meanwhile the agents of Heraclius in Syria were working frantically to secure allegiance and cavalry recruits from the Ghassanid Arabs whose territory marched with Syria and Palestine. The army which Heraclius sent south in 636 to free the two provinces from the Arabs carried many classic hallmarks of defeat before it even struck a blow. It was under the dual command of Theodore and Baanes. About 100,000 strong, it was over three times the size of the diminutive but well-balanced field armies of the age of Belisarius only a century before; quantity had come to replace quality. Drawn hugger-mugger from the exhausted provinces of the Empire, the Byzantine army of 636 was a multinational force whose Greeks, allied Slavs, Armenians and Syrians hated each other as much as the Arabs, while the loyalty of the Ghassanid Arab was justifiably suspect.

Theodore and Baanes were completely outfought by Khalid, whose forces were outnumbered by two to one and probably more. Khalid only accepted battle after maneuvering the Byzantine army until it had its back to the rocky defile of the River Yarmuk. He may have been waiting for the weather to turn in his favor, because he took the risk of allowing the Byzantines to close and threaten to crush the Arab left flank. Arab cavalry meanwhile bypassed the Byzantine army and seized a vital bridge over the Yarmuk, cutting the Byzantine line of retreat. Finally, out of a sandstorm which stopped the Byzantines in their tracks, Khalid ordered a devastating charge, whereupon the Ghassanid Arabs deserted and came over to his side. The Byzantine army dissolved in a *sauve qui peut* in which thousands died as they tried to scramble down rocky precipices and recross the Yarmuk. Theodore died in the rout, which destroyed the only Byzantine field army and forced Heraclius to abandon the whole of Palestine and Syria.

On the Persian front the Arabs struck their decisive blow in 637 when about 30,000 warriors under Sa'd ibn Abi Waqqas tackled the massed forces of Sassanid Persia collected by the Empire's virtual ruler Rustam, general-in-chief to Yazdigird III. Rustam duplicated the mistake of Heraclius in putting all his eggs in one basket. His force comprised a mixed army about 100,000 strong, most of the manpower being made up of low-grade infantry levies. The Persian host included 33 war elephants. In the opening stages of the four-day battle fought at Qadisiya in May-June 637, the elephants exercised their usual deterrent effect on the charging Arab cavalry, only to be disabled or stampeded when Rustam ordered an elephant attack. The Arab commander played his master stroke by wearing out the Persians with repeated attacks throughout the third night, then launching a decisive general assault out of a sandstorm on the following morning. As at Yarmuk in the previous year, the beaten army's losses were increased by the River Euphrates at its back. Apart from the presence of elephants, the similarity of Arab tactics in the two battles is impossible to ignore. As the French General Nivelle was to claim in 1917 (with, in his case, such lamentable inaccuracy) the Arabs 'had the formula.'

After this brace of resounding victories the Arabs completed the occupation of Syria, Palestine and lower Mesopotamia, taking Ctesiphon with immense booty before the year was out. They scattered the surviving Persian forces at Jalula and chased Yezdegird III east into the uplands of Iran and Media. In 640-41 the Arab offensive leaped forward again – under new commanders, for Omar took care to prevent his victorious generals from settling as governors in the territories they conquered. Amr led the invasion of Egypt in 640; al-Muzani began the conquest of northern Mesopotamia in the following year. Amr had the easier task. The Coptic Christians of Egypt, long persecuted by orthodox Constantinople, proved especially amenable to the Arab invasion and the Patriarch Cyrus of Alexandria was a devious and ambitious governor.

After an initial Arab victory at Heliopolis the military key to lower Egypt was the confusingly named fortress of Babylon near the site of Cairo. When the Arabs trapped Cyrus there in 640 the Patriarch proved eager to bargain. He offered the surrender of Egypt as a province of the Caliphate under his continued administration. Amr agreed to a peace settlement on this basis, but when Cyrus went to Constantinople to have the treaty ratified his acts were declared void and he was banished by Heraclius, who died soon afterward (February 641). Months elapsed before Heraclius' grandson Constans II was accepted as emperor and by then it was too late to save Alexandria. Cyrus had returned to Egypt and negotiated the surrender of the city which was abandoned in September 642 after the Byzantine garrison had been evacuated.

Niharwand, the 'victory of victories' which sealed the conquest of Persia, was also fought in 642. This battle is particularly interesting because it shows how quickly an Arab army could re-cast its tactics when the original plan had failed. The huge Sassanid army assembled for the defense of Persia began confidently. Its front had been strewn with dense fields of caltrops (clusters of spikes, each cluster presenting an upward-pointing spike no matter how the caltrop lies) to disable the Arab cavalry. The Arab commander al-Muzani was killed on the first day, and during the night and the second day repeated Arab charges were made with heavy loss. No friendly sandstorm came to the Arabs' aid this time, but on the third day they resorted to a mock attack and feigned flight. The latter ruse succeeded in luring the massed Persian formations, whose most unreliable infantry levies had been chained together like galley slaves to prevent flight, beyond the deadly belt of caltrops. The Arab rally and final attacks butchered the Persians out in the open. After Niharwand the final occupation of the Persian Empire came down to a gigantic mopping-up operation spread over the next ten years. In 651 or 652 Yezdegird III was finally murdered by one of his own officers at Marv near the River Oxus, having retreated eastward as far as he could go.

The biggest problem which the Arabs faced in Persia was the furious resistance put up by some of the fortified towns of Media and Persia. Totally lacking the skills of siege engineering, the Arabs had no answer to strong walls and defiant garrisons during the first ten years of the conquest. But the only reasons for a garrison to hold out are to win time for a friendly field army to come to the rescue, or to sacrifice itself in order that a decisive counterblow may be launched against the invader somewhere else; and the Arabs' technique was to destroy all enemy field armies at the earliest opportunity. This technique, coupled with the inability of the exhausted Byzantine and Persian Empires to raise successive field armies for the relief of besieged

strongpoints, is the key to understanding the speed at which the Arab conquest proceeded.

When Caliph Omar was assassinated by a Persian slave in 644, the extent of the Caliphate already rivaled that of the Macedonian Empire at the death of Alexander the Great. The following 17 years were a mixture of crisis and consolidation in Arabia and the conquered territories, with repeated fights for the succession at home and provincial revolts abroad. These years of confusion nevertheless saw the Arabs pushing west out of Egypt along the North African coast; Barca in Cyrenaica fell in 644 and Tripoli three years later. Above all the 640s were the years in which the Arabs added sea power to their arsenal. In 645 a Byzantine fleet appeared off Alexandria and the Greek population of the city rose in support, forcing the Arabs to recapture the city from the landward side before the insurgents could put its defenses in order. To prevent similar trouble in future the Arab governor of Egypt, Abdallah ibn Sa'd, fitted out the first Moslem fleet. This fleet assisted the Syrian Arabs in the conquest of Cyprus (649). The Egypt of the Pharaohs had been a sea trading nation and a naval power; under Persian, Macedonian, Roman and Byzantine rule, Egypt had contributed fleets and seamen on the conquerors' demand. The possession of Egypt, in short, spelled instant sea power and nothing changed when Egypt passed from Byzantine to Moslem

rule. Moslem sea power, once born, was destined to prey upon Christian shipping in the Mediterranean for the next 1167 years until the lingering menace of the Barbary Corsairs was finally broken in 1816.

Arab expansion reached its zenith after the establishment of the Omayyad dynasty of Caliphs, with their new capital at Damascus, in 661. The Byzantine Exarchate of Africa put up a splendid fight for almost 30 years, considerably helped by the uncharacteristic failure of successive Arab commanders to win over the Berber tribesmen of the interior. One of the worst offenders was Uqba (nephew of Amr, Syria's conqueror). Uqba established an advanced base for the conquest of *Maghreb* or Morocco – 'the West' – at Kairouan in 670. But he so infuriated the Berber chiefs by his harshness and arrogance that they joined forces with the Byzantines of Carthage, and pushed the Arabs all the way east into Cyrenaica. Hassan ibn an-Nu'man finally won the war by relying on diplomacy as much as armed force, mollifying the Berbers by his reasonable approach and leaving the Byzantines on the coast isolated. Sea power, however, sealed the fate of Carthage in 698, when the relieving ships under the Patrician John were destroyed by the Arab fleet.

Thirteen years after the fall of Carthage, the Berbers had accepted Islam and the Arab supremacy with such enthusiasm that they car-

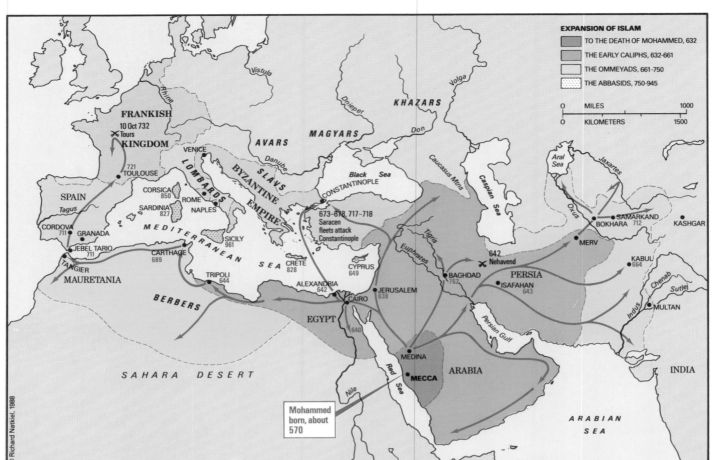

Left: The expansion of Islam from AD 570 (the birth of Muhammad) to 945.

Below: The 'Infidels' rapidly gained a reputation for treachery and surprise attacks that was to endure for centuries. Here, Saracen beggars appealing for Crusader charity mask the advance of their armed comrades (from the fourteenth century *Chroniques de St Denis*).

ried the brunt of the 'Arab' invasion of Visigothic Spain. The commander of the expedition was himself a Berber, Tariq, to whom Gibraltar owes its name – *Gebel al-Tariq*, or 'Mount of Tariq.' Considering that Berber warriors consisted mainly of fleet-footed light infantry who fought in loincloths, the Spanish expedition should never have stood a chance against the Visigoths, who were amply supported by cavalry. But the Visigothic kingdom was far gone in decline in 711, and the army concentrated on the River Lakka (Guadalete), suffered from treachery at the top. King Roderic, commanding in the center, was left unsupported by the sudden desertion of his cavalry wings, and the Visigothic center collapsed before a wild Berber charge. Arab cavalry took up the running for the all-important pursuit, invariably exploited to the full in any Arab victory. The death

of Roderic in the rout, and the fact that his seedy, demoralized host was the only effective army in the kingdom, made the almost instantaneous reduction of Visigothic Spain one of the easiest conquests the Arabs ever made.

The Arabs enter Europe

The information which the Arabs culled from their new Visigothic subjects about the sprawling Christian lands of the Franks north of the Pyrenees must have sounded as promising as it was familiar. At the height of their power in the sixth century, the Frankish Merovingian kings had ruled a mighty kingdom stretching from the Pyrenees across the Rhine into the distant lands of Germany; but now, in the early eighth century, the Merovingian royal house was even frailer than that of Visigothic Spain. It produced a seemingly unending succession of boy-kings

and weaklings presiding only nominally over an assortment of Frankish sub-kingdoms and dukedoms frequently at odds with each other – Austrasia, Neustria, Alamannia, Burgundy, Aquitaine and Gascony. And the powerful landed aristocracy who ruled the Frankish provinces had a record of successful resistance to the Merovingian official known as the 'Mayor of the Palace' who tried, with fluctuating success, to govern effectively in the king's name. From the Arab point of view all that seemed to be lacking in Francia was the familiar eastern undertow of religious discord and persecution which had served the spread of Islam so well. The Franks had no persecuted religious sects eager for Arab patronage, and its spiritual leaders did not reciprocate the inherent respect of Islam toward the prophet Jesus. The Frankish Church, so far from being a useful vehicle for another Arab

Right: Mounted archers, the backbone of successive Saracen armies, in an illuminated manuscript of AD 1307-8. Their equipment as depicted here did not essentially change until the end of the sixteenth century.

conquest, encouraged, assisted and gave its blessing to determined resistance. The Arabs arrived in Francia as temporal and spiritual aliens.

For 80 years the Arab Caliphate had flourished by exploiting weaknesses of the kind that plagued Merovingian Francia, but by the early eighth century those weaknesses were less marked than they had been in the middle seventh. The powerful Austrasian Mayor Pepin II (680-714) had reunited the kingdom with the exception of Aquitaine, the southwestern dukedom closest to Spain. After another interlude of civil war Charles, illegitimate son of Pepin, restored the unity imposed by his father and gained the allegiance of Eudo, Duke of Aquitaine (719). Thus instead of making a promising start by enlisting the willing support of the Aquitanians (as he seems to have hoped) the Arab governor of Spain, al-Samah, was greeted with spirited resistance by Duke Eudo in 721.

Though less sophisticated than the *themata* established in the Byzantine Empire by Heraclius and his successors, the Frankish levy system operated on similar lines, involving military service in return for land tenure. The Franks relied mainly on unarmored infantry spearmen carrying round shields, with the *seax* (long knife) for close-quarter work. The battle line of spearmen could be packed tight to form a shield-wall perfectly capable of withstanding Arab cavalry, and was covered by mail-clad cavalry lancers. The latter vital elements enabled Duke Eudo to encircle al-Samah's invading force at Toulouse and break it after a gratifyingly short action, al-Samah being killed in the battle.

Eleven years later the Arabs launched a second invasion with what was evidently a larger army and a substantial cavalry component, commanded by Abd ar-Rahman. He defeated Duke Eudo's Aquitanians near Bordeaux, but this was not the decisive battle with which so many Arab armies had sealed the outcome of previous campaigns. Eudo's conception of duty did not demand pointless death in a lost battle. He got away to organize further resistance, riding northeast to join Charles and urge the muster of the army of united Francia.

The decisive Frankish-Arab clash took place in 732 between Poitiers and Tours, south of the Loire, and its dominant feature was the concern of the Arabs to protect the withdrawal of their plunder-laden wagon train. Such was the keynote of what has been hailed as one of the decisive battles of European history: intercepted invaders trying to get away with the loot, rather than gallant patriots resolved to fight and die for the defense of Christendom against the infidel. Charles took no risks. He formed his infantry in close order on high ground, beat off repeated Arab cavalry charges, then sent off a cavalry force which broke into the Arab camp and started to loot the baggage train. This caused an instant Arab withdrawal which degenerated into flight as word spread that Abd ar-Rahman had been killed. Charles did not pursue the beaten Arabs, being more than content to return to Tours with the spoil recovered from the invaders. The Arabs evacuated Aquitaine virtually unmolested.

The Arab defeat at Tours in 732, the centenary of the Prophet's death, was only one among a number of indications that the Arabs had, for the moment, reached a high-water mark. No more easy options beyond their outermost frontiers beckoned the Arabs to fresh conquest. Successive Arab naval expeditions (670, 674-8 and 717-18) had besieged Constantinople only to recoil without success; abortive attacks on Sicily (667, 720) had also failed. The Arabs had only reached the line of the Caucasus after heavy fighting against the Khazars, while far to the east the last major advances had been made under Walid I (Caliph 705-15). These had carried Islam as far as Bokhara, Samarkand and Ferghana in Transoxiana; Kanadahar, Kabul and Ghuznee in Afghanistan; and the line of the Indus in Sind and the Punjab. When the Omayyads of Damascus were supplanted by the Abbasids in 750, the break-up of the Arab world into independent emirates – Spain and Morocco being the first – had already begun.

The Arab conquests

Though the Arab conquest was triggered off by the achievement of Muhammad in uniting the Hedjaz tribesmen, it owed its rapid success to the enfeeblement of the Byzantine and Persian Empires after nearly 50 years of war. Lacking any advantage either in weaponry or weight of numbers, the Arabs exploited their mobility to the full and developed an admirable resilience in their combat tactics – surprise attacks, feigned flight and so on. Masters of the pursuit, they excelled in beating the enemy field army at the earliest opportunity, which relieved them of the need to develop orthodox siege tactics.

The Arabs were quick to realize the benefits of sea power which they acquired early in the career and used to deny reinforcements to the Byzantine garrisons in North Africa. After the Arab conquest Moslem sea power in the Mediterranean, plus the unshaken Moslem domination of the Middle East 'land bridge' to the Far East, exerted a powerful influence on the development of world history. Frustrated after centuries of failure to break that domination by orthodox military operations, the sea powers of Western Europe would finally take to the oceans in efforts to find a way round by sea.

47

Charlemagne and his Heirs

For his victory over the Arabs at Tours, the Frankish Mayor Charles was remembered as 'Martel' – the hammer of Christendom's foes. But his most important achievement was reunification of the Frankish domains and the maintenance of a powerful alternative ruling dynasty capable of replacing the effete heirs of the Merovingian royal line. Ten years after Charles Martel died in 741, his son Pepin II finally made the transition from hereditary court official to ruling monarch. The rapid advance of the Frankish kingdom toward imperial status under the Carolingians, the heirs of Charles Martel, had begun. And on Christmas Day 800, only 68 years after Tours, Martel's grandson Charles the Great, supreme warlord of Christian Europe, was crowned 'Emperor of the Romans' in St Peter's at Rome.

The fact that Charlemagne's empire was a temporary phenomenon which split, like a swollen and overripe fruit, within three years of his death in 814, never diminished his aura over the following centuries. Though the authority of the Christian Church meant that Charlemagne could never be accorded the divine status assumed by the emperors of old Rome, posterity gave him neo-Biblical and mythical honors, ranking Charlemagne among the 'Nine Worthies.' For the latter were, as Caxton put it in his Preface to Sir Thomas Malory's *Morte d'Arthur* (1485):

. . . the best that ever were. That is to wit three paynims, three Jews, and three Christian men. As for the paynims they were tofore the Incarnation of Christ, which were named, the first Hector of Troy, of whom the history is come both in ballad and in prose; the second Alexander the Great; and the third Julius Caesar, Emperor of Rome, of whom the histories be well-known and had. And as for the three Jews which also were tofore the Incarnation of Our Lord, of whom the first was Duke Joshua which brought the children of Israel into the land of behest; the second David, King of Jerusalem; and the third Judas Maccabaeus: of these three the Bible rehearseth all their noble histories and acts. And sith the said Incarnation have been three noble Christian men stalled and admitted through the universal world into the number of the nine best and worthy, of whom the first was the noble Arthur, whose noble acts I purpose to write in this book here following. The second was Charlemagne or Charles the Great, of whom the history is had in many places both in French and English; and the third and last was Godfrey of Bouillon [King of Jerusalem after the recapture of the Holy Sepulcher in the First Crusade].

The concept of the Nine Worthies was, of course, a literary conceit of the Christian West; hence the exclusion of such Byzantine giants as Justinian or Heraclius. But the Worthies are a reminder, if nothing more, that medieval thinkers did worry a little about how the teachings of Jesus squared with the waging of wars. It was in the Middle Ages that the idea of the 'just war' was born in defense of the establishment – Church leaders and lay princes alike. The Nine Worthies were held up as the leading examples of warfare for noble ends and fulfillment of the divine plan. Thus Hector had been the mighty champion of the legendary Trojan Empire at bay; Alexander and Caesar stood for world conquest, pioneers of the imperial dream, workers for world order and peace. The Old Testament heroes added religious motivation to the waging of war, an element almost totally lacking in the wars of pagan antiquity. It was under divine orders that Joshua had led the Israelites into Canaan, the warrior King David had founded the city of Zion and Judas Maccabeus had led the Jews in their first impassioned war of liberation. And of course all these beginnings and precedents had been inevitably fulfilled in the Christian era. Arthur of Britain, it was said, had nobly defended his embattled realm against the pagan Saxon invaders. Charlemagne, as the champion of the Church of Rome, had added pagan Saxony to his other conquests before receiving his crown from the Pope. Godfrey the Crusader, liberator of the City of David and the Tomb of Christ, was clearly in a class of his own as a champion of Christendom. Defense – conquest – crusade: that was the triple ideal implied in respecting the Nine Worthies, and Charlemagne's qualifications for a niche in their hall of fame was never in question.

The growth of the Frankish kingdom

In strictly historical terms it is true that Charlemagne's wars created a temporary empire which enforced a permanent unity – that of the Roman Church – on Western Europe. But it is equally true that Charlemagne's achievement was not all his own work. His conquests were not the result of an imperial master plan; they were largely opportunist, the result of historical accident. Like Alexander the Great, Charlemagne had inherited all the right tools for the job from the reign of his father. In fact it is hard to see how Charlemagne's wars could have followed any other course.

By the second half of the eighth century the Frankish kingdom and the Church of Rome were moving into an increasingly close alignment. Charlemagne's father, Pepin 'The Short' (751-68), needed the Pope's blessing to legitimize his ousting of the Merovingians; the Papacy needed a powerful ally to prevent Rome from going under to the Lombards. The contemporary Byzantine Emperor Constantine V had his hands full with the Arabs; he could not prevent the Lombard king Aistulf from destroy-

ET SYRIAM SOBAL · ET CONVERTIT
IOAB · ET PERCVSSIT EDOM INVAL
LE SALINARVM XII MILIA ·

Below left: Carolingian horsemen, from the ninth century illuminated manuscript known as the *Golden Psalter.* Note the typical mail 'byrnies,' 'winged' spears, round shields and 'wyvern' standard.

Right: The marble Throne of Charlemagne, in Aachen (Aix la Chapelle), Germany. It was used for imperial coronations throughout the Middle Ages.

ing the Byzantine Exarchate of Ravenna in 751, let alone from besieging Rome and exacting tribute. In 754 Pope Stephen II took the extraordinary step of traveling to Pepin's court to beg for military aid. As a *quid pro quo* the Pope not only formally anointed Pepin King of the Franks but gave him (quite unauthorized) the Byzantine title of Patrician.

Pope Stephen had done his homework on the Franks and their institutions, for he arrived in January. This gave Pepin over two months in which to prepare the ground for an Italian campaign, and those two months were needed. The military power of the Frankish kingdom was derived from the provincial call-up (*Heerban*) of land tenants for the military service they owed their lords, and which the lords in turn owed the king. The actual period of military service, though unspecified, was necessarily limited by the seasonal tug of agriculture. If the provinces were starved of manpower at harvest time, there would be no crops and no revenue. When the Frankish counts assembled with their contingents for the annual national muster known as the *Marchfeld* or 'Field of March,' they came ready to oppose any long-term military adventures which the king might be contemplating – and that definitely included campaigning in Italy. Thus the true 'strength' of a 'strong' king was measured by his success in persuading his vassal lords to fall in with the royal plans.

Having persuaded his lords at the 754 *Marchfeld* to agree to a limited campaign in Italy, Pepin had the great good fortune of winning an encouragingly rapid victory. When the Franks drove his northern outposts out of the Mont Cenis Pass in 754, Aistulf submitted without further ado and promised to hand over Ravenna and the Exarchate to Rome. When the Franks had gone home, Aistulf held on to Ravenna and

continued to pressure Rome. Pope Stephen then prompted a second Frankish invasion, this time by using naked spiritual blackmail. Calling the Franks the 'adopted sons' of St Peter, the Pope assured them of heaven if they came to his help and damnation if they refused. It worked. In 756 Pepin led the Frankish host into the Po valley and trapped Aistulf in Pavia, extorting a heavy tribute for himself and the Exarchate for the Pope. Eleven hundred years of tortuous Italian history was thus inadvertently set in motion by the creation of the central Italian Papal State, the survival of which depended on military power from beyond the Alps.

Apart from the Italian front, Pepin found his other wars comparatively easy to 'sell' to the Frankish warlords at the *Marchfeld.* The first of these was the conquest of Septimania, the coastal strip of Provence between the Rhone and the Pyrenees. Once the Spanish Visigoths' last territory in Gaul, Septimania had passed under Moslem rule with the Arab conquest of Spain. Pepin reduced Septimania after repeated campaigns between 752 and 759, helped by the cooperation of the Visigothic population to whom he promised the retention of Visigothic law. As recovering Septimania from the Moslems amounted to a holy war against 'infidels,' these campaigns only helped strengthen the ties between the Frankish court and the Papacy. Pepin certainly found Septimania an easier nut to crack than the defiant Duke Waifar of Aquitaine, against whom Pepin launched annual unsuccessful campaigns from 760 to 768, when Waifar died and the Aquitanian nobles finally submitted. Even then Pepin was obliged to grant Aquitaine generous privileges to make sure of its allegiance to the Frankish kingdom, which had thus been pushed south to the line of the Pyrenees by the time Pepin died in September 768.

The third arm of Frankish expansion under Pepin did not involve a military offensive. It was the tradition of missionary activity in heathen Frisia and Saxony, a heroic chapter in Church history, carried out since the end of the seventh century by devoted and gallant churchmen from England – Wilfred, Willibrord and finally St Boniface (from 716 until his martyrdom in 754). These missions were themselves an offshoot from a general pursuit of Church reform in the seventh and eighth centuries, a movement supported and sponsored by both Pepin and Charlemagne. Royal patronage of the reformed Frankish Church ensured the Papal blessing for wars against the Saxons, whose raids imperiled the lucrative trade route of the Rhineland. Thus the conquest and conversion of the Saxons, in itself an objective worthy of pursuit because of the increased security and profit it would bring, became another holy war in which Charlemagne was to enjoy the consistent support both of his own magnates and of the Papacy.

Charlemagne inherited three other war fronts from his predecessors. The first of these was Bavaria, the eastern equivalent of Aquitaine, a fiercely independent duchy whose rulers had, for the past century, put a most elastic interpretation on their nominal allegiance to the Frankish crown. Both Bavaria and eastern Austrasia were prone to raids by the neighboring Slav tribes of the Sorbs (or Wends), the Bohemians, Moravians and the Avar kingdom of the Central Danube. And away in the west there was the irritation of Lesser Britain or Brittany, whose inhabitants represented the last stand of the ancient Romano-Gallic population against the Teutonic invaders. Across the Channel the Bretons' kinfolk of Cornwall and Wales continued to resist, in similar fashion, the southern kingdoms of Saxon England.

When Pepin died in 768, therefore, the Frankish kingdom had acquired a selection of military commitments on all fronts. These included Italy, Aquitaine-Spain, Frisia-Saxony and Bavaria, quite apart from the need to quell the aggressive Slav tribes of central Germany. The steady growth of these commitments had kept pace with the growing authority of the Carolingian mayors and kings and it forced a significant change on the Frankish army. Exactly like the imperial Roman army back in the third and fourth centuries, the former dependence on infantry troops had to go; the need for intensified campaigning against fast-moving enemies demanded an expanded cavalry arm. During Pepin's reign, in about 754, the date of the *Marchfeld* annual muster was put forward from March to May to allow the growth of enough grass to feed the army's horses (transport animals as well as cavalry mounts). Within a century of Pepin's death, Charlemagne's grandson Charles 'The Bald' had issued the decree that all Franks owning or able to buy a horse must bring it when reporting for military service.

This increased mobility did not, of course, transform the Frankish army overnight. Nor did it relieve Charlemagne of the need to enlist allied aid, by means of diplomacy or subsidies – Ibn Ar-Arabi of Saragossa in his Spanish campaign, the bishops of Bavaria against Duke Tassilo and the Obodrite Slavs east of the Elbe. But it did enable Charlemagne, after his brother died in 771 and the unity of Pepin's Frankish kingdom was restored, to wage virtually non-stop campaigns on one front after the other, a grandiose program which had not been seen in the West

Left: Frankish infantry and cavalry from the *Golden Psalter.*

Right: The Shrine of Charlemagne, Aachen. It was completed in 1215.

Below right: A gold and jewel-encrusted sword, reputedly that of the Emperor Charlemagne.

since the collapse of the Roman Empire: Italy 773-4; Saxony 775-7; Spain 778; Saxony 782-5; Italy 786; Bavaria 787; Avars 791; Saxony 792-5; Avars 795.

Charlemagne's campaigns

These were the campaigns which molded Charlemagne's empire on to the firm base of united Francia. There was nothing to distinguish them from earlier Frankish campaigns in that the army was mustered in May, campaigned through the summer months, dispersed for harvest and winter, and reassembled for the next campaign in the following spring. As Pepin had found against the Aquitainians and Charlemagne found against the Saxons, this seasonal pattern meant that several years were normally required for the reduction of a really determined enemy. Winter campaigns had been known during the European wars of the Roman Empire, though the summer months were naturally preferred for the greater ease which they lent to the movement of armies. In medieval Europe, however, summer campaigning became accepted as the norm and remained so until the revolutionary wars at the end of the eighteenth century.

In so far as Charlemagne had a 'grand strategy,' it consisted of surrounding Francia with a comfortable belt of conquered or allied territory – like the basic Soviet strategy since the end of World War II. A notable feature of Charlemagne's empire at its zenith was the ring of new frontier provinces or *marks* – the Spanish Mark against the Moslems, Breton Mark against the Bretons, Pannonian Mark against the Avars, Friulian Mark against the Illyrian Croats. In the wars which led to the establishment of these territorial buffers Charlemagne usually acted as his own commander-in-chief, reviewing the army at each spring's muster and leading it on campaign.

Charlemagne never attempted to plant fortresses and leave costly garrisons all over the territories he conquered; he did not have a long-service professional army and the provinces could not endure the withdrawal of farming manpower which prolonged foreign service demanded. Instead he tried, wherever possible, to seal each successful offensive with a permanent *political* settlement, reaching an accommodation with the defeated magnates. Other victors pursued this policy throughout the Middle Ages; in the first two years after Hastings, for example, William of Normandy held out the

most generous terms to the surviving leaders of Saxon England. There was nothing generous or humanitarian about this policy. It was common sense, a coat designed very much by the shortage of military cloth.

Charlemagne's first campaign, his invasion of Lombard Italy in 773, could be called the exception which proved the rule. It comprised an unusually prolonged string of sieges in which the Franks' lack of equipment forced them to starve out their victims. Desiderius, the Lombard king, clearly considered that Aistulf's surrender at Pavia in 756 had been a wanton failure to push the Franks – very much strangers in a strange land – to the limit of their patience and endurance. The ostensible reason for Charlemagne's invasion in 773 was to protect the Papacy from renewed Lombard pressure, but Charlemagne had another motive. When his brother Carloman died in December 771 Carloman's widow and sons had fled to Lombardy. Charlemagne was anxious to prevent his nephews from growing up to head a Frankish 'government in exile.' Avoiding pitched battle, Desiderius shut himself up in the northern cities and forced the Franks to sit down for a winter of siege warfare. Unfortunately for him, Charle-

magne refused to give up and go home. Verona, where Carloman's widow and sons had taken refuge, fell at the end of 773 and Pavia followed suit in 774. When Desiderius capitulated to Charlemagne at Pavia the Lombard war was over, for Charlemagne took the throne of Lombardy for himself, confirming all the territorial concessions to the Papacy made by his father Pepin.

An early solution on the Italian front freed Charlemagne to tackle the Saxons who had steadily intensified their raids on eastern Austrasia since his accession. As punitive raids into Saxon territory had no effect, Charlemagne decided on piecemeal conquest. After three campaigns (775, 776 and 777) he had advanced to the River Lippe, strengthening his hold on the slice of Saxon territory thus occupied by building a string of palisaded camps. The 'Mayfield' of 777 was held at Paderborn and by 778 Charlemagne considered the new Saxon *mark* secure enough for him to turn his attention to the Spanish front.

Charlemagne's Spanish expedition of 778 was an attempt to fish in troubled waters for the security of his Pyrenean frontier, plus (hopefully) a large portion of Spanish territory and the

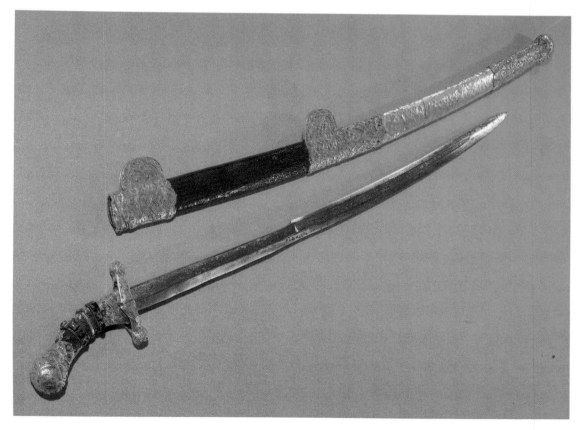

Left: The coronation of a Frankish king, believed to be Charlemagne's father Pepin the Short, from a ninth century illuminated manuscript in the Bibliothèque Nationale.

incidental advancement of the frontiers of Christendom. The troubled waters were provided by a civil war between the Moslems of Saragossa under Ibn Ar-Arabi, who solicited help from Charlemagne, and the Emir Abd-ar-Rahman I. There are interesting similarities between the invasion of Spain by Charlemagne and that by Napoleon 1030 years later; both underestimated the difficulties of campaigning in Spain and both were forced to quit the Peninsula because of trouble breaking out in Germany. Though the Frankish army reached the Ebro valley Charlemagne failed to take Saragossa. The threat to his western flank and communications posed by the hostile and, then as now, isolationist Christian Basques of Navarre, plus the disconcerting

strength brought against him by Abd-ar-Rahman, would probably have caused Charlemagne to cut his losses; but the arrival of news that the Saxons were in revolt made a prompt Frankish retreat essential.

While the Frankish rearguard and baggage train were pulling back through the Pass of Roncevaux they were ambushed and wiped out by a surprise Basque attack, the dead including Count Roland of the Breton Mark (about whom nothing else is known). The chronicler Eginhardt soberly recorded the disaster along with its date – 15 August 778 – adding merely that Eggihard, the king's seneschal, and Anselm, Count of the Palace, fell with Roland 'together with a great many more.' At the time the massacre at

Roncevaux must have seemed almost appropriate, the dismal tailpiece to an ill-starred campaign. And yet, human nature being what it is, admiring stories began to be woven about the supposed gallantry of the rearguard in its last stand – almost exactly like those instances of nineteenth-century military lunacy, the Charge of the Light Brigade and Custer's Last Stand. Two hundred years later the Roncevaux myths were enshrined in the splendid epic poem known as the *Chanson de Roland*, allegedly chanted by the Norman minstrel Taillefer, the first man to strike a blow at Hastings in 1066.

The *Chanson de Roland* is a classic example of the old adage 'when in doubt between myth and fact, print the myth.' It begins with Charlemagne, a snowy-bearded 200-year-old (he was 38 at the time) storming the Moslem stronghold of Cordoba after a seven-year string of victories in Spain. Most of those victories have been won by the valiant Roland, the Champion of Christendom, Charlemagne's 'right hand.' The black-hearted, devil-worshipping Saracens under King Marsile, advised by the traitor Ganelon – Roland's wicked stepfather – feign surrender, paying tribute to induce Charlemagne to withdraw from Spain and leave Roland exposed with the rearguard. Though confronted by impossible odds, Roland scorns to sound his horn and bring Charlemagne's army to his aid. Thus Roland and his men die because Roland is too brave to live – but Charlemagne avenges them with a splendid slaughter of the Saracen army, and the traitor Ganelon is pulled apart by wild horses as a lesson to all renegades.

In its way the *Chanson de Roland* was the most important military legacy of Charlemagne's reign, despite being the fruit of one of the emperor's biggest strategic miscalculations. The poem reached its peak popularity in the eleventh century which, as we shall see, was the heroic age of the Christian West, ending with the crusading army taking Jerusalem. It was also in the eleventh century that the ideals of knighthood and chivalry began to take recognizable form, with far-reaching effects on the theory and

Above right: The Iron Crown of Lombardy (part of the Frankish Empire), from the Cathedral Treasury of Monza.

Right: A Norse 'byrnie' of riveted mail. This was comparatively rare, highly prized armor for a Viking warrior, but became gradually more common throughout the Frankish Empire, until by 1066 it was the standard military dress of early Norman knights.

practice of medieval warfare. The absurd exaggerations of the *Chanson de Roland* were, therefore, more than mere embellishments on the Charlemagne legend. The poem remains a master document to understanding the so-called 'age of chivalry,' which produced the first attempts at civilized rules for warfare.

There was little chivalry about Charlemagne's conquest of Saxony between 779 and 785. 'War upon rebellion,' T E Lawrence has remarked, is 'messy and slow, like eating soup with a knife.' And this was a brutal and bloody war, made worse by the resilience of Saxon heathenism and Charlemagne's bull-headed determination to make the Saxons accept Christianity or death. Here was the seamy side of holy war, made more prolonged by the Saxons having found a national leader in Widukind. The Saxons could not match the heavy Frankish cavalry but were adept at ambushes and surprise attacks on isolated units and lines of communication. Very few great commanders have ever found a successful formula to overcome guerrilla warfare. Charlemagne never did. By 782, after four campaigns, he had marched and counter-marched through Saxony as far as the Elbe, killing, burning villages and setting up Frankish mission stations which were attacked and destroyed as soon as the Frankish army moved on. Charlemagne nevertheless repeated his earlier mistake and believed that Saxony was sufficiently cowed to be divided into Frankish counties, Widukind having fled north to Denmark. Then Charlemagne sent a Frankish column through Saxony to punish the Wends on the upper Elbe. The Saxons rose in revolt and cut the Franks to pieces.

Charlemagne retaliated with another punitive expedition in force which he led himself and crowned with the biggest atrocity associated with his reign: the massacre of 4500 Saxon prisoners at Verden on the River Aller. Apologists have suggested that this crime never took place; that some blundering scribe weak in his spelling wrote *decollare* (behead) when he really meant *delocare* (deport). Certainly Charlemagne did resort to deportation in his last Saxon wars, but the mud of the Verden massacre has stuck. After Widukind finally capitulated and accepted baptism in 785 the Saxons were subjected to ferocious laws, with the death sentence for continued heathen observance or offenses against Church property and clergy. This finally provoked the last Saxon revolt of 792. The Saxons found Charlemagne's persecution particularly hard to bear because of his two-faced attitude toward their existence and traditions. He turned a blind eye to the heathenism of his Slav allies, the Obodrites of modern-day Mecklenburg, and favored them with generous grants of territory evacuated by deporting the native Saxons. From 795 to 804, when the northern Saxons of Holstein submitted, Charlemagne relied increasingly on population deportations to break Saxon

Charlemagne's cavalry had completed the scattering and final dissolution of the Avar supremacy. The huge new 'Pannonian Mark' screening Bavaria and northeast Italy led in time to the consolidation of German Austria.

Charlemagne's surprise coronation by the Pope on Christmas Day 800 led to one of the last wars of his reign. He had no complaint at being crowned emperor but strongly resented the implication that he owed his imperial dignity to the Pope, whose hands had crowned him. It turned out to be an explosive precedent, for the most aggressive of Charlemagne's imperial successors were to find the principle no more congenial and the struggle for supremacy between pope and emperor was destined to brew repeated wars throughout the Middle Ages. Even Napoleon, 1000 years after Charlemagne, would make great play with crowning himself Emperor of the French while the Pope looked on. For Charlemagne, being crowned 'Emperor of the Romans' meant new problems as well as a new title. Until this was recognized by the Byzantine Emperor of 'New Rome' – Constantinople – Charlemagne would look like a barbarian usurper.

In 800 there seemed little chance of such recognition. Constantinople resented and distrusted the new Frankish supremacy in Italy, even though this had been the direct result of the Byzantine failure to give the Roman Papacy effective military aid against the Lombards. Charlemagne tried to improve his bargaining position by making a formal claim to Venice, Istria and Dalmatia, all of which had been subject to the old Western Roman Empire. He finally ordered Pepin of Italy to force the Byzantines' hand by capturing their dependency of Venice. The latter war may be seen as a neat parable on the futility of war. It failed, but this defeat nevertheless gave Charlemagne the objective he wanted. Pepin's failure to capture the islets of Venice in 809-10 enabled Emperor Nicephorus to demand that Charlemagne renounce his claim to Venice, Istria and Dalmatia – in return for formal recognition of Charlemagne's imperial title. After this the Republic of Venice, protected on its islets by the Byzantine navy, was left free to develop under Byzantine patronage.

resistance. By the end of his reign, after immense suffering, this had been achieved and Saxony remained a province of Christian Germany.

When it came to overcoming the opposition of Duke Tassilo of Bavaria, a Christian duchy, Charlemagne had an easier task. Tassilo had to be brought to heel because of frequent border clashes between Bavaria and the River Adige frontier of the Kingdom of Italy where Charlemagne's son Pepin had been installed as king in 781. What beat Tassilo were the earlier victories of Pepin and Charlemagne over the Lombards in Italy which had invested the king of the Franks with the role of the Papacy's sword. The bishops of Bavaria refused to support Tassilo in his continued attempts to reject Frankish suzerainty, and in 787 Tassilo swore formal allegiance to Charlemagne. In the following year Charlemagne coolly accused Tassilo of treason and deprived him of his duchy, using the Byzantine trick of condemning him to become a monk.

Charlemagne's bloodless coup against Tassilo completed the reduction of the eastern German lands which had plagued Frankish Austrasia for the past century. It was accomplished during a lull in the Saxon war and had been preceded (786) by a royal expedition to southern Italy to receive the oath of formal submission from Arichis, Lombard Prince of Benevento. Charlemagne had no ambition to conquer the whole of Italy. He was content to leave the Benevento Lombards as subservient vassals, forming a territorial cushion between the Papal lands in central Italy and the Byzantine enclaves in the extreme south of the peninsula.

The annexation of Bavaria, however, obliged Charlemagne to put an end to the recent spate of Avar raiding against Bavaria and northeast Italy. The Avars had greatly declined since the days when they had terrorized Constantinople a century and a half before; their home territory had been compressed by the rise of the Bulgars on the lower Danube. By the 790s the Avars had little left but the nuisance value of long-range raids but this was considerable – and intolerable. Charlemagne led one Frankish reprisal raid as far as the Raab in 791, then turned the final offensive over to Eric, the 'Mark-Count' (Margrave) of Friuli and the young King Pepin, his deputies in Italy. In 796 Eric crossed the Danube and captured the huge circular encampment which the Avars called the 'Ring,' and which served them as a capital; Pepin took over for the mopping-up in the following year. By 800

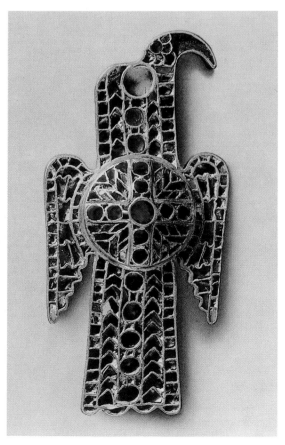

Charlemagne's empire, like that of Alexander, was a unique, over-sized prodigy destined for inevitable partition after his death. The emperor never had any intention of creating a united realm fit for the inheritance of a single heir. Such a bequest was impossible under Frankish custom, which insisted that every son must receive a share of his father's inheritance. The break-up of the empire was accelerated by the reign of his son Louis (814-40), remembered by the significant nickname of 'The Pious.' The mildness of his reign was matched in direct proportion by the fierceness of the rivalry between his sons. The latter was made all the worse by the fact that Louis produced sons by two successive marriages.

The biggest battle of the resultant civil wars took place at Fontenoy (25 June 841). The Emperor Lothar with his Austrasians, supported by Pepin of Aquitaine, tried to break the united opposition of Charles 'The Bald' of Neustria and Louis 'The German' of Saxony, Swabia and Bavaria. This was a stand-up killing match between the levies of the East and West Franks, remembered for a wickedly high casualty list (40,000 men from the two sides combined). It was noted that the worst losses were suffered by the armored nobility who provided the cavalry element – not the unprotected foot, as in so many battles of the later Middle Ages. Thus Fontenoy invites comparison with the carnage of Mursa five centuries before – but whereas Mursa was followed by Constantius' reunification of the Roman Empire, Fontenoy was followed by the formal dissolution of the Carolingian Empire. Mursa had been fought by professional troops, but the rulers of neither the West nor the East Franks, recruiting from the annual *Heerbann* call-up, could contemplate a prolonged war of attrition with losses of such a scale. After a triple partition between Charles, Lothar and Louis at Verdun in 843, a second partition between the West and the East Franks at Meersen in 870 – not 60 years after Charlemagne's death – gave medieval France and Germany their first recognizable joint frontier.

The tactic of annual warfare

Charlemagne's wars pursued relatively limited objectives, in each case with sufficient strength to make defeat highly improbable even if outright victory was not always won in the first year's campaign. Non-stop campaigning was out of the question without a professional standing army, but the increasing reliance on armored cavalry provided a high degree of mobility.

As the Saxon wars proved, a really stubborn enemy left Charlemagne with no choice but to give up or batter away at his objective in repeated campaigns. Waging war in deliberate annual slices, however, left Charlemagne with the strategic flexibility to pursue different objectives on different fronts. The first Spanish campaign, the submission of Benevento, the cowing of Duke Tassilo, the defeat of the Avars and the establishment of the Spanish March – all were interleaved with Charlemagne's top military priority, the conquest of heathen Saxony.

Charlemagne was neither the first nor the last warlord to be strictly a 'land animal.' His lack of sea power in the Mediterranean led to his failure to take Venice and Dalmatia from the Byzantines; and the failure to establish bases for operations along the Channel left a free hand for the Scandinavian fleets which punished the Christian West in the two centuries after his death.

The Viking Phenomenon

The tremendous era of Scandinavian expansion known loosely as the 'Viking Era' spanned the ninth and tenth centuries, faltering and falling away by the second half of the eleventh. Thus the Viking attacks on Christian Europe were a much more prolonged phenomenon than any of the other runaway conquests of the Middle Ages – much longer in duration than, say, the Arab or Mongol conquests. This alone would have rendered the Viking onslaught likely to be remembered more often than most, but there is another obvious reason. The race memory of sheer terror implanted by the Vikings will never wholly die, sublimated though it is today into hackneyed images of hairy blond giants with horns on their helmets, rape, pillage and blood everywhere. With world-famous public exhibitions, archeologists and historians have striven in vain to set the record straight by showing the creative and artistic side of the Viking world. Such efforts invariably tend to be greeted with polite skepticism, almost with disappointment. The race memory is too deep and 'Viking' remains a popular synonym for barbarian greed, cruelty, pillage and blind destruction.

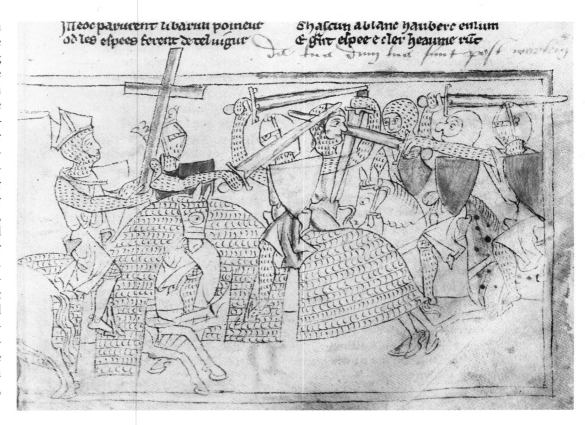

Above: A thirteenth century manuscript illustration showing a scene from the *Chanson de Roland.* Charlemagne is on the right, partly obscured by Bishop Turpin's cross.

Left: The Viking long ship from Oseberg in Norway. Fast, capacious and of very shallow draught, such vessels could cross oceans or explore rivers to penetrate deep inland.

Right: A Viking 'byrnie' of riveted mail links, forming a defense both strong and flexible.

Below right: Detail of the carved prow of the ninth century Oseberg ship.

round the Spanish and Provençal coasts the expedition arrived at the Italian coastal city of Luna, which the Viking leaders Hasteinn and Bjorn mistook for Rome, only to be foiled by the city walls. The sequel was the Viking era's equivalent of the Wooden Horse of Troy. Hasteinn was carried to the city gate as if dead, his comrades asking for the dignity of Christian burial for the 'dead' chief. This was granted – but once Hasteinn's funeral procession was inside the city, Hasteinn sprang from his bier and killed the presiding bishop while his men produced their weapons and proceeded to sack the city. The punchline of this ever-popular Viking epic was the rage of Hasteinn when he discovered that he had not taken Rome after all. Even when allowance is made for embroidery, the story captures all the typical Viking traits of ambition, ingenuity, treachery and ferocity.

At its height the scale of Viking operations outlined above shows that the populations of Norway and Sweden must have been at bursting point for so much manpower to have been on the loose at the same time. If the Gokstad ship – the best-preserved Viking longship – is taken as the norm, we find that it has 16 rowlocks a side, meaning a minimum crew of 32 oarsmen and a steersman for all-round efficiency under oars as well as sail. There is plenty of room for at least ten more, which meant that 40 to 50 men – and all of them fighting men, for the Vikings did not

This is appropriate, for terror was not the least of the Vikings' military stock-in-trade. Their reputation for terror was established right at the beginning of their career, with their first devastating raids on the monastic centers of civilization in Western Europe.

Scandinavian expansion overseas

The overall growth of overseas expansion from Scandinavia took the form of two distinct surges, one in the ninth century and one in the tenth. The second surge followed the same sequence as the first with isolated raids, then attacks by roving armies, then attempts at outright conquest and settlement. Each surge ended with an outer ripple of colonizing voyages across the Atlantic to Iceland around 900, to Greenland in 986 and from Greenland on to 'Vinland' – Newfoundland and probably New England – around 1000. The mastery of the sea which enabled the Scandinavian settlers to cross the Atlantic also enabled their warriors to strike where they chose at an enemy coast, but this was not all. The wonderful versatility of their oared, shallow-draught longships enabled them to penetrate as far up the rivers of Europe as there was enough water in which to float. At this point they would beach their ships, protect them with a rampart and garrison, then take off to ravage the surrounding hinterland before returning to embark with their spoils.

This skill afloat gave the Vikings a tremendous range and choice of targets. In 860, for instance, Viking raiders were active on every river of Francia – Rhine, Scheldt, Somme, Seine, Loire and Garonne – the coastline of Moslem Spain, Provence and Italy, plus the Irish Sea, North Sea and the Channel, whence one raiding army plunged confidently inland to plunder Winchester, capital of the strongest kingdom of Saxon England. It was also in 859-60 that a Viking expedition set out from the mouth of the Loire to enter the Mediterranean and plunder Rome, the 'White Christ's' capital. After looting its way

Left: This early seventh century iron helmet, excavated from the Sutton Hoo ship burial, is clearly derived from the late Roman *spangenhelm.*

Right: Helmet from an eighth century pagan burial at Vendel in Sweden.

Below right: Detail of the carved animal head post found with other artifacts in the Oseberg ship burial.

Charlemagne, vividly captured the horror of the occasion in a famous letter to King Ethelred of Northumbria which included the telling admission 'nor was it thought that such an inroad from the sea could be made.' Alcuin adds that as well as cleaning Lindisfarne out of its Church plate, the raiders also carried off slaves in the form of monastic novices. But in the following year Viking raiders hit Northumbria again, 29 kilometers down the coast at Jarrow. This time, however, they did not get away unscathed. Jarrow monastery was looted, but the raiders ran into local resistance and were badly caught by the weather on an unfamiliar shore. 'One of their leaders was killed there,' records the *Anglo-Saxon Chronicle*, 'and also some of their ships were broken to bits by stormy weather, and many of the men were drowned there. Some reached the shore alive and were immediately killed at the mouth of the river.'

Across the North Sea, Charlemagne was well aware of the menace, quite apart from the remonstrances of Alcuin (who used all his influence to persuade Charlemagne to recover the prisoners taken at Lindisfarne). Charlemagne's arch-enemy Widukind had been sheltered by the Danish King Guthrodr during the Saxon wars. Later Guthrodr not only raided Charlemagne's Obodrite allies but built a defensive rampart across the Schleswig isthmus to keep out the Franks. But in 810 Guthrodr raided the Frisian coast with a fleet of ships numbered at 200 by the Frankish chroniclers. Guthrodr's seaborne army fought three successful engagements with the Frankish forces stationed in Frisia by Charlemagne with an eye to coastal defense, finally demanding a tribute of 100 pounds in silver. This humiliation stung Charlemagne into deploying more land and naval forces along the North Sea

use slave rowers – is a reasonable estimate for a single ship's complement. Even a modest fleet of 20 ships could therefore unleash a raiding force of up to 1000 fighting men, capable of inflicting immense damage in a very short period. Much more important, there was little or nothing that could be done to discourage the first Viking raiders from coming back for more, as likely as not in greater strength once the news of rich and easy pickings had been put about. For there were no patrolling fleets to intercept the raiders at sea and no standing armies which alone could have brought the raiders to rapid action ashore.

Ironically, the first Viking raid on record was an abortive affair. It happened in Saxon England in the year 789 when, according to the *Anglo-Saxon Chronicle*, 'three ships of Northmen' made landfall on the south coast near Portland. They do not seem to have accomplished much; certainly they raided no Church property, for if they had the ecclesiastical records of the day would have lamented the outrage to the heavens. But in nearby Dorchester Beaduheard, the reeve or steward of King Brihtric of Wessex, heard of the strangers' arrival and rode down to the coast to question them. When Beaduheard tried to bring the Vikings to the king's residence, they killed him and re-embarked, possibly disconcerted by so early an appearance by the local authority.

Four years later, however, it was a very different story. In 793 Lindisfarne, the most famous monastery in the English kingdom of Northumbria, was 'miserably destroyed' by 'the ravages of heathen men' (*Anglo-Saxon Chronicle*). The scholar Alcuin, friend and counselor of

Left: The Viking ship from Gokstad in Norway, showing the strong keel and clinker-built construction.

Right: The eighth century Vendel helm.

Below: Grave goods from Vendel. Besides his helmet, the warrior's sword, shield, spear and archery equipment were also found.

In the following year two island monasteries in the Bay of Biscay, Noirmoutier and the Ile de Rhé, were sacked by Vikings.

It was in the 830s, when the Danes at least must have been well aware of the increasing discord between the heirs of Charlemagne, that the tempo of Viking attacks began to accelerate. In 834 a Viking fleet headed up the Rhine and destroyed the rich Frankish trading city of Dorestad which was sacked three more times over the next six years. Danish 'inside information' about the internal troubles of the Franks is understandable enough, but it was equally accurate about affairs in England. There King Egbert of Wessex, overlord of the southern English kingdoms, was campaigning against the 'West Welsh' or Cornishmen. In 836 a Viking fleet of 35 ships suddenly appeared on the coast of Somerset, clearly in support of the Cornishmen. King Egbert intercepted the Viking force at Carhampton and was beaten there – or, as the *Anglo-Saxon Chronicle* puts it, 'the Danes had possession of the battlefield.' Two years later Egbert got his revenge by a resounding defeat of a combined Viking-Cornish force at Hingston Down.

The Viking flood really broke loose in 840, savaging both sides of the Channel. A fleet under Asgeirr drove up the Seine as far as Rouen and St Denis, while the West Saxons won a victory at Southampton, but suffered a later defeat at Portland (possibly against the same fleet). In 841-3 the English suffered raids from the Lincolnshire and East Anglian coast to the Thames estuary and Kent. On the other side of the Channel Quentavic, near Etaples, suffered 'a great slaughter'; Nantes was raided with terrible losses (the city was packed with celebrants for the feast of John the Baptist), and a new Viking base was set up on the now-abandoned monastery island of Noirmoutier.

and Channel coast. They were maintained in the early reign of Louis the Pious and proved their worth in 820, beating off raids on the Flanders coast and the Seine estuary. These were the only occasions in the early eighth century when Vikings were beaten by coast-defense forces specifically deployed to frustrate raiding – but the Frankish victories had no deterrent value at all.

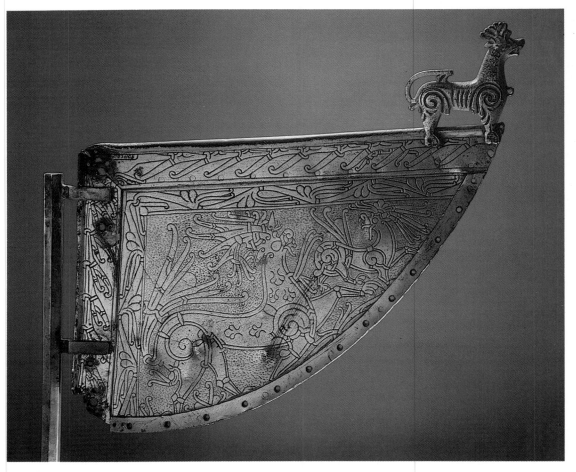

In these years by far the most effective resistance was mounted by the English. Their kingdoms' provinces, known as shires, were governed by *ealdormen* – the equivalent of the Frankish counts – who in emergency raised the shire *fyrd* or levy of freemen. If the king was in the area the resulting force would come under royal command; if not, the *ealdorman* (and, as likely as not, the local bishop as well) would lead the *fyrd* against the enemy. Though the basic *fyrd* armament and deployment was probably little more than a hedge of spears and hatchets, its fighting value was surprisingly high. Of the seven pitched battles fought between Viking armies and Saxon *fyrdmen* between 840 and

851, the *Chronicle* records that the English won four. Such an efficient mobilization of the defense can only have been made possible by an early-warning system. Most likely this took the form of beacon-chains, the value of which for flashing simple warnings over long distances was again surprisingly high. (During the 1977 celebrations of Queen Elizabeth II's Silver Jubilee, the nationwide network of beacons took precisely five minutes to cover the 250 kilometers between Windsor Great Park and Haytor on Dartmoor – and that on a night lashing of rain and generally indifferent visibility.)

By 851, moreover, the West Saxons had made their first successful experiment with coastal sea

patrols. In that year Athelstan, King of Kent and Alfred the Great's eldest brother, took a naval force to sea and captured nine Viking ships in a fight off Sandwich – the first recorded naval victory in English history. None of these English successes, however, prevented the Vikings from converting warfare into an immensely profitable business by exploiting their victims' inability to keep armies in the field indefinitely. In the 840s the Emperor Lothar recruited Viking mercenaries for his wars against his brothers and was the first ruler on record to cede land (the island of Walcheren) in a bid to purchase Viking loyalty. Contrary to popular belief, the English did not invent the sytematized protection money known as *Danegeld*. This was first paid by the West Franks under Charles the Bald in 845, a sum of 7000 pounds of silver; a further payment was extorted in 852.

When looked at as a sort of premature tribute to bribe the enemy to go away, such payments were not unprecedented. What was new was the technique of raising *Danegeld* amounts by a national war-tax, an extraordinary source of royal revenue which outlived the Viking era. This was also pioneered by Charles the Bald: a tax levied on all merchants, churches and farms in 860. Five years later came the first recorded English payment, which incidentally proved that *Danegeld* was by no means a guarantee of immunity. Quailing before a Viking army encamped on the Isle of Thanet, the Kentishmen negotiated a *Danegeld* settlement – but the raiders reneged on the deal and its accompanying truce. 'Under cover of that peace and promise of money the army stole away inland by night and ravaged all eastern Kent,' records the *Chronicle* with a puff of indignation.

The following year, 866, the picture changed completely. To put maximum pressure on the English, previous Viking forces had wintered on the Isle of Thanet in 851 and the Isle of Sheppey in 855; but in 866 a 'great heathen army' landed in East Anglia and established its winter quarters there after extorting a peace and tribute from

Above left: A gilt-bronze masthead vane from a Viking ship, from Heggen in Norway. It is furnished with holes for streamers and metal pendants.

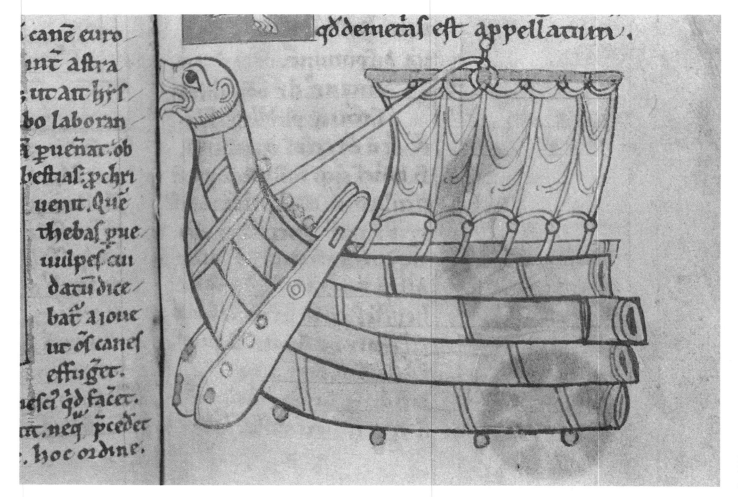

Left: A mid-twelfth century manuscript calendar, showing the stern (with rudder oars) of a Viking ship.

Right: An eleventh century masthead vane from Häisingland, Sweden. These were often reused on churches, hence this survival.

Below right: A *stela* (memorial stone) from Sweden showing the god Odin's eight-legged horse and a square-rigged Viking ship.

King Edmund of the East Angles. This army was led by the sons of the semi-legendary Viking Ragnar Lothbrok, 'Hairy-Breeches,' who had sacked Paris with a fleet of 120 ships back in 845. Terror cloaked their names: Halfdene and Ivar 'The Boneless,' the leading Viking of the age, said to have gristle instead of bone because his father had raped a menstruating woman. Legend had it that Halfdene's and Ivar's motive was to punish the English for the inglorious death of their father, for King Aelle of Northumbria had captured Ragnar and thrown him alive into a snake-pit. Certainly Northumbria and not East Anglia was the principal objective of the 'Great Army's' campaign.

Having spent the winter of 866-7 in rounding up every available horse in East Anglia, the Great Army rode clean across the Midland kingdom of Mercia, crossed the Humber into Northumbria, and headed for its capital, York. The Danish leaders seem to have known that the Northumbrians were currently engaged in a civil war, belatedly suspended by the rival sides to cope with the new joint menace. The Army stormed into York, ensconced itself inside the old Roman walls and shattered the Northumbrian forces which tried to expel the Danes.

For the next ten years the Great Army moved as it pleased, to the pattern established in its first Northumbrian campaign. Each year it moved at great speed to a new region of the island and established fortified winter quarters. The English rulers were forced to dance to the Army's tune, pursuing with armies of *fyrdmen* who objected to long-term service far from home and melted away as each year's harvest time approached. Though the Army's movements were carried out on horse-back it fought on foot, its tactical objective being to lure the English to attack and destruction either against the Danish shield-wall or the fortifications of the army's winter quarters.

The total lack of any effective joint defense agreements between the English kingdoms was the Great Army's biggest asset. Only once did one English kingdom march to the aid of

another. This was in 868, when King Ethelred of Wessex and his brother Alfred led the West Saxon army north to join forces with King Burgred of Mercia. The two armies besieged the Danes in their fortifications at Nottingham, only to let the Army off the hook by making peace and raising the siege as harvest time approached. The piecemeal destruction of the English kingdoms proceeded relentlessly. East Anglia went in 870, Mercia in 874, Northumbria in 875; only Wessex held out. Ethelred and Alfred, who succeeded his brother as king in 871, decided that the only hope was to fight and keep fighting until the Great Army had had enough and left Wessex alone. When the Army invaded Wessex in 871 the West Saxons gave the Danes such fighting as the invaders had never seen since their arrival in England. There were nine field engagements, of which the West Saxons could only claim victory in two. One of these was Ashdown, when Alfred launched a surprise uphill attack with his division of the army, Ethelred only entering the fight – by accident, at the crucial moment – when he had completed his eve-of-battle devotions.

After the rough handling it received in 871 the Great Army left Wessex alone and proceeded to the conquest and initial settlement of East Anglia and the northern kingdoms. In 875 the Army split, one division, Halfdene's, marching north into Northumbria and the other, under Guthrum, remaining in East Anglia. It was Guthrum who attempted the conquest of isolated Wessex in 876-8, leap-frogging farther and farther west

with Alfred's army doggedly pursuing. Guthrum then came within an inch of victory by demonstrating the Viking flair for treachery. He agreed a fake peace with Alfred, evacuated West Saxon territory – then, in the midwinter of 877-8, struck at Alfred's winter residence while the West Saxon host had dispersed for the winter. Alfred escaped to set up a guerrilla base in the Somersetshire marshes at Athelney, then staked everything in a surprise attack of his own with the *fyrd* of only Somerset, Wiltshire and part of Hampshire. Virtually no details are known of the decisive action at Edington on the northern fringe of Salisbury Plain save that it was another day long killing match which ended in a Danish rout, after which Guthrum accepted baptism and agreed to evacuate Wessex.

The defense measures of Alfred the Great

Having agreed a comparatively stable peace with Guthrum and negotiated a settled frontier between Danish-occupied and unoccupied England, Alfred planned a new defense structure for the security of Wessex and its dependencies. By putting the *fyrd* call-up on a rota basis, Alfred ensured that there would always be an English field army able to campaign at any time of the year. Local defense was entrusted to the new system of *burhs*: enclosed and fortified areas in which town and country folk could seek shelter during a Danish attack, holding out behind their defenses until the English field army came to the rescue. For coastal defense Alfred improved on

Above left and above: These memorial stones afford us a glimpse of the visual impact and terror the Viking longships must have instilled in their victims.

Right: Another (particularly fine) eighth century *stela* from Gotland in Sweden.

Left: A sword from the battle site of the Danish victory at Reading in 871.

Below: A *scramasax*, usually a form of knife, but its size indicates that this example was a fighting weapon.

his brother Athelstan's earlier experiment in fighting the Danes at sea, beginning the construction and maintenance of a fleet not only capable of engaging a Danish invasion force at sea but also of supporting the operations of the English land army. He set a heartening example in 882 by taking a squadron to sea and intercepting four longships, two of which surrendered while the crews of the other two fought to the death.

The true versatility of Alfred's defense measures was shown after the tremendous campaigns against the Danish army which crossed to England from France, and marched the length and breadth of the country during the last 15 years of Alfred's reign. Alfred's successor Edward 'The Elder' turned his father's defense system inside out and used it with brilliant economy to reconquer occupied East Anglia and Mercia from the Danes. This was a key chapter in the history of fortification, for Edward used the *burhs* as an offensive, not a defensive weapon. He would start the year with a modest advance into Danish territory, halt and construct a new *burh*, then cram it with a powerful garrison capable of taking the field. The local Danish earl, unable to ignore the new menace in his territory, would gather his forces and try to crush the *burh* – whereupon Edward's field army would advance to catch the Danish army between two fires. If the Danish commander tried to deal with the field army first, the *burh* garrison would sally out for the decisive battle. Thus within 40 years of the near-defeat of Wessex by the Great Army, the English had succeeded in robbing the seaborne invaders of every element of surprise and mobility which had previously served the Vikings so well.

Above left: A silver Carolingian cup found in Denmark, probably traded or looted by the Vikings.

Left: The Lindisfarne Stone from Holy Island, Northumbria (first attacked in 793). These seven warriors are thought to represent Viking raiders.

Right: Vikings attacking a Saxon *burh*, from a twelfth century English manuscript.

Below: A fine Anglo-Saxon silver-inlaid sword, perhaps from one of Alfred's campaigns, found at Abingdon in Berkshire.

Right: The 'Alfred Jewel,' an Anglo-Saxon enameled gold masterpiece bearing the inscription 'Alfred had me made,' from Athelney Monastery, Somerset.

For the West Franks as for the English, the last two and a half decades of the ninth century were the worst. The Vikings' elusiveness and speed of movement, plus their excellence in fighting as close-order infantry, largely canceled out the Frankish advantage in being able to field armored cavalry. The Franks, moreover, failed to produce national leaders of the high caliber of Alfred of England. It was in the reign of Charles 'The Simple' (893-923) that the Norse leader Rolf extracted the cession of Normandy from the Frankish crown.

The middle tenth century was the eye of the hurricane. Settled dynasties brought a new measure of security to the Norwegian and Danish homelands, while the powerful new English kingdom successfully broke the attempts of Norse adventurers from Ireland to rule as kings in York. The last of these Viking kings of York, Eric 'Bloodaxe,' was a thoroughgoing

67

Viking warrior born a century too late. He would have been perfectly at home in the middle ninth century; to the Northumbrian people he tried to rule, he was a jarring anachronism in the middle tenth. But the very prosperity enjoyed by the English in the tenth century proved their undoing. The revival of trade, culture and monastic learning was paid for by an inevitable softening of the taut readiness which had characterized the English under Alfred and Edward.

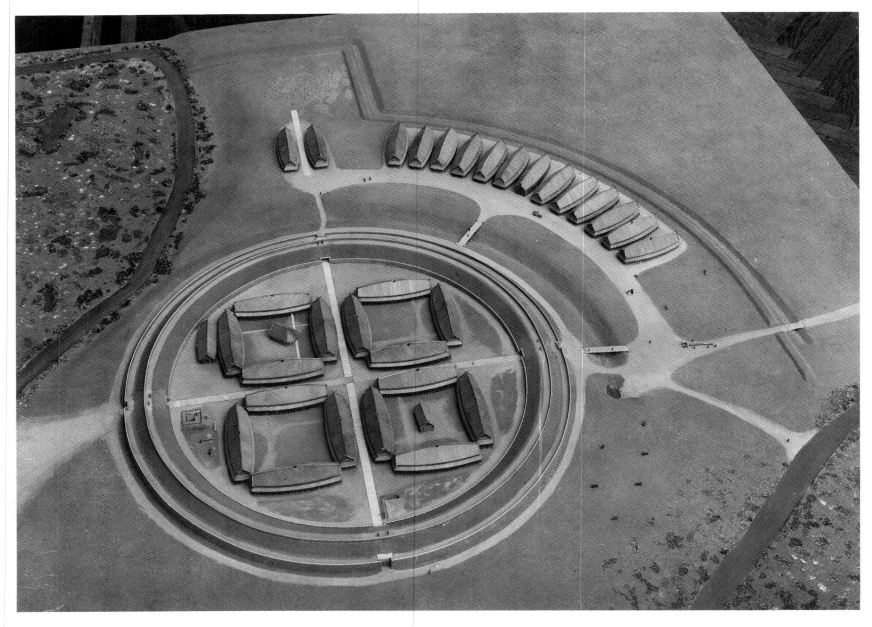

Renewed Viking attacks on England during the feckless reign of Ethelred 'Evil-Counsel' (978-1016) encountered a rich and ill-defended land ruled by a coward who would rather pay *Danegeld* than fight. The cycle of increasingly heavy raids began again. Ethelred's supreme act of folly was to order a massacre of Danes in the eastern shires of England – the 'Danelaw,' as it was known – whom he regarded as potential fifth columnists (1002). This prompted King Sweyn 'Forkbeard' of Denmark to launch a series of reprisal campaigns in England, finally (1013) driving Ethelred into exile in Normandy. Ethelred was recalled when Sweyn died in 1014, and the next two years passed in a breathtaking duel up and down the country between the massive Danish forces loyal to Sweyne's son, Cnut, and the English led by Ethelred's son, Edmund 'Ironside'. Edmund's own death in November 1016 left the English magnates with no choice but to submit to Cnut as their new king.

It was Cnut who demonstrated that the Viking era of conquest and terror was drawing to its close. King of England as well as Denmark, the unchallenged overlord of the Scandinavian world, he nevertheless astonished all Europe by developing as a devout Christian monarch able to talk on equal terms with pope and emperor. Having paid off his armies and sent them home, he reduced the size of the fleet and refused to treat England as a financial milch cow for the benefit of Denmark. When he died in 1035 the heyday of the Viking raider, enemy of mankind, already seemed remote.

Far left: A silver penny (face and reverse) of King Ethelred of Wessex, made in the Canterbury Mint, *c*870.

Left: A bronze former used to make decorative silver plaques for helmets from the eighth century.

Above right: The front and back of a Viking shield from Gokstad showing its construction.

Left: Model of the Trelleborg Viking camp in Denmark.

Right: The detail of the carved wooden portal from Hylestad church in Norway depicts Regin the Smith reforging the sword of Sigurd's father (twelfth century).

The 'invincible' Vikings

As with the Arabs, the Vikings profited greatly from the inability of their victims to mount a sufficiently mobile and long-term defense. Like the Japanese in Word War II, the Vikings won a spurious reputation for invincibility with their early successes; but their attacks on Church property, horrifying though they were, did not mean that the Vikings shared the Arabs' religious drive. The tough heathenism of Scandinavia instilled contempt rather than hatred toward the milder precepts of Christianity; a well-endowed monastery spelled loot galore and zero resistance – any pirate's dream.

Viking armies invariably operated from a fortified base and only fought when they had to. Requisitioning horses gave their armies high mobility across country but the Vikings fought on foot, their speciality being the tight-packed shield-wall, preferably on high ground. They were adept at choosing positions where cavalry attacks were difficult if not impossible and were able to cope with the Franks' armored cavalry.

Despite their ferocity and skill in combat Vikings were by no means invincible but they were amazingly resilient, being seldom if ever persuaded to withdraw from their chosen victims' land by isolated defeats. The only way of 'seeing them off' was determined and sustained resistance, forcing the invaders to fight repeatedly without easy profit. Even this was only a partial solution, for there was never any guarantee that fresh invaders would not renew the menace. Alfred of Wessex saved his kingdom from Guthrum in 877-8, yet 20 years later his reign approached its close amid four desperate years of non-stop campaigning against the enemy of Haesten. Under Alfred and Edward the English discovered the way to recover Danish-occupied territory by the planting of fortified *burhs* and limited offensives by a rota-based field army. But a mere 80 years later the English also discovered that too long a period of peace, prosperity and run-down defenses is a sure-fire recipe for national disaster.

Left: A twelfth century manuscript illumination from Bury St Edmunds (Suffolk) of the martyrdom of King Edmund in AD 870.

One of the Vikings' most impressive attributes was the excellence of their intelligence. Their raids on Francia in the 840s coincided perfectly with the wars between Charlemagne's grandsons. In England the Great Army of 866 neatly exploited the chronic lack of joint defense preparations between the Anglo-Saxon kingdoms, while the Army's first offensive in England

Left: King Edmund martyred by the Danes; a fifteenth century wall painting in Pickering church, Yorkshire. The Vikings had a strong tradition of archery.

Right: A mounted warrior in the Viking tradition, from a thirteenth century tapestry fragment found in Baldishol church, Norway.

Below: A Viking sword made in England (or influenced by English craftsmanship) but found in Skane, Norway. It dates from about the year 1000.

Below right: This figure on a tenth century Anglian cross from Middleton in North Yorkshire represents a Viking warrior as laid out for a pagan burial with his weapons.

caught Northumbria right in the middle of a civil war. The renewed Danish attacks on England at the close of the tenth century similarly exploited the reign of an abnormally unwarlike and vacillating king. Both in England and in Francia, Viking leaders learned that the deadliest moment to strike was just after the harvest, when the winter food stocks had been gathered and most rulers were desperate to pay *Danegeld* rather than see their lands (and revenues) destroyed by famine. Conversely, as the summer months wore on, a Viking army on campaign knew that the opposition was bound to dwindle as harvest time approached and the Christian part-time soldiers went home to their fields.

By the middle of the eleventh century, however, Scandinavian rulers had lost this intuitive sense of timing, and seemed no longer to possess accurate information about their enemies' strengths and weaknesses. The abortive invasions of England by Harold Hardraada in 1066 and by Sweyn of Denmark in 1067-71 were sorry affairs compared to the onslaught of the previous two centuries.

Perhaps the most fascinating contrast in the entire Viking era is that between the Danes in eastern England and the Norsemen in northern France. The former were reconquered and absorbed into a new English kingdom; the latter retained a defiant individualism destined eventually to conquer its way to the Holy Land. Had it been the Franks who reconquered Normandy instead of the Saxons who reconquered the Danelaw, the history of medieval Europe would have followed a totally different course.

The Normans

The unique history of the Normans began in the year 911 with a treaty between an embattled Carolingian king and a Viking chieftain. The Carolingian king was Charles 'The Simple,' ruler of the West Franks or French; the Viking chieftain was Rolf 'The Ganger,' one of the most powerful raiders operating along the west Channel coast.

The treaty was agreed at St Clair-sur-Epte on a tributary of the lower Seine. It was a formal grant to Rolf (or 'Rollo,' as the Franks called him) of the *Deuxième Lyonnaise* – the province of Rouen, subsequently extended westward to include the Cotentin peninsula. Rolf was given Charles' daughter in marriage, and for the price of swearing homage to Charles became the effective ruler of his new lands. All this was a typical piece of *realpolitik* thrown up by the long Viking wars, in that Charles was buying the services of a tough new ally who he hoped would be capable of repelling future Viking attacks where Charles himself could not. In fact there was little of novelty in the deal. Just as Charlemagne had done, Charles needed a powerful buffer between central France and Brittany. By handing the *Deuxième Lyonnaise* over to Rolf and his followers, Charles was getting up a 'Northman's Mark' intended to contain the Bretons as well as shield Paris from more Viking attacks. Whether he realized it or not, Charles was also following a tradition dating back over 500 years to the Roman emperors of the fourth century by permitting a limited settlement of barbarians in order to keep more barbarians out. Thus Rolf the Ganger was not only the first duke of Normandy, he was the last of the great barbarian *federati*.

The Norman gift of adaptation

In 911 there was no reason to believe that Rolf's enlistment as a Frankish ally and nominal subject would bring more than temporary relief to a battered and increasingly anarchic kingdom. No previous agreement with *federati* had remained stable for long – but this one did. The Norse and Danish settlers in Norway were able to bring in all the reinforcements they needed from home (mostly from Denmark); but as Viking expansionism continued to wane the settlers were not subjected to sustained pressure from other would-be conquerors. Moreover the Normans, as descendants of Rolf and his original band are known, turned out to have an uncanny knack of making things work, usually to their own advantage. The essence of their achievement in the tenth and early eleventh centuries was a highly efficient amalgam of all that was best in the Scandinavian and Frankish social and military orders. Precisely how the Normans did this will never be known; the course of policy they followed was never chronicled in detail at the time. But the fact remains that by the time Cnut died in 1035 the Normans were already emerging as the most aggressive and efficient soldiers in the world.

A list of the main ingredients in the 'Norman formula' reads as follows. Along with the language of the West Franks, the Normans rapidly adopted the Frankish aristocratic structure of counts holding land from the duke, and owing him military service in return. Also from the Franks, the Normans learned all the advantages of fighting as well as riding to battle on horseback, developing a cavalry capable of fighting on foot if necessary.

This cavalry was formed by the knights, whose small manorial holdings (*feoda* or 'fees') formed the broad base of the landholding pyramid with the duke at its peak. The knight's manorial revenue paid for the weapons and equipment not only of himself but of the men he was required to bring to his lord's service on request. The most expensive single item of equipment was the mail-armor *hauberk* of linked iron rings, a long-sleeved tunic ending in a loose skirt at the knees which could be fastened securely behind each knee with straps. The better-off could afford the additional expense of mail extensions for the lower leg (*chausses*). A *coif* or 'balaclava helmet' of mail protected the head and neck beneath the simple conical helmet with its jutting *nasal* or nose-guard. But armor, once obtained, could be handed down from father to son and was only one of the expenses which a knight was expected to meet.

Almost as important was the warhorse or *destrier*. The mount was a highly-trained beast, fed when possible on expensive grain fodder to keep him in peak condition. A knight whose *destrier* could not be relied upon to run straight and wheel at the precise moment of command, time after time regardless of fatigue, was a useless liability on a battlefield. The *destrier* provided the solid platform for the knight's attack which usually took two main forms. There was the shock attack, pressed right home with the lance couched or tucked firmly under the knight's right arm; and the missile attack, a galloping approach followed by a volley of javelins at the enemy line before wheeling and retiring.

Apart from the lance or javelin the Norman knight's main weapon, in the saddle or on foot,

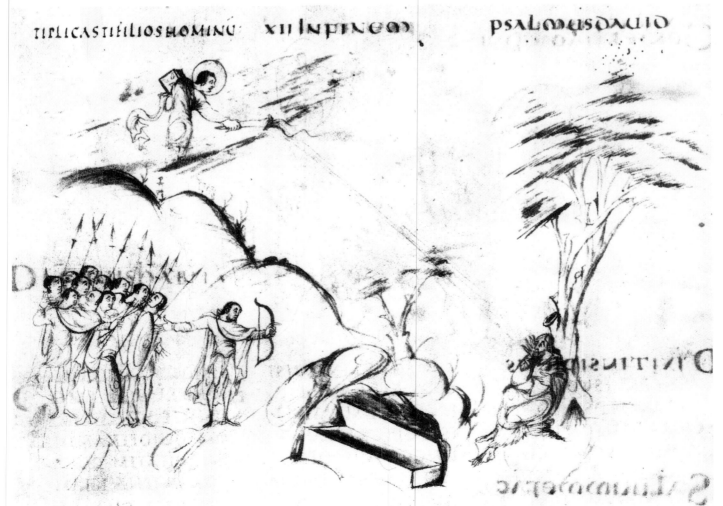

Left: A page from the *Utrecht Psalter* (c832) depicting the Resurrection of Christ; note the Carolingian-style winged spears and the short bow.

Above right: The castle of Dinan in Brittany surrenders to William of Normandy, and Harold is knighted by the ceremonial bestowal of arms. Both are scenes from the Bayeux Tapestry, worked after 1077.

Right: Norman knights outside Rennes, the fortified capital of Brittany. The Bayeux Tapestry is a primary source for our knowledge of the military equipment and strategy of the Norman Conquest.

was the heavy tapering longsword, a direct legacy of the Viking wars. Here was the most natural marriage between Viking and Frankish custom, because the two cultures produced the best swords in the world (as acknowledged by Arab sources). Viking swords were not only works of art, they also were the products of high technology, laminated from bars of various strengths of iron and steel to provide great strength in all climatic conditions. (A modern analysis of one of these longswords showed that it had been forged from 58 separate pieces.)

Another blend of Viking and Frankish military custom was shown by the Norman use of infantry archers to supplement the infantry spearman line. Though the Vikings only drew their bows to the chest and not 'all the way' to the ear, they produced skilled marksmen, and the so-called 'Danish' bow remained a standard weapon throughout the tenth and eleventh centuries. The Danish bow, however, had a notably short range and it could not be relied upon (as modern tests have shown) to penetrate mail at ranges over 45 meters. This forced a secondary

role on the foot archer, who was forced to shelter behind the mass of the shield-wall against charging cavalry or even infantry armored with the shorter *hauberk* or *byrnie*. Operating out in the open at such short range spelled suicide for the archer, who would hardly have time to let off one arrow before the enemy was on him. In the tenth century, however, an answer to the problem was found in the crossbow.

Thanks almost entirely to the reputation later established by the English longbow, the crossbow remains one of the most misunderstood weapons of all time, not just of the Middle Ages. It consisted of a short laminated bow of great strength, mounted horizontally on a stock, and capable of firing a heavy bolt in an accurate flat trajectory at ranges beyond the capability of orthodox stave or composite bows. Like the early musket, the crossbow was a heavy weapon which could be used as a club when its ammunition ran out, a decided advantage over the bow. The crossbow principle had been used in siege artillery throughout the Greek, Roman and early Byzantine eras. Details of its first use in the West

as a one-man infantry weapon are unknown, but it made its first appearance in Frankish use in the early tenth century, apparently in long-range sniping during sieges of walled towns. Crossbows are recorded at the siege of Senlis in 949 and again at Verdun in 985.

The crossbow's deficiencies were obvious enough. It demanded more strength, and took far longer to cock and fire than any bow; its rate of fire was necessarily low; wet weather slackened its string and made it useless. But the crossbow did not require months of practice before its user could be certain of hitting the target, and for all its faults it remained for over 500 years the standard infantry weapon against armored troops at long range. This makes the crossbowman the medieval ancestor of the modern infantryman capable of knocking out a tank with a rocket missile. It goes without saying that the crossbow's range and punch were almost immediately appreciated by the Normans, and a squad of crossbowmen became one of the best contributions a Norman knight could make to the feudal levy.

If the crossbow was of Frankish derivation, the Norman development of the castle was an unmistakable product of the Viking wars. Time and again, English and Frankish assailants had recoiled baffled from the banks and palisades with which Viking armies protected their base camps on campaign. Continental defenders of the walled cities had learned that the best way of frustrating a marauding army was to sit out repeated sieges until the army had eaten up the surrounding countryside's supplies and had to move on. As the English had discovered during their reconquest of the Danelaw, establishing a fortified base to dominate a chosen region was the ideal preliminary to a permanent occupation of the area.

It is at least possible that Rolf and his Normans began to consider the implications of this from a very early date. Normandy was a natural refuge for dispossessed Danes who chose to go overseas once their former territory in the Danelaw had been overrun by Edward the Elder's lengthening chain of *burhs*. We know from the *Anglo-Saxon Chronicle* that in 916, after

Above: Edward the Confessor is throned (left) while Harold Godwinson leads a hunting party (right).

Left: Henry II (AD 1154-89) as depicted on his Great Seal.

Edward had advanced into Essex and planted his latest *burh* at Maldon, the Danish earl Thurcetel 'went across the sea to France along with the men who were willing to serve him.' It is not too fanciful to picture Thurcetel in Rolf's hall, telling the founder of Normandy how the English had contrived an irresistible method of winning wars by controlling terrain.

Early Norman castle design

Whether or not it was developed in deliberate imitation of the English *burhs*, the classic Norman defense complex – the *motte-and-bailey* castle – served precisely the same purpose. The basic idea was to defend an outer perimeter which enclosed an area taking up at least half of the overall ground plan. This outer area, the bailey, acted like a watertight safety compartment in a ship's bottom. If an attack proved too strong for the castle garrison to hold the bailey perimeter, the surviving defenders withdrew up a wooden catwalk into the inner, main defensive area, the keep. To the Danes who settled in Normandy this idea of an outer bailey and inner keep

Right: The reverse side of Henry II's Great Seal shows him equipped as a Norman knight.

Below: The Bayeux Tapestry's depiction of the difficulties of embarkation aboard Viking-style ships.

would have been familiar; the massive ramparts of the late Danish camp at Trelleborg on the flat island of Zeeland clearly follow the same format. But the Norman motte-and-bailey was designed to give attackers an uphill fight, even when the castle had to be sited on the flat. The soil from the ditch surrounding the castle was used to make a motte or mound (or add to the height of the knoll at the chosen site), on top of which stood the keep. The motte provided an all-round view of the fortifications, and enabled archers and crossbowmen to shoot down at enemies who had penetrated the defenses. The Bayeux Tapestry, that invaluable documentary of the eleventh-century Norman war machine in action, has a scene of a motte being thrown up for a Norman castle at Hastings.

But the Tapestry not only shows castles, it also demonstrates how the Normans attacked them. The scene of the Norman assault on Dinan castle is particularly explicit. The most vulnerable point of the defenses is the long catwalk or bridge connecting the outer bailey gate with the keep on its motte. While squadrons of Norman

knights gallop up the castle's approach ramp and keep up a distracting hail of javelins, two dismounted knights in armor creep up the motte and set fire to its encircling palisade with torches.

It is in England that most examples have survived of how imaginative the Normans could be when it came to siting castles. At Porchester and Pevensey, for instance, they used the massive curtain wall of the old Roman 'Saxon Shore' fortress as the bailey perimeter, siting the keep in a corner. Father inland, at Old Sarum, they used the much earlier ring of the Iron Age hill fort as the bailey perimeter and sited the keep plumb in the center, like the bull's eye of a target. But this flexible approach was not merely an intelligent use of existing facilities, it was yet another direct throwback to earlier Viking practice. The Great Army of 866, for instance, had readily dug its own defenses when it had to, but had been equally swift to make use of earlier defenses such as the Roman city walls of York and Exeter. In their typical fashion, the Normans applied superior method to established ideas in fortification; they no more 'invented' the castle than they

created the medieval English monarchy.

In its first 90 years of existence Normandy had the luck to to be ruled by four powerful dukes in a row: Rolf (911-27), William *Longespée* or 'Longsword' (927-42), Richard I (942-96) and Richard II (996-1026). In the same period neighboring France went through eight reigns and a change of dynasty, the latter being established with the accession of Hugh Capet, supported by Duke Richard I of Normandy, in 987. The internal disarray of the French kingdom naturally worked to Normandy's advantage, but although the absorption of French influences continued apace (with Duke Richard I marrying Hugh Capet's sister), its ties with the Scandinavian homeland were not severed. When Viking attacks on England began again in the 980s enough of the raiders were given temporary hospitality in Normandy for Anglo-Norman relations to be frayed to breaking point. By 990 Pope John XV was moved to negotiate a peace treaty between England and Normandy which, when signed at Rouen in March 991, provided that in future neither the English king nor the Norman

Above: Mounted Norman knights finally break through the English 'shield wall' at Hastings.

Left: As shown in this Bayeux Tapestry scene, William's first concern upon landing in England was to erect a wooden motte-and-bailey castle.

duke should entertain the other's enemies. In the year 1000, however, the Danish fleet which had spent the previous year punishing southeast England passed the summer in Normandy before heading across the Channel to ravage the western shires. It was in hopes of preventing future Norman assistance to Danish armies that Ethelred of England married Emma, sister of Duke Richard II, in 1002. For the duke's sister to marry the king of England was a splendid dynastic coup for Normandy, showing how rapidly the duchy was climbing in the 'pecking order' of Western Europe by the early eleventh century. Like the founding treaty of St Claire-sur-Epte back in 911, the English marriage of 1002 was a move of immediate benefit to both parties, and little more. There was no way of knowing that within 50 years the Norman ducal line would, thanks to the marriage of Ethelred and Emma, be a strong contender for the throne of England itself.

The Normans in Italy

By the time that Ethelred and his son Edmund died in 1016, leaving the field free for the unopposed accession of Cnut in England, the population of Normandy was rising fast. The feudal share out of manors in Normandy had reached saturation point and there was a definite surplus of fighting men itching for land of their own to conquer. It was in this year, 1016, that a party of Norman pilgrims to the Mediterranean returned to the duchy with electrifying news – the growing opportunities for good fighters in Italy.

In 1016 Italy south of the Papal States was a seven-ring circus of interstate wars between principalities, duchies and city-states struggling either for independence or for the subjection of their nearest rival. The Byzantine Greeks of Calabria claimed traditional rule over the Lombards of Apulia, who were prepared to fight for independence with the help of the Lombard principalities of Salerno, Capua and Benevento. At the same time the Holy Roman Empire of Germany and the Papacy repeatedly used southern Italy as a battleground in their long-standing quarrel over temporal supremacy. In short,

southern Italy was a happy hunting ground for landless mercenaries willing to switch allegiances at the drop of a hat, and for the next half century there was a steady flow of military emigrants from Normandy to the Mediterranean.

The men who went to Italy were usually younger sons with no hope of inheriting their father's manor in Normandy, if the manor was too small to be divided among a number of sons. Thus the otherwise totally undistinguished Tancred de Hauteville, whose manor lay in the Cotentin peninsula, sired four counts and one duke of Apulia, one count of Sicily and a

daughter who became countess of Aversa. (The highest climbing de Hauteville was Tancred's grandson Bohemond, destined to lead the Italian Normans in the First Crusade and become Prince of Antioch.) All this came to pass within decades of the first Norman appearance in southern Italy in 1017, when a force of some 250 Normans fought for the rebel Apulians against the Byzantine general Boioannes. It was not a promising debut. The Normans ended up on the losing side at, of all places, Cannae, site of Hannibal's murderous defeat of the Romans in 216 BC. But a single defeat was nothing. There were

Above right: Old Sarum in Wiltshire, where an Iron Age fort was used as the site for a Norman castle.

Right: The curtain walls of Porchester in Hampshire, where the Normans utilized the existing Roman fortifications for their own castle.

plenty of alternative employers for Norman swords, defeat only meant more profitable service with the winning side, and the Norman mercenaries stayed on. By the late 1020s the acknowledged Norman leader in Italy, Rannulf, was milking the endemic hostility between the dukes of Naples and the princes of Capua. The breakthrough came in 1029 when Duke Sergius of Naples created Rannulf 'Count of Aversa' as an incentive to help Naples against Capua. The Normans had won their first solid territorial gain in Italy and the result, once the news reached Normandy, was a rush of Norman adventurers eager to match and surpass Rannulf's achievement.

By 1040 the leadership of the landless Normans in Italy had passed to the de Hauteville brothers: William, the eldest, Drogo, Humphrey and Robert nicknamed *Guiscard*, 'The Crafty.' After a spell of mercenary service under the Byzantines, the de Hautevilles reverted to championing the cause of the Apulian Lombards against the Byzantines. At Monte Maggiore in 1041, 700 Norman knights and about 1300 foot soldiers tackled the main Byzantine field army of Apulia. The Byzantines apparently had a comfortable advantage in numbers and were relying on their armored infantry, which included units of the elite Byzantine 'Viking foreign legion', the Varangian Guard. The Normans allowed the Byzantines to deploy into two lines, then launched a head-on charge in separate, narrow-wedge formations. The shock of the Norman charge broke clean through the front line and drove on to scatter the second. Having thus destroyed the sole instrument of Byzantine power in Apulia, the triumphant de Hautevilles were soon accepted as the new rulers with William becoming the first Norman 'Count of Apulia' in 1043. The title then passed to brother Drogo (1046-51) and on to Humphrey (1051-7).

But the Apulian Lombards had not bargained for the ferocious efficiency of the Normans, not just as soldiers but as rulers. Under Count Humphrey, driven mad by tax collectors who not only demanded payment in full and on time, but who could not be bribed either, the Apulians revolted again. Led by Argyrus, son of the rebel Melo who had first appealed to the Normans for armed assistance back in 1016, the Apulians placed the city of Benevento under the suzerainty of Pope Leo IX, and appealed to the Pope to liberate them. Leo arranged a joint expedition with the Byzantine court, whose forces were to march up from the Byzantine ports of Bari and Brindisi, while his own army of Italo-Lombard horse and foot, including 700 Swabian infantry mercenaries from the Empire, invaded Norman Apulia from the Papal States. Pope Leo had been correct in diagnosing the menace of growing Norman power in the south, but had no idea of the energy with which Norman leaders reacted under pressure. Count Humphrey's reply to the Papal-Byzantine pincers thus raised against him was to concentrate all available Norman forces in Apulia and Aversa and strike a decisive blow at the Papal army before the Byzantines could intervene in the campaign.

At Civitate (1053) Count Richard of Aversa, Count Humphrey and Richard Guiscard led the three divisions of Norman cavalry against the isolated Papal army. Richard's division emulated the shattering charge which had broken the Byzantines at Monte Maggiore and drove the Italo-Lombard main body clean off the field. But the Swabian mercenaries stood firm in close for-

mation, hewing at the cavalry of William and Robert which shrank from forcing its way among the Swabian two-handed swords. Only when Richard rallied his division and returned to the battlefield did the scales tip decisively in the Normans' favor. They would have been only too pleased to accept the Swabians' surrender and enlist them – but the Swabians' attitude toward oaths of loyalty, not to mention the awe at fighting under the Papal banner, lacked the inimitable flexibility of the Norman mind, and the Swabians' chose to fight to the death. It was a drawn-out killing match the like of which no Norman army was to see until Hastings 13 years later, when Norman cavalry charges would again be frustrated by resolute infantry.

Civitate marked the end of the second stage of the Norman advance in Italy, for the victors captured Pope Leo. Though treated with deep respect he was not released until he had recognized Richard and Humphrey as Counts of Aversa and Apulia. Over the next four years Richard and Humphrey both vigorously expanded their domains while the younger de Hautevilles, Robert Guiscard and Roger, embarked on the conquest of Calabria. No sooner had Guiscard replaced Humphrey as Count in 1057 than he obtained a marriage annulment from the new Pope, Nicholas II, enabling him to dispose of his Norman wife (who had already borne Guiscard a son, Bohemond). Thus unencumbered, Guiscard married the Lombard Princess Sigelgaita, sister of the childless Gisulf of Salerno. Business was equally good for Richard of Aversa. In 1058 he took Capua. At Melfi in 1059 Pope Nicholas formally invested Richard as Prince of Capua, and Guiscard as Duke of Apulia, Calabria and Sicily – the latter of which, held by the Moslems, had still to be conquered.

If Pope Nicholas hoped that Guiscard's new honors would tempt the Norman adventurer to overreach himself, the Melfi settlement must be considered a classic example of papal fallibility. Guiscard and Roger began the conquest of Sicily with a landing in 1060 and the capture of Messina in the following year. The Norman reduction of Sicily was a prolonged affair, repeatedly suspended by revolts on the part of Guiscard's vassals on the mainland, few of whom were prepared to accept the paramountcy of the upstart

Above left: A coin of Roger I, the Norman conqueror of Sicily, who died in 1101. He is shown as a Norman knight like those depicted in the Bayeux Tapestry.

Left: An early eleventh century carved ivory plaque of St Demetrius. He wears a *hauberk* of overlapping scales with sleeves and skirt of lamellar armor.

Right: Christ crowning Roger II, King of Sicily; a Byzantine twelfth century mosaic in a Sicilian church.

nothing less than the conquest of the Byzantine Empire.

The Byzantine failure to crush or even check the Norman adventurers in Italy was the symptom of an overall imperial decline from a peak not attained since the glory days of Heraclius four centuries before. Under the formidable Macedonian dynasty of emperors, the Byzantines had restored their sea power and *themata*-based army in the tenth century, recovering Crete, Cyprus, Cilicia and even northern Syria with Antioch in the 960s. Under Basil II *Bulgaroktonos* ('The Bulgar-Slayer') the Byzantines had crushed the Bulgarian Empire during his long reign (976-1025), restoring the ancient Balkan-lower Danube frontier of the Eastern Roman Empire.

After Basil II, however, the military supremacy of the Byzantine Empire began to crack under a scatter of brief-reigning emperors whose best generals held the Balkan frontier but were unable to retain southern Italy. Far more serious was the conquest of Iran and Iraq by the Seljuk Turks (1037-55) and the new vitality and energy which they inspired in Moslem Asia. The Seljuk ascendancy was an oriental mirror-image of Christian Western feudalism: aggressive, good at administration and above all based on landholding in return for military service. It was, in short, conquest-hungry. The first Seljuk overlord of Islam, Tughril Beg, was proclaimed Sultan at Baghdad in 1055; his successor Alp Aslan (1063-72) began to launch punishing raids on the eastern *themata* of the Byzantine Empire. Thus by 1070 the Byzantines were caught in the middle, between the Latin Christian Normans and the Moslem Turks – with the difference that as long as Constantinople could buy enough mercenary sea power to command the Adriatic, the Normans could be held in Italy. The Seljuk Turks, on the other hand, represented the same threat to Asia Minor which the Arabs had posed in the last years of Heraclius.

In 1071 the Emperor Romanus Diogenes, after prodigious efforts, raised an enormous host of regular troops and mercenaries to meet the Turkish menace head-on. On 19 August 1071 one of the decisive battles of the Middle Ages was fought at Manzikert, when the disorganized and ill-deployed Byzantine forces were cut to pieces on an open plain by Alp Aslan's Turkish cavalry. Romanus, surrounded in the center with the best of his regular troops, was betrayed by Andronikos Ducas, who deliberately withdrew with the Byzantine reserve instead of supporting the emperor. The result was the slaughter of the Byzantine Empire's regular army – a disaster with precisely the same results as those of Hadrianopolis 700 years before. The subsequent loss of Anatolia to the Seljuks

de Hautevilles. Guiscard was also completing the conquest of southern Apulia by attacking Brindisi and Bari, the last Byzantine-held ports on the Italian mainland, both of which fell to him in 1071.

To the repeated dismay of his legions of enemies, Guiscard only increased in cunning, ambition and confidence as he grew older. When Pope Gregory VII tried to bring him to heel by excommunication in 1074, Guiscard seized Salerno from Gisulf and took over the papal fief of Benevento. Jordan of Capua sided with the Pope against Guiscard in 1079, only to be beaten with ease by Guiscard with his handful of knights and mercenaries paid for with years of loot. But in June 1080 Guiscard renewed his homage to the Pope. He needed the papal sanction for the most grandiose project of his life –

Right: The Norman conquest of England and the Battle of Hastings (1066).

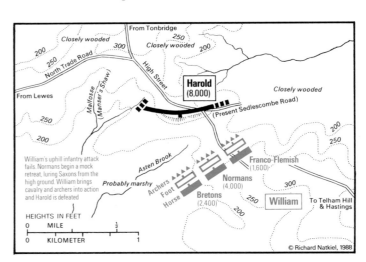

deprived the Empire of its vital recruiting grounds in southeast Asia Minor and forced it to rely on mercenary and allied troops.

To Robert Guiscard in southern Italy, Manzikert and its aftermath offered a unique opportunity. There were only two emperors in the whole of Christendom, the German and the Greek. The German emperor had already been proved incapable of ousting the Normans from southern Italy; if the Normans could cross to the Balkans and beat the Greek emperor's mercernaries there, there would be nothing to stop Guiscard from marching direct on Constantinople. While Roger de Hauteville continued to grind away at the Moslems in Sicily, Guiscard and his son Bohemond invaded Epiros with an army between 15,000 and 18,000 strong, of which the contingent of Norman knights amounted to the usual strength of less than ten percent. After taking the island of Corfu the Normans' first objective on the mainland was Durazzo, the ancient Roman city of Dyrrachium where Julius Caesar had besieged Pompeius in similar circumstances during the Roman Civil War of 48 BC. Playing Pompeius to Guiscard's Caesar was the new Byzantine emperor Alexius Comnenus, like the de Hautevilles a capable leader of mercenary-based armies, who scraped together an army of about 70,000 to throw the Italo-Normans back into the sea. This included a powerful contingent of the axemen of the Varangian Guard – elite armored infantry, all Scandinavian in origin, who rode to the battlefield but dismounted to fight.

Alexius' attempt to raise the siege of Durazzo nearly succeeded because of the refusal of the Norman cavalry to charge home against the well-drilled Varangians; but the latter advanced too far and were cut off from the Byzantine main body by Bohemond's cavalry wing. While the threat of his knights forced the Varangians to hold their position in close order, Bohemond brought up his crossbows and shot the splendid guardsmen to pieces. Alexius, however, recovered well from his defeat at Durazzo. His agents in Italy encouraged another revolt by Guiscard's vassals, and Guiscard returned to Italy to cope with the rebels. Bohemond remained to face Alexius. The Emperor survived numerous defeats, and for the next three years the rival assortments of mercenaries marched and countermarched in northern Greece. Alexius' best card was his retention of the mercenary services of the Venetian navy which imperiled Bohemond's communications with Italy – but the Byzantines were also helped by Bohemond's obsession with taking Macedonia and Thessaly as his own private domains before marching on Constantinople.

Guiscard meanwhile reduced the Apulian rebels only to be called upon to help Pope Gregory against the German Emperor, Henry IV, who had occupied Rome. In midwinter 1082, by

Left: A page from the *Chronicle of Petrus de Eboli*, depicting the forces of the Emperor Henry VI (1190-97) laying siege to Naples. Note the importance accorded to archery (including the crossbow) as well as cavalry.

Below: William the Conqueror's invasion fleet sails for England, a scene from the Bayeux Tapestry.

a unique coincidence both emperors of Christendom were in simultaneous retreat before the de Hauteville warlords, Henry before Guiscard in Italy, and Alexius before Bohemond in Greece. Guiscard's last coup in the imperial-papal war was to take Rome (1048) which he characteristically treated to an appalling sack. Guiscard had already resumed the Byzantine war when he died in July 1085, and Alexius was saved again by Bohemond's speedy return to dispute Apulia with his half-brother Roger Borsa.

The Norman conquest of England

By the late 1080s, therefore, the achievement of the de Hautevilles in the Mediterranean could in itself be described as an outstanding testament to the Norman mastery of war. But it had, of course, been paralleled in the 1060s and 1070s

by the invasion and conquest of Saxon England by Duke William of Normandy – a venture which came closer to failure than is usually remembered.

Norman propaganda, as exemplified by the Bayeux Tapestry, always stressed that William's claim to the throne was not only sound but approved by the ageing Edward 'The Confessor,' last of the Saxon kings. William, however, had great trouble in raising support for his invasion in 1066; his vassals in Normandy only considered themselves bound to support their duke in maintaining the security of Normandy itself; and they resented being called upon to support ducal adventures in England. So far from being a popular Norman crusade, the conquest of England seemed a most unpromising military proposition. Harold Godwinesson, Earl of Wes-

sex, was the foremost soldier in England and had distinguished himself on campaign with William's army against the rebel Bretons during his visit to Normandy in 1064. Quite apart from Harold Godwinesson there was the question of Harold Hardraada, King of Norway, former Varangian champion of the Byzantine Empire and a renowned warrior.

The well-known events of 1066 normally concentrate on praising Harold's race north to shatter Hardraada's invasion of Northumbria before returning to confront the Norman invasion in the south. The former achievement, however, owed much to the magnificent fight put up by the northern English earls Edwin and Morcar at Fulford. Hardraada inflicted a crushing defeat on the northern earls and his army was lying at ease when Harold arrived only four days after the battle, catching many of the Norwegians without their armor at Stamford Bridge. The other popular controversy of the 1066 campaign is whether or not Harold should have taken the time to raise more troops in the south before marching on to engage the Norman expeditionary force – about 5000 strong, of which about 2000 were knights and sergeants trained to fight on horseback – which landed at Pevensey on 29 September. Here the point surely is that Harold had fought with William and his Normans. He was acutely aware of their mobility, of the speed with which they were likely to reinforce their beach-head in England and their remorseless prowess at 'conquest by castle.' Apart from these urgent considerations, Harold had at his disposal an army 'with its tail well up' after the defeat of Hardraada and was clearly confident of the outcome of an early battle with the invaders in the south.

The barest examination of the course of events at Hastings (14 October 1066) shows that this confidence was largely justified. William's initial charges against the shield-wall formed by Harold's armored 'house-carls' were repulsed and even the most slavish pro-Norman chroniclers admit that the Norman army came close to panic at one stage. William won the battle by playing on the indiscipline of Harold's supporting *fyrdmen*, who fell easy victim to feigned flights during the afternoon. Having destroyed the cohesion of the *fyrdmen*, William began the destruction of the house-carls with missile fire from archers and (according to at least two French sources) crossbowmen, though the latter are not depicted in the Bayeux Tapestry. Harold was *not* 'shot in the eye' at Hastings. The Tapestry clearly shows him being cut down amid the wreckage of the shield-wall by a mounted knight's sword. His insistence in fighting on foot shows the baneful legacy of Scandinavian military honor; Alfred the Great would never have left himself without a line of retreat from a lost battle.

As it was, the deaths of Harold and his brothers Gyrth and Leofwine at Hastings wiped out the ruling Godwinesson family and left the field clear for William. All Hastings gave him was control of Sussex and Kent, but the fighting potential of northern England had been scotched by the losses suffered at Fulford and Stamford Bridge; and the last surviving male heir of the Old English ruling house was a frightened boy of 13. The initial tendency of the English magnates to resist William was curtailed by the 'frightfulness' of the circuitous Norman march on London – a well-calculated piece of policy with much the same results as the German bombing of Rotterdam in May 1940. The magnates of the English *Witan* submitted and on Christmas Day 1066 William was crowned King of England.

It was after an uneasy, two-year honeymoon that the north broke out in three flares of revolt – but the lack of an English national leader enabled William to show his true colors as a warlord. William knew all about fighting rebels as he had spent the 20 years before Hastings doing little else in Normandy. Baffled by the raw new Norman castles and overwhelmed by the speed of William's movements, the rebels were crushed piecemeal. William rubbed in the lesson by his terrible devastation of Yorkshire from sea to sea (1069-70) before turning south to eliminate the guerrilla leader Hereward amid the swamps of Ely. By 1072 William was the unchallenged master of all England.

The Norman strength – an eye for a strategic opportunity

Like the Viking conquests of the ninth century, the widespread Norman conquests of the eleventh were characterized by the lack of any central direction. There never was a Norman equivalent of Charlemagne since the authority of the Norman duke outside Normandy proper was strictly limited. Nor were the Normans invincible. It took time for them to learn the correct formula of cavalry plus missile power, and this could only be learned the hard way. What the Normans did have was an unerring eye for strategic opportunity, coupled with a refusal to accept any man's superiority that could not be made good in battle. Both qualities were amply revealed in the subsequent chapter of their story, the best-remembered of them all: the wars of the Crusades.

Right: Weakened by archery and javelin attacks, the English 'shield wall' gives way to William's cavalry, while on the left Harold is cut down by a mounted Norman knight.

The Age of the Crusades

Military history abounds with lost causes, glorious blunders, the rapid collapse of freak runs of conquest and the inevitable failure of over-ambitious plans. But the Crusades, while meriting all these depressing labels and many more, nevertheless remain a unique interlude in the history of warfare. In practical terms the Crusades mark the attempt of the Christian West to seize and hold the confines of the eastern Mediterranean, taking over a function which the Byzantine Empire had, by the end of the eleventh century, proved unable to perform. The military operations of the Crusading era began with the great quadruple expedition of 1096-9, which captured Jerusalem, and ended 200 years later with the loss of the last pockets of Crusader territory on the coasts of Syria and Palestine. But the spirit of the Crusades proved far more durable than the temporary conquests it inspired. Perverted though it was by opportunism, ambition, greed and treachery, the spirit represented an attempt to come to terms with the fundamental immorality of war.

No twentieth century nation which considers itself bound to rely on force for the ultimate defense of its interests has the right to sneer at the notion of 'just' or 'holy' wars. It was alive and well and brandished by all major combatants in the two world wars of 1914-18 and 1939-45, and has made its most recent appearance among the Moslem defenders and Soviet Russian invaders of Afghanistan. Holy war was not invented by or for the Crusades, it was a far older concept. The first people on record to butcher and conquer in obedience to divine orders were the Israelites in the twelfth century BC. Roman imperialists argued from Virgil's *Aeneid* that conquest in the name of Rome (itself semi-divine) was thoroughly justified by divine ordinance. Eastern Roman and Byzantine emperors considered themselves heirs to a Christian world empire constantly at war amid a sea of heretical or pagan enemies while the Arabs, beginning their career of conquest in the early seventh century, believed it their mission to convert the world – by force when necessary – to the acceptance that 'There is no God but God, and Muhammad is his Prophet.'

If the Crusades represented no new attempt to justify war, they were an attempt to divert the making of war into a new course. Brute force, might, the law of the sword, *force majeure* – under whatever name it had always existed and according to Scripture it always would, until the

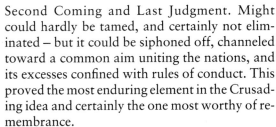

Second Coming and Last Judgment. Might could hardly be tamed, and certainly not eliminated – but it could be siphoned off, channeled toward a common aim uniting the nations, and its excesses confined with rules of conduct. This proved the most enduring element in the Crusading idea and certainly the one most worthy of remembrance.

As the eleventh century drew to its close, a pattern was emerging which indicated that some form of Western military intervention in the eastern Mediterranean could not be long delayed. In the western and central Mediterranean the power of Islam had been palpably failing for decades. In Spain, the southward expansion of the Christian kingdom of Castile had led to the capture of Toledo from the Moslems in 1085, and the legendary success of Ruy Diaz, *El Cid* (who, like his Norman contemporary Robert Guiscard in Italy, was not over-scrupulous as to which side retained his services). In 1016 the fleets of Genoa and Pisa had expelled the Moslems from Sardinia; they provided mercenary assistance for the Normans during the latter's steady advance in Sicily and in 1087 captured and sacked the Moslem naval base at Mahdia in Tunisia.

All these successes assisted the flow of pilgrim traffic from Western Europe to the Holy Land and the Christian shrines in Palestine from which the local Moslems drew considerable profit. Pilgrimages to the Holy Land were actively encouraged by the eleventh century reform movement in the Latin Church known as the 'Cluniac Revival,' but after the Seljuk Turks conquered Syria the pilgrim traffic fell victim to brigandage and extortion on the part of local Turkish chieftains and had been virtually cut off by 1090. The restoration of pilgrim facilities – by first the liberation, then the defense of the Holy Sepulcher in Jerusalem – was one of the major objectives of the First Crusade.

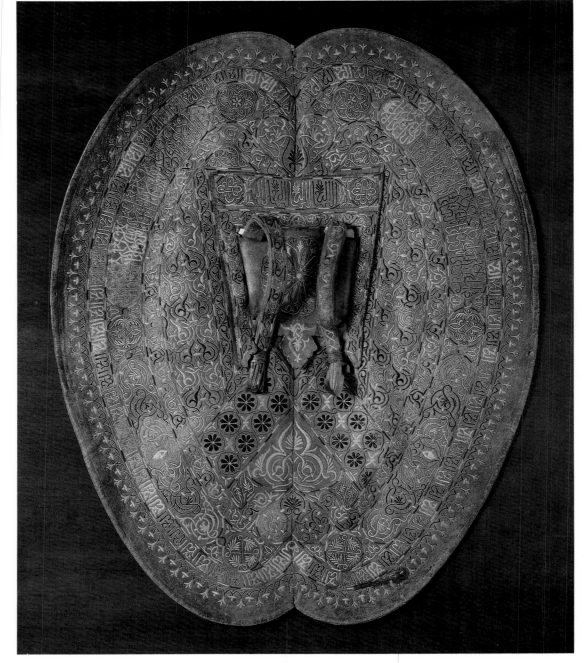

quasi-independent provinces, Alexius lacked the troops with which to profit from the situation and recover the lost provinces of the Empire. Finally, in 1095, he took the step of appealing to Pope Urban II for Western troops.

Alexius hoped that this appeal would attract a straightforward mercenary force which would be safely on his payroll, under his orders and control. When the fighting was over and the Empire's frontiers had been restored, the Western mercenaries would be paid off and sent home. Instead the emperor found himself confronted by the biggest crisis to endanger the Byzantine Empire since the reign of Heraclius 470 years before.

For Pope Urban's reaction was not to send an appeal to the rulers of Western Christendom, asking for warriors to fight in the Eastern Emperor's service. Instead, at the Council of Clermont (27 November 1095) he preached holy war as it had never been dreamed of before. In an impassioned public appeal Urban unfolded the vista of a wholescale pilgrimage of the Cross (*Kreuzzug, Croisade,* Crusade) to redeem the Holy Sepulcher in Jerusalem, and drive the infidel beyond the ancient Christian frontiers of the East. This pilgrimage, he promised, would be replete with chances of advancement and profit in this world and would carry the assurance of heaven in the next. '*Deus vult*' ('God wills it!') was adopted as the Crusading battle cry.

Here we are concerned principally with the military reaction, rather than the popular response to Urban's appeal – the massacre of Jews in the Rhineland and the lemming-like 'People's Crusade' of deluded peasantry whom Peter the Hermit and Walter the Penniless led to destruction in Asia Minor. For fighting men of every rank, the Crusade offered a short cut to material fulfillment. A lowly crossbowman might dream of commanding the garrison of a castle in the East; a penniless knight (or armored man-at-arms who could not even afford a *destrier* and groom) might dream of winning a castle to hold for a lord like Bohemond de Hauteville, to whom the winning of a new principality or even kingdom in the East was an itch in the blood. It was, in short, the military 'have-not's' dream. To the 'haves,' the ruling establishment of Western Europe (monarchs and tenants-in-chief), the Crusade was a fantastic scheme, to be left well alone. It had one decided advantage. This crazy pilgrimage would siphon off all the surplus (landless) fighting men who would otherwise be tempted to look for profitable trouble at home.

Another key element in the build-up to the First Crusade was the Papacy's increasing reliance on vassal military aid in its temporal struggles with the German Empire. Again, there was nothing new about this. As we have seen, Pope Stephen II had used naked spiritual blackmail to bring Pepin's Franks to his aid as far back as 756. In the ninth century Popes Leo IV (847-55) and John VIII (872-82) had both affirmed that soldiers who died fighting for the interests of the Church would have their earthly sins remitted and go straight to heaven. But by the end of the eleventh century the process had been taken much further. The Papacy was now promising that soldiers who fought with the blessing of the Church would go to heaven whether or not they got killed in the process and they would be allowed, as Papal vassals, to keep the lands they conquered. To warlords like the ambitious but still landless Bohemond, the son of Robert Guiscard, here was a far more compelling motive than being assured of Paradise or building a world safe for peaceful pilgrimages.

The real catalyst, however, was the Byzantine Empire's military bankruptcy after the Manzikert disaster in 1071 which ended the Empire's traditional role as defender of eastern Christendom. Since its last breach with the Greek orthodox Church in 1054, the Papacy was more than willing to sanction expeditions to conquer Byzantine provinces and enlarge the domains of the Latin Church. The first military reaction to the Eastern Empire's weakness was the attempt by Robert Guiscard and his son Bohemond to conquer Macedonia (1081-85). The Emperor Alexius survived by adroit generalship and skillful exploitation of his opponents' weaknesses – the vassals in southern Italy who challenged the supremacy of the de Hautevilles and the fierce rivalry between the de Hautevilles themselves after Guiscard's death in 1085. But the narrow slice of Asia Minor left under Byzantine control after Manzikert was insufficient recruiting ground for the creation of a new Byzantine regular army. When the Seljuk ruler Malik Shah died in 1092 and the Turkish Empire split into

Above left: One of Richard I's bishops dressed for battle, from the thirteenth century *Chronicles of the Kings of England.*

Above: Christ leading the Crusades, a scene from a thirteenth century manuscript.

Left: A fifteenth century Moorish shield of traditional form and decoration.

Right: Embarking for the Crusades as depicted in a fourteenth century miniature.

Tancred. Neither of the two de Hautevilles considered themselves the inferior of any of the other leaders.

Though Pope Urban could persuade all these leaders to pledge their support for the pilgrimage and agree on a rendezvous at Constantinople by the end of 1096, he could do no more than order that all private feuds and quarrels be suspended for the duration of the pilgrimage. This was, in fact, no mere pious hope; given the multinational forces involved it was a principle of sound common sense. But when it came to agreeing on a sensible command structure and a joint strategy for the expedition, the leaders were necessarily left to settle it among themselves. It was an incredibly half-baked start to one of the most difficult campaigns in military history. The Crusaders lacked a commander-in-chief whom all were content to follow, they had no secure base, no guaranteed lines of communication or source of supply once they had passed beyond Byzantine territory, no reserves and no accurate information about the enemy's overall numbers, let alone about the terrain in which they would be fighting. Hitler's invasion of Soviet Russia in 1941, even the Franco-British invasion of the Crimea in 1854, seem models of forethought and planning by comparison with the First Crusade.

The Crusaders were relying on the irresistible massed charge of knights which, they were confident, would guarantee victory in any stand-up fight. If the Turks refused to fight (unlikely though this seemed, given their record since Manzikert) the Crusaders would be granted an unopposed march into Syria and Palestine. The basic Turkish tactics were easy enough to foresee: provoke the Crusading knights into repeated charges until their horses were worn out, then close and fight it out hand to hand. The Turks were certain to try to exploit their superior maneuverability on horseback, luring the Crusading knights away, then rushing in to cut down the foot people, and loot camp or baggage train. Here the superior range of the Western crossbow would be a decided asset in making the Turkish horsemen keep their distance. Though the light bow carried by the Turkish horsed archers could not penetrate a Western knight's mail, it could certainly kill his horse – and *destriers* trained to charge in the 'Frankish' manner were unobtainable east of the Adriatic.

The First Crusade

The leaders who rallied to Pope Urban's appeal by raising forces for the pilgrimage were all far down in the monarchical pecking order – Count Hugh of Vermandois, Count Raymond of Toulouse, Duke Godfrey of Lorraine and his brothers Jiustau and Baldwin, Count Stephen of Blois and Count Robert of Flanders. Their best asset, as potential leaders of the Crusade and the new order which it sought to establish in the East, was the nobility of the ruling houses which had produced them. Duke Robert of Normandy, eldest son of William the Conqueror, was an unknown quantity. Feckless and spendthrift, he lacked any recognizable political flair or ambition for command but there could be no doubt of his enthusiasm for the Crusade. To raise the cash for his share in the pilgrimage Robert pawned his birthright, leasing Normandy to his brother William II of England for three years for 10,000 marks of silver. Most formidable of all the Crusading leaders was Bohemond de Hauteville, the only leader with experience of campaigning east of the Adriatic, seconded by his nephew

Above left: An eleventh century manuscript illustration depicting the armory of Christendom: crossbow, sword and lance. The figure of 'Justice' rides in the bottom right corner.

Left: European crossbowmen assault a city in this scene from the *William of Tyre* manuscript (1250-60).

Right: In this fourteenth century manuscript illustration, heavily armored European knights clash with Moslem cavalry.

Below right: This thirteenth century carved stone relief depicts Seljuk Turks in full war panoply.

The prologue to the Crusade proper was the advance to Constantinople, the agreed venue for the muster. Godfrey and his brothers took the northernmost overland route, from Regensburg on the upper Danube south through Hungary, Serbia and Bulgaria. Raymond of Toulouse and the Papal Legate Adhemar of Puy, with the Provençal contingent, opted for the immensely difficult overland march round the head of the Adriatic and southeast through the mountain passes of Dalmatia, suffering badly from ambushes by the Slavonian mountain people. Bohemond, and lastly Robert of Normandy, both chose the simplest route of all: the sea crossing from southern Italy. Encamped outside Constantinople by Easter 1097, the Crusading leaders reached agreement with the apprehensive Emperor Alexius, despite some vicious clashes between Greeks and Latins during the negotiations. Alexius offered supplies, guides and a lavish share of the loot recovered from all former imperial cities which the Crusaders might recapture for him in Anatolia. For the Crusading leaders, knowing that their joint forces were momentarily superior to any expedition which Alexius could possibly send against them, swearing allegiance to the 'Greek emperor' was not too much of a bond; it guaranteed them help which would otherwise have to be fought for without doing any damage to the Turks.

The first operation of the Crusade, the siege of Nicaea (May-June 1097), was a joint exercise with the Byzantines on Constantinople's doorstep, which ended with the Turkish governor concluding a private treaty with Alexius and depriving the Crusaders of a lucrative sack. Alexius kept faith with his allies, however, content to have recovered this key city intact, and the Crusaders moved on from Nicaea well supplied with provisions and the shared-out spoils of the city. At the end of June 1097 – most probably, after all the losses already suffered, no more than 30,000 strong at the most optimistic

count – the Crusaders began the invasion of the Seljuk kingdom of 'Rum,' Turkish-held Anatolia. The pilgrim army marched in two divisions, the van being the Normans under the joint command of Bohemond and Robert and the rear the Provençals under Godfrey and Raymond. The first objective was the road junction at Dorylaeum from where the Crusaders could choose their main line of advance toward southern Armenia and Antioch.

Dorylaeum (1 July 1097) was the first battle which the Crusaders fought on their own, without Byzantine assistance or advice, and it nearly ended in disaster. Bohemond's division was surprised in camp by the main Turkish army under the Sultan Kilij Arslan of Rum (possibly 100,000 strong, but surely not the 350,000 claimed by some Western sources). Bohemond, who had fought the elusive Patzinak horsed archer mercenaries of Alexius, tried to fight a dismounted

NORWAY
SWEDEN
SCOTLAND
ESTONIANS
IRELAND
DANES
LITHUANIANS
ATLANTIC OCEAN
WALES
ENGLAND
LONDON
POMERANIA
Vistula
PRUSSIANS
RUSSIA
Rhine
HOLY
POLAND
1147 'Lisbon Crusade': English fleet en route to Holy Land takes Lisbon from the Moors
Richard I
ROMAN
REGENSBURG
Frederick I (Barbarossa)
VÉZELAY
FRANCE
EMPIRE
VIENNA
Dnieper
1071 Byzantines defeated by Moslem Turks, who then conquer Jerusalem and Anatolia
Richard I's fleet
LYON
BUDA PEST
HUNGARY
Philip II
LEON AND CASTILE
NAVARRE ARAGON
VENICE
GENOA
CROATS (To Venice)
ZARA
Danube
Black Sea
June 1190 Barbarossa dies on way to Holy Land
SINOPE
GEORGIA
PORTUGAL
KINGDOM OF ALMORAVIDS
MARSEILLES
PISA
SERBS
BULGARIANS
ADRIANOPLE
CONSTANTINOPLE
ICONIUM
COUNTY OF EDESSA
LISBON
CORSICA (To Pisa)
ROME
NAPLES
BARI
BRINDISI
EASTERN EMPIRE
ANGORA
ICONIUM
ARMENIANS
EDESSA
Tigris
PRINCIPALITY OF ANTIOCH
SARDINIA (To Pisa)
SICILY
APULIA
ATHENS
ANTIOCH
Euphrates
MEDITERRANEAN SEA
MALTA
Richard I
RHODES
CRETE
CYPRUS 1191
TRIPOLI
COUNTY OF TRIPOLI
Philip II
CRETE
ACRE 1191
KINGDOM OF JERUSALEM
JERUSALEM
NOMADIC ARAB TRIBES
CAIRO
Nile
1099 Crusaders capture Jerusalem. Kingdom established (retaken by Saladin, 1187)

ROUTE OF FIRST CRUSADE
ROUTE OF THIRD CRUSADE
BOUNDARIES, 1100 (AFTER THE FIRST CRUSADE)
CRUSADER STATES
0   NAUTICAL MILES   500

First crusade 1096-99 Supply fleet provided by Venice and Genoa

Third crusade 1189-92 Large fleets from Atlantic states appear in the Mediterranean for the first time

©Richard Natkiel, 1986

Left: The First and Third Crusades resulted in the establishment of the Crusader states.

action, sparing his knights' horses and luring the Turks to destruction by his crossbowmen, but the harrying archery of the Turkish attacks forced him to get his knights mounted and try to drive the enemy back. All attempts to press home even one destructive charge against the Turks failed, and the knights fell back into the camp perimeter where the guy-ropes of the tents inhibited the Turks' horsemanship, if not their archery. Kilij Arslan, however, had mistakenly believed that he had trapped the entire Crusading army, and had committed his entire force to the attack when the second Crusading division arrived at just the right moment, catching the Turks between hammer and anvil. The Turks dissolved in rout, allegedly losing about 35,000 men to the Crusaders' 4000.

Though Dorylaeum was a most heartening victory, it nevertheless cost the Crusading army irreplaceable losses in trained warhorses, and confirmed the shortcomings in Frankish tactics – the extreme difficulty of catching Turkish horsemen with a decisive charge and the infantry's vulnerability without constant cavalry protection. The most important consequence of the battle was the near-total demoralization of the Turks in eastern Anatolia, leaving the Crusaders free to advance southeast on Iconium and Heraclea, reaching the borders of Cilicia and Armenia. Once the barrier of the Taurus Mountains had been passed by a long detour the Crusaders found Christian allies in the Armenians. The two landless aspirants, Tancred and Baldwin, both led small expeditions through the mountains to the coastal Cilician plain around Tarsus, where they came to blows. Tancred, having the smaller force, was obliged to give best to Baldwin, who set off to conquer a county for himself with the aid of the Armenians. This piece of opportunism and brute force ended with the foundation of the first Crusader state: the County of Edessa, spanning the Euphrates. It was a chance gain of im-

Left: A miniature by Matthew Paris (*c*1250), showing the harness and weapons of a thirteenth century knight. Note the helm in the top right hand corner which was worn over the knight's mail coif.

mense strategic importance because the new county acted as a territorial barrier between the Moslems of Kurdistan and Upper Mesopotamia, and the Turks of Syria. Just as important from the viewpoint of the main Crusading army, Edessa and the friendly Christian principality of 'Little Armenia' along the Cilician coast also prevented any Byzantine attempt to move against Syria by land.

The Crusaders began the siege of Antioch in October 1097. At first sight it seemed an impossible nut to crack. The city was surrounded by a 13-kilometer curtain-wall, studded with towers, and sited on rising ground which ruled out any effective assault with siege engines. The Crusaders lacked the manpower to impose an all-round siege, and though they were able to reduce the Turkish intake of supplies to a trickle it seemed more than likely that the besieging army would starve first. But Antioch had to be taken. It was the capital of Syria and lay squarely across the line of communications which the Crusading army would leave behind it as it advanced south into Palestine.

By the New Year of 1098 the army was suffering from extreme hunger and frustration, despite the precarious opening of a supply route down the coast to the little port of St Simeon, where Genoese traders brought in supplies at exorbitant prices. Foraging expeditions inland, however, brought in just enough provisions to maintain the siege. Fortunately the Moslem states were as divided by rivalry as the contingents of the Crusading army, and launched no joint expedition to raise the siege. Karbogha, Sultan of

Above right: The Crusades were often pursued with unimaginable savagery. Here, besiegers catapult the severed heads of their enemies into a beleaguered city (from *Les Histoires d'Outremer,* thirteenth century).

Right: The colorful pageantry seen here in a thirteenth century illustration from the *Romance of Alexander* shows the other side of warfare during the era of the Crusades.

Mosul, spent the spring of 1098 vainly trying to evict Baldwin and his followers from Edessa and its satellite castles before leading his army south against the besiegers of Antioch at the end of May. But it was too late. The persistence of the Crusaders had at last borne fruit, and Bohemond had stormed Antioch, aided by treachery from inside, on 2 June. Only the morning before, Count Stephen of Blois had abandoned the pilgrimage in disgust and set off back to Anatolia with his contingent.

Not yet masters of Antioch, with survivors from the massacred Turkish garrison still holding out in the citadel, the Crusaders now had to defend the city which they had besieged for the past eight months. It was precisely because there were too few Crusaders in Antioch to contain the pocket of resistance in the citadel *and* man the huge expanse of curtain-wall that Bohemond now urged a novel and daring plan on the joint war council. This was to deploy the whole Crusading army (apart from a 200-strong masking force to watch the citadel) outside the city, providing an apparently weak force to lure the Turks into an attack. The 1000-odd force of mounted knights was parceled out into three divisions, the main objective of their charge being the Turkish camp. Bohemond provided for the inevitable Turkish counterstrike against the Crusading infantry by making the latter deliberately strong in dismounted knights, whom he commanded in person.

The result (28 June 1098) was the decisive victory of the campaign, won as much by the steadiness of Bohemond's infantry reserve as by the charge of the knights. The victory outside Antioch destroyed the only Moslem field army capable of preventing the Crusaders from marching south into Palestine. For Bohemond the victory was particularly sweet. The Turkish garrison in the citadel insisted on surrendering to him and not to Raymond of Toulouse, who had commanded the citadel blocking force while Bohemond commanded in the field. With the approval of the other Crusading leaders overriding the objections of Raymond, Bohemond took Antioch as the capital of his own principality – not as a vassal of Alexius, as had originally been understood. The Principality of Antioch was the second of the new Crusader states to be established in open defiance of the Byzantine emperor; but its foundation took Bohemond and a sizeable proportion of his Apulian Normans out of the main Crusading host. The others followed Tancred when the march on Jerusalem began in January 1099.

The road to Jerusalem

The Crusaders' invasion of Palestine from the north was made easier by the fact that the year before the Fatimid Caliphate of Egypt had invaded Palestine from the south, expelling the waning power of the Seljuks from all key cities. This meant that once again, as after Dorylaeum, the Crusading army was left unmolested on its march south. The command was now shared between Godfrey, Raymond and Tancred, with Robert of Normandy making an amiable but unforceful fourth. They were acutely sensitive of the need to capture at least one major seaport to assure their line of supply, as had been found necessary during the siege of Antioch. The problem, however, was the same as at Antioch: the massive Byzantine and Roman fortifications guarding the landward approaches to the major ports, which ruled the idea of reducing them one by one completely out of the question.

Left: The taking of Nicaea by the Crusaders in 1097 (from a lost window in the Abbey of St Denis).

Below left and below: A late medieval plan of the walled city of Jerusalem, and a twelfth century plan of its most sacred shrine, the Church of the Holy Sepulcher.

From March to May 1099 the army invested Acre, watching its vital horses reach peak condition as the spring grass grew. As the experience of the past two years dictated, the army's condition would rapidly decline through the baking summer months. As Acre, which could take in an unlimited flow of supplies by sea, would take far longer to reduce than Antioch, the audacious decision was made to 'go for broke,' forget the seaports and march straight on Jerusalem.

Perhaps few other decisions in medieval warfare were so prompted by considerations of morale. This was no ordinary feudal army. It was held together by a web of loyalty oaths, by no means all of them pledging the swearer to stay with the army until Jerusalem had been redeemed. Many had sworn to come East merely to fight the infidel; or follow their lords in fighting the infidel; or accompany the pilgrimage to the Holy Land, a vague abstraction already satis-

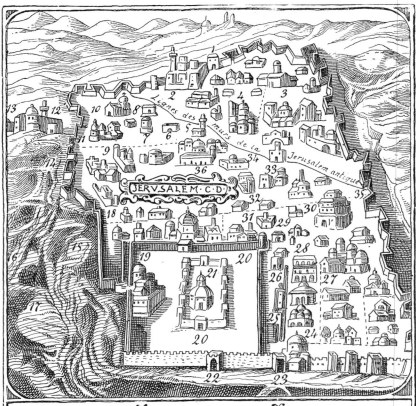

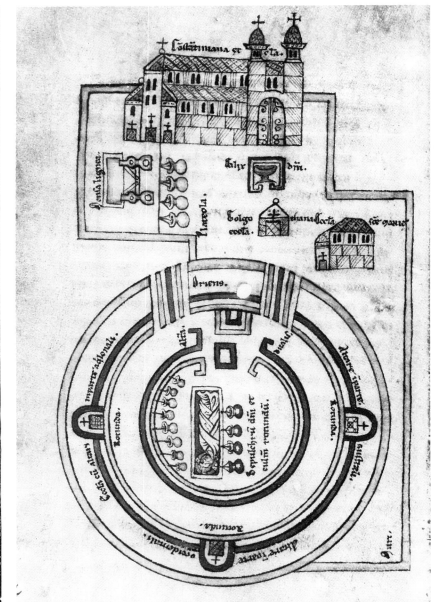

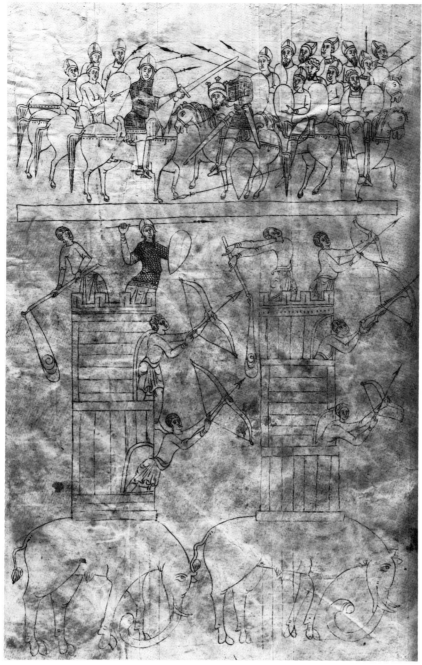

Right: A page from the tenth-eleventh century *Bible of Rhodes* showing siege tactics; the Crusaders (well acquainted with classical modes of warfare) used mobile wooden towers to storm and finally take Jerusalem in 1099.

Right: A portrait miniature of Saladin, whose crushing victory over the Crusaders at Hattin (1187) led to the recapture of Jerusalem and the loss of the Crusader states.

fied merely by having shared in the capture of Antioch. The eight-month ordeal before Antioch had been a climacteric as well as a heart-breaking experience. The desertion of Count Stephen of Blois – who, like many others, could claim that he had fulfilled his vow by having fought at Dorylaeum – was vividly remembered. In this, the Crusade's third year, it was tacitly agreed that the army could not survive another prolonged setback. Jerusalem, however, was a supreme objective. Its capture would inflame the whole of the Christian West and assure a flood of reinforcements from home. Nor was Jerusalem a 'Holy City' to Christendom alone; it was deeply revered by Moslems and its loss would be a shrewd blow to infidel morale. The morale factor set aside, it is possible to see, in the decision to march on Jerusalem, an instinctive recognition of the so-called 'modern' principle of *Blitzkrieg*: throw away the rule book, forget about a secure base and line of communications and strike with concentrated strength at your most important objective.

The latter consideration was shown by the haste with which the siege of Jerusalem was pressed. The city was stoutly walled and garrisoned, yet where Antioch had held out for eight months Jerusalem fell in under six weeks (6 June-15 July 1099). The acute shortage of heavy timber for building siege catapults with which to batter the walls, as much as the abhorrence against a time-wasting 'full-dress' siege, led to the initial reliance on scaling the walls with ladders. The first attempt (13 July) failed because the ladders were too short to reach the top of the curtain-walls, and the Crusaders suffered their first outright repulse since they had raised the siege of Acre. Five days later, however, came the electrifying news that a Genoese fleet had taken the seaport of Jaffa, only 65 kilometers away, bringing not only provisions but timber suitable for building siege engines. It was from the upper storeys of the movable towers or *malvoisins* ('bad neighbors') that the Crusaders finally stormed into the city on 15 July 1099, accomplishing the pilgrimage with a thoroughly typical blend of looting, piety and slaughter:

...seizing gold and silver, horses and mules, and houses full of all sorts of goods, and they all came weeping from excess of gladness to worship at the Sepulcher of our Savior Jesus, and there they fulfilled their vows to Him. Next morning they went cautiously up on to the roof of the Temple and attacked the Saracens, both men and women, cutting off their heads with drawn swords.

Within a week the conquerors of Jerusalem had realized that they were adventurers in an alien land whose first priority must be to defend what they had taken. None of the leaders had the presence to style himself 'King of Jerusalem'; Godfrey de Bouillon, when elected, took the title 'Defender of the Holy Sepulcher.' To help him live up to this title and repel a Fatimid counter-invasion, Godfrey had about 12,000 fighting men, less than ten per cent of them mounted knights, while Vizier Afdal came up from Egypt with an army at least 20,000 strong. Godfrey marched from Jerusalem to meet Afdal head-on, catching the Fatimid army on the coast at Ascalon. The resulting battle (12 August 1099) was a gift for the Crusaders. Instead of grouping his cavalry on the flanks, Afdal stupidly massed it behind his 3000-strong front rank of Sudanese infantry archers, who were thus left unprotected to take the full shock of the Christian charge. On

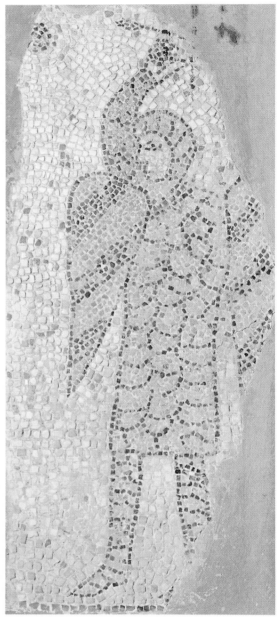

the tortuous terrain of the hinterland such a deployment might have made sense; as it was Afdal's wretched archers barely had time to get off one flight of arrows before the knights were on them, driving clean through, and scattering the entire Fatimid army beyond hope of a rally. The Crusaders in Palestine could now prepare to defend and extend their gains with no threat of immediate danger from the south.

By the New Year of 1100 the new order in Syria and Palestine was rapidly taking shape. Daimbert, Archbishop of Pisa, had come out as the new Latin Patriarch of Jerusalem, confirming Baldwin as Count of Edessa, Bohemond as Prince of Antioch, and Godfrey as King of Jerusalem. To Raymond, who had set about the reduction of the coastal strip between Beirut and Markab, went the title 'Count of Tripolis.' (There was an early reshuffle when Godfrey died in 1100 and was replaced by Baldwin, his brother.) On the map, the Crusader states could

not disguise that they really were an attempt to make permanent the terrain covered by an army's line of advance, a narrow belt of territory fragmented by individual dynasticism. In theory Edessa, Antioch and Tripolis were vassal states of the Kingdom of Jerusalem; in practice the vassalage was fragile at best and always subject to untimely lack of cooperation. As each state had its own army there was no joint defense structure or strategy, save when it suited two or more princes to join forces. And yet, in the first 45 years of existence, the Crusader states flourished, capturing every major seaport on the east Mediterranean coast, wiping out inland pockets of resistance, and pushing east to occupy as many vital ridges and passes as could be taken and held with the massive castles which remain the Crusaders' greatest monuments.

Reduced to its simplest terms, the story of the Crusader states shows the attainment of a peak of success under the fourth king of Jerusalem, Fulk of Anjou (1131-43). Then came the first disaster: the loss of Edessa in 1144 and the rapid Moslem conquest of that vital bastion, prompting the abortive Second Crusade of 1147-9. Over the next 35 years the surrounding Moslem principalities were finally united by Saladin, who by 1185 was overlord of the central Moslem world from the Gulf of Tripoli to upper Mesopotamia. Saladin's crushing victory at Hattin in 1187 was to the Crusader states what Manzikert had been to the Byzantine Empire a century before – a disaster beyond redemption. It led to the loss of Jerusalem and forced the Crusaders back to the coastal strip. The famous Third Crusade (1189-92) led by Philip of France and Richard of England, failed to recover the ground lost since Hattin. From then on it was downhill all the way until the final evacuation of Acre in 1291.

The Crusades against the Byzantine states

The story of the Crusades is commonly described as 'the wars of Cross and Crescent.' It is no less accurate to call the Crusades 'the wars of Latins and Greeks.' The fate of the Crusader states was really settled by the events of the First Crusade, characterized as this was by the mutual distrust of Eastern and Western Christendom. Far from winning the Byzantine Empire as an invaluable ally, the First Crusade permanently alienated the Comneni emperors at Constantinople. A workable 'triple alliance' between Constantinople, Edessa and Antioch would have prevented the loss of Edessa; the sea power of the Empire, if used on the Crusaders' behalf, would have guaranteed them all the supplies and reinforcements they needed. But such an alignment was never remotely likely. Constantinople could never have tolerated the domination of the eastern Mediterranean trade routes by the Latin West. Hence the rapid corrosion of the original Crusading ideal – that of the West marching to the aid of the Christian East – into open hostilities. The indignities visited on the French and imperial forces of the Second Crusade were amply avenged by the infamous Fourth Crusade of 1204 which was directed not against the infidels in the Holy Land but against the Byzantine Empire itself. The Fourth Crusade conquered Greece, Thrace and the city of Constantinople, creating a 'Latin Empire' which endured from 1204 to 1261 – 100 years too late to be of any use to the now-vanished Crusader states of Syria and Palestine, for which the Fourth Crusade was a cheap and greedy substitute.

If there was any one man who was personally responsible for the continued feud between the Latin and Greek worlds, so fatal as this was to the survival of the Crusade states, it was Bohe-

mond of Taranto and Antioch, greatest leader of the Norman 'heroic age' in the Mediterranean. Bohemond's stubborn refusal to acknowledge Alexius as his overlord for Antioch was only part of the story. He had never abandoned the feud with Alexius begun with Guiscard's invasion of Greece back in 1081, and his ultimate dream of replacing Alexius as emperor survived two humiliating setbacks in Syria. The first, in 1100, was his capture and brief imprisonment by the Turkish Emir of Cappadocia, an accident which happened sufficiently close to the triumphs of 1097-9 for his release to be speedily negotiated. Then, in 1104, Bohemond joined forces with Baldwin II of Edessa to repel a Turkish assault on Edessa, which was under siege. A fascinating battle resulted at Harran, in which the Christian and Moslem armies each kept a concealed force in ambush and relied on feigned flight to lure the opposition to destruction. Unfortunately for the Christians Baldwin's men fell into the trap prepared for the Turks and were routed by the Turkish ambush; Bohemond meanwhile emerged from *his* ambush, scattered the forces opposed to him, only to be caught up in the flight of the Edessans and chased from the field. But only a de Hauteville would have reacted to these humiliations in the manner displayed by Bohemond. In 1105, leaving his nephew Tancred to hold Antioch for him, Bohemond sailed for his original power base in southern Italy. His aim was to raise a new 'crusading' army – for the planned invasion of the Balkans and conquest of Constantinople.

The irony was that Alexius was now far stronger than he had been 20 years before, thanks largely to the Crusaders' victories in which Bohemond had himself played so prominent a part. As soon as Bohemond's small force landed at Valona in October 1107 it was tightly blockaded by land and sea. Before the year was out Bohemond had been starved into an armistice which forced him to acknowledge Alexius as the suzerain lord of Antioch and to hand over the seaports of Cilicia to the emperor. This crowning humiliation after over 30 years of scheming and campaigning finally broke Bohemond's spirit, and he went home to Taranto to die in 1111. After the death of Alexius in 1118 his imperial successor John Comnenus kept up the pressure on Antioch and conquered Little Armenia, Antioch's Christian ally to the west, just before the Moslems took Edessa. The double loss of Armenia and Edessa exposed the southern Crusader states to attack from the north as well as the east and south.

Given Byzantine hostility and their reliance on the distant sea republics of Venice, Genoa and Pisa, could the Crusader states have survived on their own? The answer seems to be that they could have, but that the geographical odds were so heavily stacked against them that there was no margin for error. The first authority to look at the Crusades with the terrain of Syria and Palestine foremost in mind was T E Lawrence in 1909-11, when he was researching his famous thesis *Crusader Castles*. Lawrence brilliantly summed up the geographical factors working for and against the Crusaders in a little-known letter to his friend Leonard Green, from which the following extracts are taken:

What I felt most myself in Syria, put shortly, was the extreme difficulty of the country. Esdraelon, & the plain on which Baalbek lies, are the only flat places in it. The coast road is often only 50 yards wide between

hills and sea, and these hills you cannot walk or ride over, because they are strewn with large & small boulders, without an inch of cultivated soil; also numberless small 'wadies' (torrent-beds) deep and precipitous: not to be crossed without a huge scramble. In one day's march, from Lake Huleh to Safed, one ascends & descends 16,000 feet in hills and valleys, often 1500 feet deep & only 200 yards or so across, and in all the way only a single track path on which one can ride without fear of smashing horses' legs. *Make a point that for heavy-armed horse, operations in such country are impossible: they can march in single file, but cannot scout, or prepare against surprise:* the battlefield of Hattin (near Tiberias) is like a dried lava-flow, or the photograph, only in rock, of the pack-ice of the Arctic seas . . .

The next point is the rivers: the Jordan is hardly passable except at three points: just below Lake Huleh (Castle Jacob or Le Chastellet in the Crusade authorities) a bridge & ford. Another ford just below Lake Tiberias, and one more (very difficult) near Jericho. The first two were available for or against the Damascenes. From Lake Huleh northwards is a swamp & the river Litani, until the hills get steep enough & high enough to be impassable: and then (very quickly) comes the Orontes, which is nearly impassable (from Riblah downwards) to Esh Shogr, on the road from Laodicea to Aleppo. There is a ford there, and after a bridge near Antioch (the Iron Bridge). Above Antioch came a large lake and then very hilly ground from the Kara Su to Alexandretta. So you see W. Syria is pretty well defended . . .

While the Crusaders held Edessa, which is a tremendous fortress of Justinian's, they were unassailable except through the Damascus gap, and one opposite Homs extending to Tripolis. This last gap . . . is a nearly sea-level pass between Lebanon & the Nozairiyeh hills. It was defended by three tremendous Crusader castles (Krak des Chevaliers, Safita – Chastel Blanc in the French authorities – and Aarka, just above Tripolis). These three places made this gap tolerably harmless, except from Arab raids: these were continuous, but only did temporary harm; still they neutralised the force of the County of Tripolis from 1140 onwards. The Damascus gaps were also blocked: the northern one by Banias (beyond Huleh), by Hunin (above the lake), by Safed, and by Chastel Jacob, just beside the ford, which last castle only existed a few

months . . . The southern ford, below Lake Tiberias, was defended by the town of Tiberias by Kaukab el Hawa (one of the Belvoirs, just above Beisan) and by an outpost, el Husn, occasionally held beyond Jordan: it is not marked on any map. The Jericho ford was never very important.

The whole history of the Crusades was a struggle for the possession of these castles: the Arabs were never dispossessed of Aleppo, or of Hamah, or of Homs, or of Damascus, and so they had all possible routes open to them: they had unlimited resources to draw upon, as soon as the Mesopotamians had recovered Edessa, which the Crusaders could not hold on account of its isolated position (Euphrates 10 feet deep, 150 yards wide, very rapid & often flooded, much difficult hill thence to Seruj & even nearer Edessa) and the shiftiness of the Greek Armenian population, who were allies, at times, but fighting men not at all: more harm than good usually . . . Any counter stroke in the nature of ambush against the Arabs was impossible, since half their people were spies. Then in the hills above Safita lived the Assassins (Haschishin) sometimes at war with the Arabs, more often than not confederate, and linked with them by an Orontes-bridge at Shaizar. They could not attack Tripolis because of the 'gap' castles (see before) and Markab, a huge fortress north of Tortosa (another stronghold): but they could and did hold Antioch in check from the south, while the Aleppines pressed on the Iron Bridge, and the Greeks and Arabs attacked by Alexandretta & Beilan & Bagras (the two last big castles). So Antioch could only just hold its own, and the Tripolis castles, and when Damascus joined with the north, and added Egypt, Syria was ringed round.

The Battle of Hattin was lost in an attempt to relieve Tiberias, the second of the great 'gap' fortresses. Banias, the first, was lost (in 1164).

For most of the occupation the Latin sphere of influence was limited to their castles; the peasantry paid them taxes, & wished for the Mohammedans to come; and come they very often did, to plunder such Christian villages as were left. So far as one can see they spared the Mohammedans. Latin Syria lived on its fleets.

For sheer economy, Lawrence's summing-up of the geographical factor in the defense of the Crusader states has never been bettered. There were, of course, other important considerations, not the least of them being the declining quality of Crusader leadership after the First Crusade. Edessa did not fall in 1144 merely because of its geographical isolation, but because Count Joscelin II of Edessa failed to emulate his predecessors and maintain a garrison strong enough to hold out until relieved. As for the calamitous reign of King Guy de Lusignan (1186-92), the brains behind the disaster of Hattin and the loss of Jerusalem, it was consistent only in its resolute military incompetence.

The Crusader states

It must be admitted that the first five kings of Jerusalem, down to 1150, had an easier task than their successors. This had nothing to do with the rally of the Moslem world and the eventual emergence of the capable Saladin. The rise of the powerful and privileged Orders of Crusading

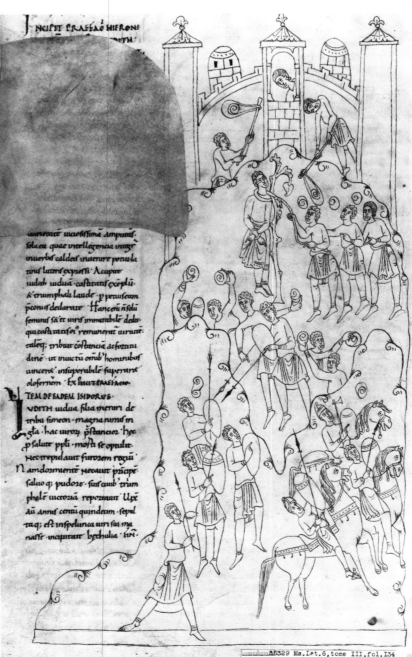

Above left: The Temple Church in London, built by the Knights Templar to a similar ground-plan to the Church of the Holy Sepulcher in Jerusalem.

Left: Illustration of contemporary foot soldiers in the tenth-eleventh century *Bible of Rhodes.*

Right: The biblical Battle of Maccabees in the *Bible of Rhodes,* illustrated (apart from the war elephant) as if it were a contemporary battle with Saracens.

Knighthood – the Knights of the Temple (Templars) and of the Hospital (Hospitallers) – dated from the 1120s and 1130s. It created military freemasonries within the Crusader states under grand masters answerable directly only to the Pope and owing no compulsory military service to the King of Jerusalem and his vassal rulers. The field contingents supplied by the Templars and Hospitallers deprived the Crusader rulers of direct, uncomplicated military command, and the Orders created as much instability in the region as they contributed loyal and reliable military aid.

Even more serious was the instability provided by the worst of the 'robber barons' who came out to *Outremer* ('overseas,' as Crusader territory was known in Europe) in the twelfth century. To an extent this phenomenon was not new in that it resembled the persistence in the tenth century of Viking heroes who would have been better suited to the ninth, like Eric Bloodaxe – men for whom the world had changed too fast. The worst of them all was Reginald de Châtillon, a ruthless land-pirate whose best epitaph was spoken by the man who eventually had him executed, Saladin: 'That man has exceeded all bounds.' Reginald's true niche in history was clearly that of Robert Guiscard's a century before. Most fittingly, Reginald married Guiscard's great-granddaughter Constance, the heiress of Antioch, in 1153. As Prince he gave Antioch one of the stormiest decades in its brief history as a Crusader state before marrying again (1175), this time becoming Lord of Transjordan, the frontier province east of the Dead Sea. From his castles of Kerak and Montreal Reginald extended his flair for brigandage as far as the Red Sea, preying with particular gusto on the Moslem pilgrim route to Mecca and becoming the most hated 'Frank' in the Moslem world – a one-man *casus belli*. Another adventurer from home was Guy de Lusignan, who married the sister of the leper-king Baldwin IV of Jerusalem (1174-83), becoming king himself when Baldwin's young brother died in 1185.

Within a year of Guy's accession all the weaknesses of Latin Syria had combined to bring about the disaster of Hattin. The most powerful of the subordinate Crusader princes, Raymond of Galilee and Tripolis, had stood for a policy of accommodation and fair dealing with Saladin, with whom Raymond had concluded a four-year truce. Raymond refused allegiance to Guy, seeing that the new king was a tool of the war-minded 'hawks' – particularly the Grand Masters of the Templars and Hospitallers, Gerard de Ridefort and Roger des Moulins. In the spring of 1187 the truce with Saladin was deliberately violated by a raid on a Moslem caravan by Reginald of Châtillon. Raymond demonstrated his non-involvement in the drift to war by allowing Saladin to send a 6000-strong reconnaissance in force through Raymond's lands in Galilee. Completely on their own initiative, the two Grand Masters attempted a surprise attack on the Moslem force at Cresson (1 May 1187), but the 140 Templars and Hospitallers were wiped out together with Roger des Moulins. Gerard de Ridefort escaped to goad King Guy into mustering his entire army for war. In June the Crusader army assembled at Suffuriya, midway between the Sea of Galilee and the coast, where there was good water and grazing. Raymond, his hopes for peace wrecked, suspended his feud with Guy to join the muster against Saladin.

The rival armies seem to have been about the same in strength with about 25,000 men each. If the fiasco at Cresson had taught anything, it was that the days when the Frankish charge could sweep away anything in its path were over. Raymond advised Guy to keep the army at Suffuriya, where it was bound to obstruct any serious advance by Saladin. The latter's opening move was to besiege Tiberias with half his army, an obvious 'invitation gambit' because Raymond's wife was in the castle. Raymond, however, knowing Saladin's high moral code and chivalrous behavior, was not to be drawn; he knew that even if Saladin took Tiberias he would behave with generosity toward his captives, and urged Guy to hold his ground. Instead Guy chose to listen to Gerard de Ridefort, ordering an advance across the waterless and convoluted plain of Toran to relieve Tiberias. The Crusaders

began their march across the desert to Tiberias on 3 July in three divisions: Raymond with the van, Guy with the center and Gerard de Ridefort with the rear.

The attempt to relieve Tiberias condemned the Crusader army to a painful and increasingly thirsty crawl across murderous terrain, harried all the way by Moslem light-horsed archers shooting from the flanks. Apart from the superior mobility of the Moslem cavalry, the Crusaders were caught in an immediate dilemma. If their army was to retain cohesion it must not leave the infantry behind – yet speed was vital to drive away the strong Moslem detachments holding the approaches to the all-important wells east of the plain. On 3 July the Crusaders encamped only halfway to Tiberias, having covered no more than eight kilometers during the whole day. On the morning of the 4th, with

Left: A fifteenth century impression of siege warfare in the Holy Land. The thirteenth century Crusaders had no cannon, however, but relied upon wooden siege engines, towers and scaling ladders.

the army now desperate for water, Raymond's van formation was cut off from the center and rear after making a charge which the Moslems countered by opening their ranks to let the knights pass through, dealing out heavy losses as they passed. Concluding that he had no chance of rejoining the army, having suffered three wounds and the capture of one of his sons, Raymond led the survivors of the van north to make sure of holding Tyre.

The surviving knights, trapped within the enveloping wings of Saladin's advancing army, pulled back on to one of the two hills known as the 'Horns of Hattin' (the other had already been occupied by the demoralized infantry). The trapped knights fought back gallantly until overcome by exhaustion, the latter being augmented by a 'smoke attack' inflicted by the Moslems firing the parched scrub of the plain. The total demoralization of the Crusaders was completed when the Bishop of Acre was killed in action and Saladin's nephew Taqi ad-Din captured the 'True Cross,' the holy standard of the Crusading host. Saladin's rich haul of prisoners included King Guy, Gerard de Ridefort and Reginald de Châtillon. Having destroyed the main field army of Latin Syria as a fighting force and rendered Jerusalem totally isolated, Saladin could well afford to spare Guy and Gerard. Yet the 260-odd Templars and Hospitallers captured at Hattin, whom the Moslems had come to regard very much as the Allies regarded the *Waffen* SS in World War II, were executed along with Reginald de Châtillon. Jerusalem finally surrendered to Saladin on 2 October.

Among the most dramatic events of the twelfth and thirteenth centuries were, of course, the joint Crusading expeditions sent out from Europe to retrieve the disasters and setbacks suffered by the Latins of *Outremer*. Given the time it took for news to travel from Syria to Italy, for the reigning Pope to arrange political truces between the Western monarchs, for the Western

monarchs to raise the necessary finance and troops and for the resultant multinational contingents to march or be shipped to the eastern

Mediterranean, the relief Crusades inevitably arrived years after such setbacks as the loss of Edessa or the Hattin débâcle. When (frequently

Left: Crusaders attacking Saracens, from a fourteenth century manuscript (note the game of chess in progress below).

Right: The course of the Fourth Crusade (1202-04).

Fourth crusade 1202-04
Crusaders assemble in Venice, where they are promised transport in return for help in recapturing Zara, which is taken in 1202. Venice gains vital strongpoints in the Aegean

if) they arrived, the current state of affairs in Syria and Palestine then had to be assessed and some form of acceptable joint plan agreed, which might or might not suit the rulers of the Crusader states. Everyone had his own axe to grind: the Crusader leaders and their mutual rivalry, the Italian princes and sea republics called upon to supply shipping who decided where the seaborne expeditions would go, and always the Byzantines, caught as usual in the middle and seeking to foment the natural divisions among their Latin enemies. In view of all these obstacles it is amazing that any of the relief Crusades ever set out at all. Yet the paramount example of the First Crusade was proof of what could be achieved against all odds, and between 1147 and 1272 no less than seven Crusading expeditions were mounted. With each of them the dominant common factor was the immense difficulty of reaching the eastern Mediterranean in the first place.

The Second Crusade of 1147-9 involved King Louis VII of France and Conrad III of Germany,

Right: An army on the march, with wagon-loads of supplies and equipment; from the *Maciejowsky Bible* (c1250).

the first reigning monarchs to take the Cross. Conrad preceded Louis on the old overland route to Asia Minor, encountered the same troubles with the Byzantines as had occurred in the First Crusade, then took a terrible beating from the Turks at Dorylaeum. He retreated to Nicomedia where he met Louis and the French. The Crusaders then traversed Asia Minor to the port of Attalia, where there was not enough shipping to embark all their troops; most of the troops left behind ended up as Turkish captives. Conrad then sailed to Acre, Louis to Antioch. Instead of joining forces against Nur-ad-Din of Mosul the two kings resolved to attack Damascus, only to be dissuaded by the Latins of Jerusalem to whom Damascus was a useful buffer against the Turks of Mosul. Fiasco was a kind word for the Second Crusade. 'I must call him blessed who is not scandalized thereby' lamented St Bernard of Clairvaux, the instigator of the Crusade.

The Third Crusade (1189-92) was preached by Popes Gregory VIII and Clement VII after Hattin and the loss of Jerusalem. The three strongest monarchs of the West – the Emperor Frederick 'Barbarossa,' Henry II of England and Philip 'Augustus' of France – agreed on a joint expedition, but Henry and Philip were locked in a struggle for the control of Normandy which was only suspended by Henry's death in July 1189. His successor, Richard I, whose heart was set on the Crusade, made an uneasy truce with Philip. Meanwhile the Crusade had got off to the usual disjointed start with King Guy of Jerusalem breaking his pledge of peace with Saladin and laying siege to Acre (August 1189), only to be besieged in turn. The Emperor Frederick, with unbelievable perversity after the experience of the Second Crusade (in which he had marched with Conrad), followed the overland route again; after the routine trouble with the Byzantines it was not until 1190 that the imperial forces advanced into Seljuk Rum. After storming Iconium, the Seljuk capital, Frederick advanced into Cilicia where he was accidentally drowned (June 1190), his much-reduced forces pressing on to Antioch and Acre.

Philip and Richard came out by sea via Marseilles and Genoa and spent the winter of 1190-1

Below: The Seal of King Richard I, 'The Lionheart' (1189-99).

in Messina, still wrangling over the terms of their truce. Philip sailed for Acre in April 1191 but Richard spent the whole of May conquering Cyprus from the Byzantines and did not join the Crusaders before Acre until 8 June. The reinforcements he brought tipped the scale and Acre was finally taken on 12 July, but the Crusaders remained divided by the feud between Richard and Philip. The two kings took opposite sides in the opposing claims on the kingdom of Jerusalem, Richard supporting Guy de Lusig-

nan, and Philip Conrad de Montferrat. Pleading ill-health, Philip returned to France with the bulk of his troops in late July, leaving the effective command of the Crusade to Richard, who marched south from Acre in August.

Richard's handling of operations was impressive and showed a long overdue readiness to learn from Moslem tactics. He followed the line of the coast, shielding his inland flank with a hedge of crossbowmen and dismounted knights who prevented Saladin's horsemen from break-

Richard's last throw before sailing for home (and the indignity of being captured and held to ransom by his former ally). The Third Crusade ended with a whimper. After all the cost and effort, the Crusaders were left with nothing more than the coastal strip from Ascalon to Acre and the guarantee of pilgrim access to the religious center of Jerusalem.

With Richard's departure from Palestine in 1192 and the death of Saladin in the following year, the 'heroic age' of the Crusades came to its end. The predatory thirteenth-century adventures which disgraced the Crusading ideal met with the failure they deserved – a failure due, in the last analysis, to political rivalry rather than military inadequacy.

The holy wars of expansion

At bottom, the Crusades were a natural extension of the eleventh century wars of Latin expansion eastward in the Mediterranean. The unique inspiration of the Crusading ideal – the reconquest and retention of the Holy Land for the Latin Christian Church – was never powerful enough to eradicate the crippling feuds and rivalries which robbed the Crusaders' military efforts of so much effectiveness.

Throughout the period the Crusaders relied on their 'Sunday punch': the massed charge of the armored knights, whose armor was proof against the lightweight missile power of the Moslem opponents. In general, however, the Moslems' lighter cavalry had the advantage of being able to maneuver over terrain inimical to their more ponderous opponents, and usually managed to get the best out of the terrain of Syria and Palestine.

The Crusades also recognized the immense value of castles, both for controlling key areas of a conquered land and for 'pegging' a campaign by holding out, sometimes for months, until a relief army could come to the rescue. The lessons in military architecture adopted in Europe transformed castle design, resulting in much more powerful defense complexes designed for garrisons of economical size.

ing up the Crusader host as they had done at Hattin. At Arsuf (7 September 1191) Richard was robbed of what could have been a decisive victory over Saladin by a premature charge by the Hospitallers of the rearguard which caused the Moslems to pull back just as Richard was preparing for a decisive counterstrike. As it was he lost only 700 men to the Moslems' 7000, and marched on to take Jaffa two days later. If only the Crusader leaders could have sunk their differences the Third Crusade would probably have ended with the recapture of Jerusalem. Richard's forces approached to within 20 kilometers of the city by the end of the year, but were compelled to fall back on the coast. Another effort in the following year, equally unsupported, was

The Mongol Invasions

Left: Hungarian knights in battle against Mongols (note the mounted archers of the latter).

Below left: The nomadic warlord Jenghiz Khan in his tent, surrounded by attendants.

In comparison with the basic stability of Asia in the ancient world, the Middle Ages were remarkable for three great eruptions of horsed warriors from the wastes of central Asia, all of which profoundly affected the established order of the civilized world. The first of these eruptions had been the Huns, driving west in the fourth century AD and propelling the Goths through the overstretched perimeter of the Roman Empire like a man being pushed through a window. The second was the Magyars of the late ninth and tenth centuries, whose superficial resemblance to the Huns earned them their Western name of Hun-garians and gave the name of Hungary to the lands they conquered north of the Danube. But the third and greatest onslaught was the landslide of Mongol conquests in the thirteenth century which in five decades struck at every focus of civilization in Eurasia.

No such phenomenon had been known before and nothing like it has ever been seen since. Across the entire land mass of Eurasia came the Mongols in their disciplined thousands, commanded by ruthless and gifted leaders driven by the motive to destroy all opposition and conquer the world. They fell upon the ancient empire of China and conquered it; they overran the whole of central and southern Russia; they reduced the heartland of the Moslem world to servitude; and they pushed into Western Europe and smashed its armored hosts in pitched battle. They seemed like an elemental, almost supernatural force, able to ride, fight and butcher in all extremes of climate and terrain. (It may be noted that the Mongols are still the only military invaders on record to have coped successfully with the Russian winter.) To a world in which the idea of waging war according to chivalrous rules (written and unwritten) was beginning to emerge, the Mongols presented the reality of *total* war in a manner destined only to be surpassed 700 years later in the anti-civilian bombing raids of the two world wars.

Like the Magyars and Huns before them, the Mongols owed their military supremacy to the unique blend of mobility and missile power represented by the horsed archer. As we have seen, the Byzantines were the last civilized power to attempt the training of horsed archers as regular troops – an experiment abandoned by the seventh century because of the abundance of nomad tribal horsed archers suitable for recruitment either as allied or mercenary troops. By the time of Charlemagne's reign in the late eighth century the armored lancer, direct descendant of the Palmyran, Sassanid and late Roman cataphract, had become the standard heavy cavalryman of the Western world and was to remain so for the next 800 years.

The Magyars enter Europe

The westward surge of the Magyars from the Ukraine in the late ninth century forcibly reintroduced the west to a menace it had not known since the heyday of Attila 400 years before: the mounted horde of horsed archers, only this time wearing armored protection equal to that of Western cavalry and using fluid tactics which were not mistaken imitations of Western models. The seven Magyar *voivode* or hordes were made up of clans, about ten to 15 clans per *voivode* and each clan consisting of 1000-2000 warriors at maximum strength. Estimating the strength of a Magyar horde is almost as impossible as estimating that of a Viking army. Both varied widely and were almost certainly never as great as the improbable totals recorded by their victims' chroniclers. Certainly the Magyars never relied on numbers alone. Their tactical specialities were a daunting charge to unleash an arrow-storm, screaming their unearthly '*hui-hui!*' warcry, followed if necessary by a feigned flight to lure the incautious enemy off his chosen ground into enfilade fire.

Right: A Mongol horseman, from a miniature in the Victoria and Albert Museum, London. Note the archery equipment.

Below: Mongol horsemen sweep all before them in this Persian miniature. Note their swords, the long, slightly curved *saif* of the Arabs.

Left: 'The Four Horsemen of the Apocalypse' by Albrecht Dürer, 1500. The impact of the Mongol hordes was long-lived in Europe, and was probably the inspiration for the image of 'War' (extreme right) in this woodcut.

Right: The tented encampment of Jenghiz Khan; the warlord's personal tent was always pitched to give him an unobscured view of the horizon.

What the longship was to their contemporaries the Vikings, the horse was to the Magyars. Their endurance in the saddle, boosted by the practice of riding with spare mounts, gave the Magyars a tremendous speed and range of operations. In the half-century 895-955, Magyar hordes set off on devastating annual expeditions, spanning half Europe in their career. The most ambitious of the Magyar raids, launched from their chosen homeland north of the middle Danube, rivaled and indeed surpassed the famous invasion of Gaul by Attila the Hun back in 451. In 899 they broke into the Po valley and drove west as far as Pavia; in 907 they reached the Rhine, crossed it and advanced south into Provence; in 947 they raided Italy as far south as Apulia.

The Magyars' appearance on the military scene in 895-6 was a direct parallel with the defensive struggles of the Roman Empire in the fourth and fifth centuries. They were originally invited west of the Carpathians in 892 by King Arnulf of Germany, who wanted allies to crush the Slav kingdom of Greater Moravia. The Magyars duly obliged, but in so doing they discovered the internal rivalries and civil wars of the Carolingian Empire which they proceeded to exploit with gusto. Like the Vikings, the main objective of the Magyars was not permanent conquest. Their raids systematized warfare for profit, setting up a lucrative sequence of invasion and blackmail – Eastern Europe's equivalent of *Danegeld.*

One of the classic Magyar victories occurred in 899, during the first Magyar foray into north Italy. King Berengar I raised an army of 15,000 Lombards from which a Magyar horde of 5000 retreated at speed to the River Brenta, crossing the river and encamping on the far bank. Berengar's mistake was to try to match the Magyars' pace in his pursuit, then lower his guard at the vital moment. He was encouraged by a Magyar request for a safe conduct – a resort to fake diplomacy immediately reminiscent of the Goths before Hadrianopolis and a ploy used many

times by Viking raiders. The weary Lombards and their blown horses were resting and feeding when the Magyars suddenly poured across the river and fell on them. Those Lombards who could tried to flee the rout, only to be overtaken with ease by the Magyars on their fresh mounts. At Augsburg in 910, King Ludwig of Bavaria was obsessed with bringing the Magyars to battle and grouped his army in three divisions, but the Magyars' reaction was too quick for him. They defeated Ludwig's first two divisions piecemeal, were held off by his third division for about seven hours, then lured the Bavarians into an ambush with a feigned flight.

The Battles of Brenta and Augsburg were both instances of the Magyars eliminating the only effective enemy field army at the outset of the campaign, meeting no resistance during the subsequent rampage. No effective answer to the Magyars was found until the German kingdoms – like the English against the Danes – repaired their city fortifications and reorganized the recruitment of suitable defense forces. The first move in this direction was made in Saxony in the 920s, where the initial Magyar assault of 924 ran riot until one of the Magyar chieftains was captured. King Henry of Saxony released his prize in return for a treaty in which Saxony agreed to pay tribute for nine years in return for immunity from Magyar attacks. Henry used his time well, building fortified strongpoints and raising a force of serf troopers, similar to the English *fyrd* but trained to fight on horseback. When the treaty expired Henry refused to renew the payment of the tribute, inviting the Magyar assault for which he was now ready. At Riade near Merseburg (15 March 933) Henry exposed his infantry and serf cavalry to the approaching Magyar force, keeping his armored Bavarian and Franconian cavalry concealed for a timely ambush. Only a flat-out retreat at full gallop,

decidedly unfeigned, saved the Magyars from annihilation, but many were killed in the retreat to and crossing of the River Unstrut.

Without the example of Saxony, it is probable that the Magyars would never have been broken as early as they were. This took place with the Battle of the Lechfeld (10 August 955) after the united Magyar *voivode*, reputedly 100,000 strong, had invaded Bavaria and laid siege to Augsburg. In the face of this supreme threat all the duchies of Germany rallied to King Otto 'The Great' (936-73), who was trying to restore the Carolingian unification of Germany under his rule. The provincial contingents which joined Otto – Franconian, Saxon, Thuringian, Swabian, Bavarian and Bohemian – consisted entirely of armored cavalry, 10,000 strong at the outside. Otto began with raising the siege of Augsburg by advancing up the Magyars' line of retreat from the city. When they turned to offer battle Otto's seven divisions stood in line, shields raised against the arrows, to stop the Magyars' main frontal attack and a flank attack against the Bohemian division guarding the baggage train. Otto then ordered a general advance, which the Magyars failed to break up by feigning flight. When they found that all bridges and fords over the River Lech were strongly guarded the Magyar formations dissolved in a frantic *sauve qui peut*, with a relentless German pursuit killing thousands over the next three days.

Lechfeld shattered the Magyar supremacy for good and must be counted one of the decisive battles of the Middle Ages. The victory was the reward for a careful diagnosis of the most obvious military weakness of the Magyars – this was the limited repertoire of massed horsed archers when not given the sort of battle they wanted. Otto's most effective tactic was to refuse to be drawn and to make the Magyars come to him. The Magyar commander, Belcsu, either

had too many men to maneuver with precision, or lacked the flexibility to improvise a new plan after his flanking attack was beaten off. Admittedly the weather conditions at Lechfeld could hardly have been less favorable for the Magyars; as the battle was fought in a rainstorm, the wet must have slackened the Magyars' bowstrings and robbed their arrows of full penetrating power. Even then, ruthless archery aimed at killing or disabling the German horses would have proved disastrous for Otto, but the Magyars never seem to have attempted this; to a nation of horsemen, enemy horses were coveted prizes of war and valuable as potential remounts. Apart from that endemic military sin, over-confidence before the crucial battle, the Magyars relied mainly on their maneuverability. They lacked sufficiently heavy missile power to guarantee the defeat of well-armored cavalry; their *voivode* lacked structured and disciplined organization from troop level upwards; and they were invariably unsuccessful against well-defended fortifications. The defeat of the Magyars was the defeat of an essentially lightweight, disorganized military machine.

Not so the Mongols 300 years later, warriors in total contrast not only to the Magyars but to every other army in the history of the world. No soldiers in any age have endured more hardships, covered greater distances, fought more battles or overthrown more enemies. Hideous to look at and most terrible to fight, the Mongols imposed a unique if fleeting unity on the Moslem and Christian worlds – the unity of defeat. From the name of one of the Mongol tribes, the Tatars, and the *Tartarus* or hell of classical antiquity, the Christian West dubbed the Mongols 'Tartars': surely the legions of Satan let loose on a sinful world. With matchless and deadly efficiency they made war with the lid off, conquering from Germany to Indo-China in the space of 50 years.

The Mongol 'war machine'

The Mongol hardihood in the saddle, capacity for physical endurance and proficiency with the bow had of course existed for centuries before the time of Temujin (c 1154-1227); but it was Temujin who not only united the Mongol tribes under his rule but disciplined their natural martial talents into a world-beating military machine. It was in 1206, at a *kuriltai* ('general assembly') of Mongol vassals, that Temujin assumed the title Jenghiz Khan, 'all-mighty lord.' And the most famous description of the Mongol war machine as perfected by Jenghiz Khan was made by Marco Polo, writing in the time of Jenghiz Khan's grandson Kubilai:

They are stout fighters, excelling in courage and hardihood. Let me explain how it is that they can endure more than any other man. Often enough, if need be, they will go or stay for a whole month without provisions, drinking only the milk of a mare and eating wild game of their own taking. Their horses, meanwhile, support themselves by grazing, so that there is no need to carry barley or straw. They are very obedient to their masters. In case of need they will stay all night on horseback under arms, while their mount goes on steadily cropping grass. They are of all men in the world the best able to endure exertion and hardship and the least costly to maintain and therefore the best adapted for conquering territory and overthrowing kingdoms.

Now the plan on which their armies are marshaled is this. When a lord of the Tartars goes out to war with a following of 100,000 horsemen, he has them organized as follows. He has one captain in command of every ten [*arban*], one of every 100 [*jagun*], one of every 1000 [*minghan*], and one of every 10,000 [*tuman*], so that he never needs to consult with more than ten men. In the same way each commander of 10,000 or 1000 or 100 consults only with his immediate subordinates, and each man is answerable to his own chief. When the supreme commander wishes to send someone on some operation, he orders the

Above: A Persian manuscript illustration of Jenghiz Khan in battle with Tartar horsemen (c1198).

Left: A sixteenth century Persian manuscript illustration of a Mongol battle in 1201, from the *History of Jenghiz Khan.*

Right: Note the laminated or lamellar form of Mongol armor shown in this manuscript illustration of about 1330-40.

Below right: Jenghiz Khan fighting Chinese warriors in a mountain pass.

They are never ashamed to have recourse to flight. They maneuver freely, shooting at the enemy, now from this quarter, now from that. They have trained their horses so well that they wheel this way or that as quickly as a dog would do. When they are pursued and take to flight, they fight as well and as effectively as when they are face to face with the enemy. When they are fighting at top speed, they twist round with their bows and let fly their arrows to such good purpose that they kill the horses of the enemy and not a few of his men. As soon as the Tartars decide that they have killed enough of the pursuing horses and horsemen, they wheel round and attack and acquit themselves so well and so courageously that they gain a complete victory. By these tactics they have already won many battles and conquered many nations.

The discipline with which the Mongols underpinned their efficiency on campaign was the most ferocious on record since the floggings,

commander of 10,000 to give him 1000 men; the latter orders the captain of 1000 to contribute his share. So the order is passed down, each commander being required to furnish his quota towards the 1000. At each stage it is promptly received and executed. For they are all obedient to the word of command more than any other people in the world. You should know that the unit of 100,000 is called a *tuk* . . .

When an army sets out on some operation, whether it be in the plains or in the mountains, 200 men are sent two days' ride in advance as scouts, and as many to the rear and on the flanks; that is four scouting parties in all. And this they do so that the army cannot be attacked without warning.

When they are going on a long expedition, they carry no baggage with them. They each carry two leather flasks to hold the milk they drink and a small pot for cooking meat. They also carry a small tent to shelter them from the rain. In case of need, they will ride a good ten days' journey without provisions and without making a fire, living only on the blood of their horses; for every rider pierces a vein of his horse and drinks his blood. They also have their dried milk, which is solid like paste; and this is how they dry it. First they bring the milk to the boil. At the appropriate moment they skim off the cream that floats on the surface and put it in another vessel to be made into butter because so long as it remained the milk could not be dried. Then they stand the milk in the sun and leave it to dry. When they are going on an expedition, they take out about half a pound of it and put it in a small leather flask, shaped like a gourd, with as much water as they please. Then, while they ride, the milk in the flask dissolves into a fluid, which they drink . . .

Decimal unit breakdown was nothing new, but the one-man 'dog-tents' and preserved 'iron rations' were centuries ahead of their time. So was the use of specialized ammunition, also noted by Marco Polo, which took considerably longer to be adopted in the West:

Every soldier is ordered to carry into battle 60 arrows, 30 smaller ones for piercing and 30 larger with broad heads for discharging at close quarters. With these latter they wound one another in the face or arms and cut through bowstrings and inflict heavy losses. When they have shot away all their arrows, they lay hold of spear or club and deal mighty blows . . .

The Mongols exploited their maneuverability and fire power to the full, but in combat they did not aim at the enemy riders alone. For the Mongol archers were the answer to the perennial question about warfare in the pre-mechanized epoch: 'Why didn't they shoot the horses?'

decimations and executions of the Republican and Imperial Roman army. It was F J Veale, in *Advance to Barbarism*, who most neatly summed up the modern distaste for corporal and capital punishment: 'The attitude of the gallant Six Hundred which so aroused Lord Tennyson's admiration arose from the fact that the least dis-

position to ask the reason why was discouraged by tricing the would-be inquirer to the triangle and flogging him into insensibility.' Jenghiz Khan died six and a half centuries before such martinets as Lord Cardigan, but their objectives were fundamentally the same – both wished to make the troops fear their own officers more

than they feared the enemy. In the Mongol period, contemporary Western military discipline was a rough and ready affair, though Richard I of England had issued a pretty draconian code to preserve order during the outward voyage of the Third Crusade in 1190. But the West had nothing to match the savage punish-

Left: A sixteenth century Persian miniature of the Mongols capturing a Chinese town in 1205. Besides lamellar armor the Mongols also wore forms of coat armor, as depicted here.

Above right: In this miniature, Jenghiz tells the people of Bukhara that he has been sent as a punishment from God (an opinion shared, no doubt, by many of his victims).

ments recorded as normal among the Mongols by Marco Polo:

For a petty theft, not amounting to a capital offense, the culprit receives seven strokes of the rod, or 17 or 27 or 37 or 47, ascending thus by tens in proportion to his crime. And many die of this flogging. If the offender has stolen a horse or otherwise incurred the death penalty, he is chopped in two by the sword. If, however, he can afford to pay, and is prepared to pay nine times the value of what he has stolen, he escapes other punishment.

Marco Polo, however, was not a military man, and he missed some of the most interesting refinements of Mongol tactics and equipment. Though he noted the tough armor of boiled leather, he failed to enlarge upon the fact that only the front two ranks of the Mongols' five-deep formations were armored and carried lance and saber as well as the great composite bow. The rear three ranks were unarmored, and it was they who shouldered the task of harrying enemy formations with softening-up archery, advancing, firing and retiring behind their armored comrades until the time was right for the latter to charge home and administer the *coup de grace*. These unarmored troops wore fur or quilted tunics over undershirts of raw silk, the reason for this being that a spent enemy arrow piercing the tunic tended to be held by the silk; gentle tugging on the silk would then ease the arrowhead free and leave only a trivial flesh-wound. Nor did Marco Polo observe the excellent logistic support enjoyed by Mongol armies on the move, with separate traveling stores of bows, bowstrings, quivers, arrows and armor.

The conquests of Jenghiz Khan

Jenghiz Khan's first campaigns of conquest outside Mongolia were leveled against China, and in the early thirteenth century China was even more vulnerable to the Mongols than Sassanid Persia had been to the Arabs in the seventh century. The country was ripe for being devoured piecemeal, having split into three autonomous elements: the northern kingdom of Hsi Hsia or Tangut, then (south of the Great Wall, built a thousand years before to keep out the Huns) the Chin Empire of northern China, and the Sung Empire of the south. By 1212 Jenghiz had overrun the Hsi Hsia kingdom and was ready to embark on the conquest of the Chin Empire, a task virtually completed by the end of his reign.

Against the walled cities of China – *Khitai* to the Mongols, 'Cathay' to the West – the Mongols originally relied on blockade and starvation in the absence of siege engines and artillery of their own. They learned how to accelerate surrenders with terror tactics – the mass slaughter of men, women and children never lacked in persuasiveness – and frequently used stratagems to inflate their numbers and make resistance seem hopeless. One of these stratagems, much used during the invasion of fresh terrain, was to tie branches to the tails of their horses to kick up vast clouds of dust.

Long before he had got the upper hand in China, Jenghiz Khan had sent his first armies riding west. Eastern Turkestan, reduced by 1218, was easy meat, but beyond the appalling mountain barrier of the Pamirs (the 'Roof of the World') lay the Turkish Khwarizmian Empire: Persia and Transoxiana combined, including the rich trading cities of Tashkent, Samarkand, Bukhara and Balkh. In 1219 Jenghiz Khan broke

Ala-ad-Din Muhammad of Khwarizm in one of the most audacious campaigns of all time, himself descending on Samarkand from the north with 100,000 men while his general Jebei Noyon approached from the east through the Pamirs with 30,000. None of the immense suffering endured by Jebei Noyon's force during the crossing of the Pamirs prevented the Mongols from closing the pincers on Muhammad at Samarkand. Massacres and widespread destruction followed on the annihilation of the Khwarizmian forces, with the total of dead numbered at 180,000.

It was Jenghiz Khan's great general Subotai, entrusted with the pursuit of Muhammad with three *tumans*, who commanded the first Mongol army to operate thousands of kilometers from its homeland, obtaining its own intelligence about totally unfamiliar terrain and peoples, and supporting itself on an independent campaign lasting nearly four years. In 1220 Subotai chased Muhammad (at a pace approaching 130 kilometers a day) through Bukhara, Merv and Nish-

apur to the Caspian Sea, skirting its southern shore. When Muhammad died and Subotai's immediate mission was accomplished, they rode 1930 kilometers in under eight days to obtain Jenghiz Khan's approval of a raid round the Caspian before returning east. Having obtained the Khan's approval, Subotai then returned to his command and led it north into the mountain kingdom of Georgia (1221-2), shattering the Christian armored cavalry which, as it happened, had been mustered for a Crusading expedition. The victorious Mongol force, clearly inspired by Jebei Noyon's feat three years before, then crossed the Caucasus and pressed on to the north across the Kuban steppe to reach the Volga.

Instead of turning east and bypassing the Caspian to the north on his return home, Subotai first decided to cast west and investigate the lands north of the Black Sea to gain intelligence for future campaigns. This foray across the Volga, Don and Dniepr rivers into the southern

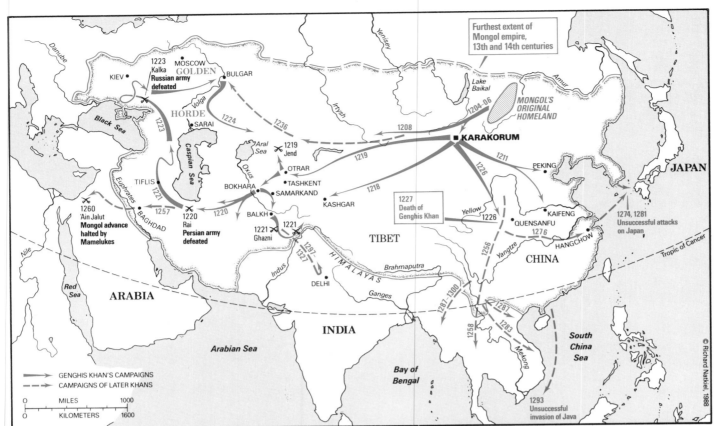

Left: The Mongol Empire in the thirteenth century.

Below: The Mongol invasion of Europe (1237).

Right: This miniature of the Tabriz School (fourteenth century) shows Mongol horsemen armed with sword, bow and mace.

Ukraine brought the Mongols into contact with the Russian Mstislav 'The Daring,' Prince of Galicia. He executed the Mongol envoys sent to him by Subotai and called on the lesser princes of southern Russia to join him by repelling the invaders. The subsequent Russian muster of 82,000 included several thousand allied light cavalry: Cumans, most recent of the Asiatic steppe peoples to establish themselves north and west of the Black Sea. In the resulting Battle of the River Khalka (1223) the Cumans fled at the first encounter, the blundering Russian armored lancers were shot to pieces and the hapless Russian foot militia, after holding out in their stockade for three days, surrendered and were butchered to a man.

Then Subotai turned for home, with the news that immense new conquests in the West were there for the taking – but Jenghiz Khan's last four years were taken up with the Chinese war. The conquest of the West was not resumed until 1236 at the order of the new Khan, Ogadai, who sent his nephew, Batu, west with a full-scale army and Subotai as joint commander. Subotai, from his earlier expedition in Russia, seems to

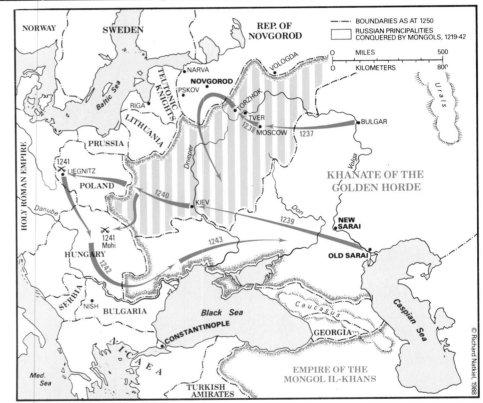

Left: A Tabriz miniature of about 1314 depicting the besieged defenders of a town advancing to do battle.

Right: A Persian miniature of Timur hunting. The dress, weapons and style of warfare employed by the Mongols influenced virtually the whole Middle East, extending across Asia to the borders of China.

have been the strategic mastermind of the immense campaign which followed. In 1236 the Bulgars of the middle Volga were broken, opening up the northern Russian principalities. Ryazan and Moscow fell in 1237; Novgorod, which the Mongols essayed in 1238, survived by virtue of the intervening swampland. The invaders headed south and west, devastating Kiev in 1240. Batu and Subotai then parted company for a parallel assault on Eastern Europe. Batu took Lublin, Krakow, and Ratibor before heading north through Breslau to annihilate the German-Polish army under Duke Henry of Silesia at Liegnitz (March 1241). Subotai meanwhile advanced into Hungary for a rendezvous with the victors of Poland at Gran near the Danube (4 April), before the utter destruction of the massed Hungarian army under King Bela V at Mohi (11 April). Subotai chased the fleeing Bela almost to the Adriatic in the follow-up slaughter after Mohi, which left central Europe open to the Mongols. The Danube had been crossed and Wiener Neustadt, south of Vienna, had already been reached when (December 1241) a message arrived that the 'Great Khan' Ogadai was dead. Batu and Subotai were required at the *Kuriltai* for the election of Ogadai's successor – and Europe was saved as the undefeated Mongol army withdrew to the east.

Under the subsequent Great Khans, Kuyuk (1242-8), Mangu (1248-59) and Kubilai (1259-94), the Mongols continued with their conquest of Sung China in the East, but in the West it was the Moslem, not the Christian world, that took the brunt. While Mangu Khan and his brother Kubilai proceeded with the war against Sung China, their younger brother Hulagu undertook the destruction of the Baghdad Caliphate. Mesopotamia, Armenia and Georgia were added to the new Mongol 'Ilkhanate' of Persia, with Baghdad falling in 1258. Hulagu also liquidated the Syrian 'County of the Assassins,' whose rulers had plagued the Latin Crusader states for over a century. But his attempt to conquer the

Mamluks of Egypt, who had gone from strength to strength since the death of Saladin 67 years before, produced the one clearcut defeat suffered by the Mongols during their rise: Ain Jalut, fought in 1260.

Admittedly, Ain Jalut was not the defeat of a 'pure bred' Mongol army, but that of a surrogate force of subject Turks, Georgians and Arme- nians officered by Mongols and commanded by the Mongol general Kitbugha. At Ain Jalut he fell into the same trap as the Magyars at Riade, storming forward against an apparently failing enemy line only to run into a fatal ambush sprung from both flanks – a fate which would never have befallen Jubei Noyon or Subotai. If Liegnitz and Mohi were the Mongol victories that should have heralded the defeat of Western Europe, Ain Jalut was definitely the battle that saved Mamluk Egypt. (The subsequent victories of Baibars Bundukdari, the victor at Ain Jalut, sealed off Mesopotamia from Syria and forced the Polos to make a long detour north through Armenia and Georgia at the start of their long journey out to China in 1271.)

Left: A Persian miniature of Bahram Gur hunting; note the thumb ring (often carved from jade or ivory) worn by the archer. This was never adopted by European bowmen, who used their fingers rather than the thumb to pull back the bowstring. The Eastern method was more effective with re- curved bows.

Right: Another Persian (Tabriz) miniature of Bahram Gur, dating from about 1330-40. He carries a mace of typical Persian form, as well as the inevitable bow, bow-case and arrows, and sword.

The Polos were by no means the only Europeans to travel through the Mongol Empire and record what they saw. They were preceded by one especially keen-eyed Franciscan friar, Giovanni di Piano Carpini, who was sent out to the Mongol capital of Karakorum by Pope Innocent V in 1245. When he got back, Carpini wrote a circular report advising the rulers of Europe on how, ideally, the Mongols should be fought. His first recommendation was missile power, strong bows and crossbows firing armor-piercing missiles. Infantry should receive the Mongol charge with long, hooked poleaxes suitable for dragging the Mongols from their saddles. Armor should be of double-strength mail; horses should also be armored; the Mongol decimal unit organization should be copied; and battle with Mongol armies should only be accepted on a flat open plain depriving the Mongols of all surprise moves. As an alternative, Carpini recommended the choice of battlefields where the Mongols would be unable to get at the defenders' flanks or rear because of a handy forest or river. Here at least the good friar was forgetting the Mongols' capacity for making any kind of terrain a battlefield ideal for their tactics. And as Ain Jalut demonstrated in 1260, merely aping the Mongol formula was no guarantee of victory.

Marco Polo observed the Mongols when they had just passed their peak and were imperceptibly beginning their decline in the 1280s and 1290s. The lands conquered by Jenghiz Khan and his successors now consisted of semi-sovereign khanates; the western khanate or 'Golden Horde' in Russia, the Ilkhanate of Persia and the Chagatai khanate of Turkestan, all nominally subject to the Great Khanate of Kubilai, which now embraced all China. But the western khanates had already come to blows on occasion, the casualties when Mongol armies fought each other being proportionately as murderous as those in the Roman Empire's civil wars. And Kubilai's armies had been twice re-

pulsed by the Japanese, though the Mongols had conquered upper Burma and pushed down the coast of Indo-China (Champa) to the latitude of modern-day Da Lat.

Marco Polo adds the interesting information of how the Mongols coped with the apparition of Burmese war elephants and the consequent panic of their 'unproofed' horses. The Mongols merely dismounted, tethered their horses and showered the elephants with arrows until the wretched beasts stampeded through the Burmese ranks – whereupon the Mongols remounted and clinched the victory in their usual style. But they ended the battle trying to capture the surviving elephants with an eye to their future use in Mongol service.

Here was the essence of the Mongols' war machine. They wasted nothing and adopted anything useful: Greek and Persian physicians, crude naphtha incendiary missiles, Western-style weight-and-counterpoise siege catapults (*trebuchets*). Unlike the earlier Huns or Magyars, the Mongols did not fight merely to plunder, destroy and extort, but to conquer and rule as well – the East's equivalent, on a gigantic scale, of the Normans. This meant adopting the most useful attributes of the people they subjugated – men like Ye'lu Chutsai of the conquered Chin Empire, the trusted Chinese minister of Jenghiz Khan. As the great Ming wars of liberation proved in China within 80 years of Kubilai's death, the Mongols preserved the nationalism of their conquered victims rather than destroying it.

The gory career of Timur or Tamerlane (1396-1404) was the last great explosion of Mongol military efficiency – but it was also a decided postscript to the true heyday of the Mongols in the previous century. Seeking to recreate the empire of Jenghiz Khan, he overthrew his master, the Chagatai khan, and progressively overran all the surviving western khanates. Timur even invaded India and penetrated Asia

Minor – but his conquests were rootless and perished with him. Had the Mongols of the thirteenth century, like Timur, been mere destroyers, the conquests of Jenghiz Khan would have melted away on his death. But they were as far superior to the earlier Huns and Magyars as the Normans were to the first Viking raiders, justly qualifying for the title of the best soldiers of the Middle Ages, and by no means the worst rulers, of all time.

The greatest of the Asiatic 'hordes'

The Mongols brought horsed archery to its highest peak of development, using it with deadly and versatile efficiency against all comers. But behind their horsemanship, marksmanship and matchless hardiness lay a structure and discipline equal to that of any age and superior to nearly all.

The suspension of the Mongol assault on Europe under the brilliant generalship of Subotai was due to an accident of history – the death of Ogadai Khan, and the decision of his eventual successor Mangu to concentrate on the Moslem rather than the Christian West. Compared with the terrain which they had overcome in Asia the Mongols would have found Western Europe an easy proposition. The military systems and techniques of the West were ludicrous in their comparative crudity, and it is impossible to see how, after Liegnitz and Mohi, they could have evolved fast enough to survive had the Mongols been able to follow up their victories.

Though the Mongols were the last and greatest of the 'Asiatic hordes' to break out of central Eurasia during the Middle Ages, they were the only one to show the will and ability to impose a genuine Eurasian *pax*. At no other time in the history of the world has it been possible, as the Polos demonstrated, to travel overland from the Mediterranean to the Pacific under the protection of a passport issued by the overlord of the entire intervening land mass.

Castles and Siege Warfare

Broadly speaking there were two types of medieval castle. There were those built at immense cost to embody the latest designs in military architecture, and those which, like Topsy in *Uncle Tom's Cabin*, 'just growed' and underwent repeated improvements and modifications. As nearly every castle started life by being built in a hurry on a site of prime strategic importance, the defenses of the castle tended to become obsolete while the importance of the site remained undiminished. Consequently the second category remained considerably larger than the first.

Designing and siting a medieval castle was very like designing a modern battle tank in that the contradictory needs of the offensive and defensive roles always produced a welter of conflicting essentials. The idea of castles possessing an offensive role often causes surprise to laymen, but in fact castle were never intended to perform a purely *defensive* function. It will be remembered that the Vikings were the first medieval people to rediscover the virtue of field fortifications which had been second nature to imperial Roman armies moving into enemy territory; and that the Saxon English, emulating their enemies' technique, had reconquered the Danelaw in the tenth century behind a deepening framework of fortified *burhs*. The primary role of the later castles, built during and after the eleventh century, was to control the surrounding countryside in the interests of the local lord (who might or might not be a loyal vassal of the king).

To exercise this control in peacetime, the castle had to be designed to permit regular sorties by the officials and troops of the lord.

Thus castles were sited to dominate the most important geographical point – road junction, river crossing or valley – in a region which was vital to guarantee the holder control of the area, which meant frustrating any enemy attempt to penetrate that area. No such enemy could succeed unless he actually captured the castle, which naturally had to be strong enough to beat off attacks until relieved.

Here again the castle's defensive function was balanced by the offensive function – or rather the potentially offensive function, in that the garrison of a bypassed castle could always sortie

Left: The massive masonry of Burgh castle in Norfolk, one of a series of Roman coastal forts built to guard against the threat of Saxon invasion.

Right: The West Gate of the old Roman fort at Pevensey in Sussex. Roman rule in Britain had already ended when the Saxon invader Aelle (later King of Sussex) landed here in 491 and massacred the local population.

Below left: A tower built on one corner of the curtain wall of Burgh castle; note the courses of flat 'tile' masonry, a typical Roman feature.

Below: Pevensey castle; the Roman outer wall was strengthened by the Normans, who also built a keep here, shortly after the Conquest.

Left: The interior of Pevensey castle, showing the original Roman masonry.

Right: This Norman motte-and-bailey castle at Pickering in North Yorkshire was originally of earth and timber, and only later rebuilt in stone. The remains of the stone keep can be seen on the right of the photograph.

to strike at the enemy's line of communication. An elusive enemy force living off the countryside would remain a menace until brought to battle and defeated. If such an enemy force had no choice but to sit down and besiege a castle, the defending field army could be given time in which to catch the enemy between the castle and the relieving army. In this way, the castle's role in the local or national counteroffensive was the

Left: The circular twelfth-century 'shell-keep' of Restormel castle in Cornwall. It was sometimes difficult to build a massive stone tower on a foundationless artificial earth mound; the shell-keep was one solution to the problem.

Right: The Norman stone keep at Rochester, 120 feet high, is the tallest in England. It was built in 1127.

same as that of the Roman walled cities in the third, fourth and fifth centuries. So far as the more immediate demands of the counteroffensive were concerned – during the siege – the castle garrison had to be able to inflict maximum damage on the besiegers in every assault made on the defenses, and whenever conditions were suitable sally out to beat up the besiegers in their camp, destroy their siege-engines, stampede their horses, burn their supplies and generally cause disruption.

The development of castle design

As already noted the Norman motte-and-bailey was the 'instant castle' *par excellence*, natural successor to the Roman marching camp, Viking field rampart and Saxon *burh*. Its most obvious limitation was the short life and vulnerability to fire of its wooden palisades, particularly the palisade girdling the castle's keep. Replacing this palisade with a circular stone wall made a shell keep, and this comparatively simple conversion was made throughout the later medieval period. To take three examples at random, the English West Country motte-and-baileys at Launceston, Restormel and Totnes were converted into shell keeps in the twelfth, thirteenth and fourteenth centuries respectively.

But the motte-and-bailey was best suited to dominating open country or small towns. It was clearly unsuitable for planting inside the walls of large towns and cities for which a dominating castle was required. The wasteful spread of the motte base took up far too great an unused area, and the keep on top was too small for the many associated functions of a city castle. Such castles usually housed not only a regular garrison but the treasury (and mint, if it was a capital city or town holding a royal licence to strike coinage) and city arsenal. As likely as not the city castle

was also used as a royal residence when the king passed through, demanding suitable living chambers, a chapel and accommodation for courtiers and leading members of the royal household.

To accommodate these extra functions the tower keep or donjon appeared in the late eleventh century. This comprised a square stone tower of several stories with battlements at the top from which the whole town could be com-

manded. The great advantage of the tower keep was that it could be built conveniently into an angle of the town walls, thus becoming the heart of the defenses. To prevent surprise attacks on the keep, access to it was prevented by a shock-absorbing ward – usually an inner and outer ward – an enclosed area performing the same function as the bailey in the motte-and-bailey.

Tower keep and ward was another combination which went through continuous extension and improvement in the late medieval period, and probably the best-known example in the

world is the Tower of London. Five hundred years after the Tower was begun, the writer John Snow summed up the roles of what must be the most famous of all medieval castles:

. . .a Citadel, to defend or commaund the Citie: a royal place for assemblies, and treaties. A Prison of estate, for the most daungerous offenders: the only place of coynage for all England: the armorie for war-like provision: the Treasurie of the ornaments and Jewels of the Crowne, and generall conserver of the Recordes of the Courts of Justice at Westminster.

London had grown around the lowest point that it was possible to bridge the River Thames, and it was at the southeastern extremity of the old Roman city wall of London that William sited his great tower keep – the White Tower – around 1078. Shielded on the east side by the city wall, on the south side by the Thames, and on the west and north sides by a simple ditch, the elegant bulk of the White Tower was one of the biggest castles in the Christian West when completed. But the original defended area was too small for comfort and its extension to the westward was begun at the end of the twelfth century by Richard I (1189-99). Under Richard's orders a new outer ditch was dug on the north and west sides, while Richard's nephew Henry III (1216-72) cut through the city wall on the east side, and added a curtain wall completely enclosing the Tower on its northern side.

By the end of the twelfth century the biggest weaknesses of castles – whether motte-and-bailey or tower keep and surrounding wall – had made themselves apparent across Europe. No matter how ingeniously they were laid out, the keep and the bailey remained separate entities, and the enemy's sudden capture of the bailey could catch the garrison before it had had time to withdraw in full strength to the keep. The best solution seemed to be the strengthening of the outer wall by studding it with towers, which projected out from the wall. From these towers garrison marksmen could shoot at any part of the wall without exposing themselves to enemy fire, preventing attackers from reaching the foot of the wall without heavy losses. The towers also acted like watertight compartments, considerably adding to the wall's defensive value as an enemy storming the wall could be counter-attacked from the towers.

Another serious problem was the structural weakness of the rectangular tower keep, which was vulnerable to battering at its corners. Wall corners were also a favorite target for mining:

driving a short tunnel under the wall, supporting the turret with brushwood, firing it and bringing down a section of the rubble-filled wall above with the tunnel's subsequent collapse.

Castle design was transformed by the experiences of the Crusades when Western armies came up against the vast tower-studded walls of cities like Antioch, Acre and Jerusalem. Western and Eastern technique with fortifications blended to produce such masterpieces as the Krak des Chevaliers, laid out like a miniature fortified city within a curtain wall with towers. The Krak was like no other European eleventh-century castle in existence. Here there was no vulnerable bailey, awkwardly tacked on to a keep – there was no keep. The Krak was a triumphal experiment in a totally new style of castle building: the concentric castle, with no one sector offering an obvious weak point to the attacker. Prodigious effort would be needed before all the outer towers and wall sections could be reduced, whereupon the attacker would immediately come under the fire of the even stronger inner defenses.

Krak des Chevaliers was admittedly an inspired prototype; other Crusader castles retained an unmistakable European stamp. At Giblet, for instance, the square tower was surrounded by a square curtain wall with square towers at its corners. And the Norman keep at Sahyun was surrounded not by a concentric wall

complex but by a mighty ditch or moat, one of the most impressive feats of rock cutting of the Middle Ages: 15-27 meters wide and 18-40 meters deep, but leaving a needle of rock in front of the main gate to carry the center span of a drawbridge. Sahyun staggered T E Lawrence, who called it 'the most sensational thing in castle building I have seen: the hugely solid keep upstanding on the edge of the gigantic fosse.'

Château Gaillard – the 'super castle'

The most famous example of how the Crusades affected European castle design was Château Gaillard, the 'saucy castle' built by Richard I at Les Andelys on the Seine in 1197-8. Apart from being the most decisive proof that Richard was a military genius and not a mere oaf who rejoiced in combat, the story of Château Gaillard is a comprehensive lesson on the role of the castle in medieval warfare. Château Gaillard was a direct product of the incessant eleventh-century wars between the Angevin kings of England and Philip Augustus of France, the Angevins trying to conquer the Vexin (the buffer zone between Rouen and Paris), and Philip trying to oust the Angevins from Normandy. Richard built Château Gaillard to command the crossing of the Seine at Les Andelys, as a bulwark for the defense of Normandy and a perfect base for offensive operations against the Vexin. He set out deliberately to build a castle which could

Above left: The White Tower, better known as the Tower of London, was begun by William the Conqueror in 1078. The keep owes its name to the fact that it was originally white-washed. This fifteenth century illustration shows the Duc d'Orléans being held for ransom.

Right: The White Tower as it is today. In its time it was (often simultaneously) a fortress, a palace, the center of government, an arsenal, a prison, and a place of execution.

never be taken and which would impede each and every French move against Normandy – the epitome of the castle's offensive-defensive role.

The siting of Richard's new castle was inspired. It was positioned on a high, rocky crag above the river from which the castle walls rose sheer, making orthodox battering and mining impossible. The configuration of the site, plus Richard's compilation of existing ideas in military architecture, resulted in a unique blend of the old motte-and-bailey and the eastern concentric layout. The castle was entered via a wedge-shaped outer ward with curtain wall and round towers, exploiting the last possible yard of the crag to bring as much of the river as possible under the castle's imperious scowl. A bridge led upwards over a deep ditch into a similarly protected middle ward, enclosing an oval-shaped inner ward around a towering *cylindrical* keep, its upper storeys strengthened with tapering downward spurs and its lower storey 'battered' – sloped outward – for even greater strength. Château Gaillard, in short, transformed the traditional European keep-and-bailey layout by grafting on the hill-crowning domination and concentric layout of Krak des Chevaliers, and the sheer walls and yawning ditches of Sahyun.

If Richard had erected nothing more than a tent and palisade at Les Andelys he would have been violating the current truce with Philip, but the prodigy of Château Gaillard was an intolerable insult – and an objective which Philip must take, if he were ever to break the Angevin hold on Normandy. For the last 18 months of Richard's life his boast – that he could hold his 'pretty child of one year' even if its walls had been made of butter – held true. But in April 1199 Richard died of a missile wound suffered while he was trying to take the castle of Chalus in the Limousin. Inevitably, Philip renewed the French pressure on Normandy. And under the disastrous military leadership of Richard's brother and successor John (1199-1216) Château Gaillard proved that there was no such thing as an impregnable castle – just as, seven centuries later, the *Titanic* was to prove there is no such thing as an unsinkable ship.

Though he had realized his dream of building a 'super-castle' proof against any conceivable form of assault, Richard had intended Château Gaillard to play the normal role of the castle in military operations, be they offensive or defensive. Nothing he could do could prevent Château Gaillard from being as vulnerable as any other castle or town to starvation in a long blockade. Its survival as the toughest Angevin stronghold south of the Channel depended on its supply line being kept open or forced open. This John failed to do when Philip invested Château Gaillard in September 1203. As the months went by without John making any positive move, all that happened was that more and more of the Norman barons made their peace with Philip to retain their lands, a vicious circle which made it increasingly harder for John to raise a reliable relief force. Finally, in December 1203, he lapsed into one of the fits of sullen inertia which fomented so much sorrow during his reign and went back to England.

But Château Gaillard's castellan Roger de Lacey refused to give up hope of eventual relief and continued to hold on. His garrison was even more isolated than the German Sixth Army after the Soviet break through at Stalingrad in November 1942 (which at least received a trickle of air-lifted supplies) and he had an acute problem in the 400-odd non-combatants – children, soldiers' wives and camp whores – who had been trapped in the castle at the commencement of the siege. To eke out the castle stores de Lacey ordered Château Gaillard's non-combatants to pack up and leave, hoping that Philip would let them through the French lines – but Philip refused. He ordered the refugees to return to Château Gaillard. De Lacey refused to let them in. For the next *three weeks*, defenseless 'troops' in the battle of morale, they were forced to camp out in the open among the rocks at the foot of the castle crag. Most of them failed to survive on their enforced diet of river water, berries, weeds and the rare frogs and fishes they managed to catch, while exposure in the increasingly cold nights carried off more by the dozen. When Philip finally relented over 200 had died, their suffering witnessed by day and heard by night by their menfolk on the ramparts of Château Gaillard. (The death toll was, we are told, boosted even more when the starving survivors got their first square meal in many months and some fatally over-ate.)

Inflicted as it was by men who had taken oaths to protect the weak and helpless, and who in peacetime made fashionable play with their devotion to the code of chivalrous conduct, this atrocity made Château Gaillard's ordeal one of the nastiest sieges of the Middle Ages. And it was all for nothing. Roger de Lacey surrendered when his provisions were exhausted on 8 March 1204. But his tenacity and its dreadful side effects during the six-month siege had not even won time in which the defense of Normandy could be assured. John's inert refusal to cross from England and take command prompted a landslide of capitulation after Château Gaillard's surrender – Falaise, Caen, Bayeux, Barfleur and Cherbourg to Philip; Mont St Michel and Avranches to his Breton allies. Rouen, the

Left: The famous Crusader castle of Krak des Chevaliers, 10 miles north of the present-day Lebanon border, was begun by the Hospitallers in 1142. It finally fell to the Moslems in 1271.

Right: Château Gaillard was built by Richard I between 1196 and 1198 to defend Normandy and the River Seine from his arch-rival Philip II. Henry IV of France ordered it demolished in 1603.

Below right: An illustration depicting siege warfare tactics in the thirteenth and fourteenth centuries. Sappers with picks attempt to undermine a castle wall; a moveable canopy called a 'sow' protects them from rocks, pointed stakes and various combustible mixtures hurled down by the defenders.

Norman capital, now totally isolated, surrendered to Philip on Midsummer Day 1204.

But the depressing circumstances of the siege of Château Gaillard could not disguise the fact that careful planning could produce an *assault-proof* 'super-castle,' and as the thirteenth century wore on the trend toward strong round towers, enclosing curtain walls and concentric defenses continued. One of the most notable features was the steady increase in the castle's fire power by adding galleries for archers and crossbowmen, sometimes incorporating a 'two-decker' arrangement with an orthodox upper gallery of crenellated battlements on top of the castle walls and a second gallery and firing-slits below. Stone *machicolations* replaced the vulnerable wooden stages which twelfth-century garrisons were wont to sling from the battlements to drop unpleasant objects – rocks, showers of red-hot sand, pots of boiling oil – on attackers at the foot of the wall. Machicolations were a permanent extension of the upper battlements, built outward from the main wall on small arches with traps in the floor through which missiles could be dropped.

Another trend was the continuing division of castle defenses into self-sufficient compartments, particularly around any castle's weakest point, the main gate. Tower gatehouses emerged, massive structures big enough to accommodate the lord, his family and a small core of trusted troops – an offshoot of the practice of hiring mercenaries as garrison troops, men whose professionalism did not preclude a healthy instinct for survival when the going got rough. Gatehouse defenses were in turn protected by *barbicans* which funneled attacks on the gate between two stone walls built out from the main curtain wall. Any attackers who penetrated a barbican could be cut off by dropping a heavy portcullis in their rear and annihilated from above like fish in a trap. Where the lie of the land was right, approach to the main curtain wall might be screened by an outer *hornwork*, a

development of the eleventh century bailey. All these refinements had the same basic aim to present the attacker with successive defenses of increasing strength, and keep his battering and ramming siege engines as far away from the main defenses as possible. These principles were destined to survive the advent of gunpowder and cannon, finally being 'codified' for troops with cannon and infantry firearms by the Frenchman Vauban in the late seventeenth century.

Easily the most impressive medieval castles anywhere in Europe were built in the late thirteenth century by Edward I of England (1275-1307) who, like Richard I, Château Gaillard's doting 'father,' had served in the Holy Land as a Crusader. One of Edward's first acts when he became king was to scour Europe for the best military architect on the market and in about 1278

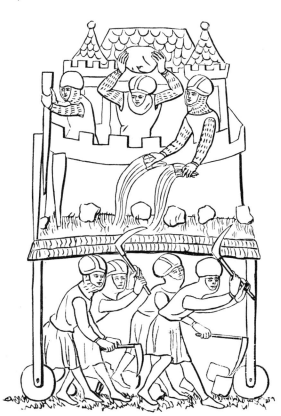

he won the service of Maître Jacques de St George, a Savoyard by birth. No other medieval craftsman on record in English state service ever earned more than Maître Jacques. He received three shillings a day, far more even than the chief justices of the kingdom. It was Maître Jacques who supervised the building of the giant castles ordered by Edward to seal the conquest of Wales, and on which Edward lavished unheard-of sums: about £14,000 for Beaumaris, the same for Conway and £27,000 for Caernarvon. Maître Jacques also had a hand in the extensive overhaul of existing castle defenses. Adding an outer concentric layer to the Tower of London's defenses, which completed the complex which the modern-day tourist sees, cost £12,000: almost as much as the Welsh giants.

Castles – costly and ingenious defenses

By the fourteenth century the castle had reached the peak of its development in the pre-gunpowder age. In its most comprehensive form – as exemplified by Edward I's Welsh prodigies – the castle had been rendered proof against direct assault and would remain so until the development of heavy battering cannon late in the following century. The concentric layout made it virtually impossible for attackers to mine under the walls or smash a breach in them with the most powerful catapults available. The main gate, once the castle's Achilles' heel, had been transformed into the strongest point of the defenses (in many cases it was far easier to take the rest of the castle than the gatehouse and barbican). In the space of a mere two centuries the castle had come a very long way from the eleventh century motte-and-bailey. Until siege cannon became an essential part of an army's weaponry, the castle's role in dominating defensive strategies remained unshakable. Against the most costly and ingenious defenses ever contrived in the history of warfare only one sure weapon has survived, the one which given time, could never fail – blockade and starvation.

Wales and Scotland: a contrast in case histories

Setting aside the nomad Asiatic, Arab and Scandinavian irruptions of the early Middle Ages, and adding the Mongol phenomenon of the thirteenth century, the most usual catalyst of warfare in the Middle Ages was feudalism. Constantly subject to both forceful and peaceful redefinition (the former more often than the latter), the so-called 'feudal system' sought to regulate society at home and abroad – an attempt to tidy an untidy world. When it came to making war, the claim that traditional feudal rights had been violated was a great conscience-saver. Whether dissected from the social, ethnic, economic or nationalistic point of view, the wars of the Middle Ages reveal either feudal lords trying to make their claimed authority real or feudal vassals claiming breach of contract and defying their feudal lords. Even the Crusades can be seen as an attempt to found new states whose rulers, via the king of Jerusalem, would owe fealty to no middleman other than the Pope.

Most conveniently in miniature, the campaigns of Edward I of England against Wales and Scotland at the end of the thirteenth century show this process at work, like a chemical reaction studied in a test tube. They show one peaceful kingdom, under an exceptionally able medieval king, resorting to force in order to assert its lordship over two weak neighbors. One of the latter, Wales, succumbed; Scotland fought

off Edward's assaults and those of his son, preserving independence. These wars against Wales and Scotland therefore present a contrast in case histories of warfare during the high noon of the Middle Ages.

Above: The gatehouse, south door and moat of Rhuddlan castle; built in 1277-82 to replace a motte-and-bailey.

Below: Rhuddlan castle, Clwyd.

Right: Caernarvon castle; the 'Eagle Tower' looking eastward. Begun in 1283 during the second Welsh war it was the center of Edward I's government in the north.

Left: Beaumaris castle on the Isle of Anglesey was Edward I's last Welsh castle; it was begun in 1294 during the last Welsh rebellion, but was left unfinished in 1296 when the war ended and Edward turned his attention to Scotland.

The Welsh campaigns of Edward I

By the 1270s the Welsh had managed to preserve their independence for some 600 years, ever since they had been pushed back into their mountains by the advancing Anglo-Saxons. Wales had stayed free for three main reasons: its mountains, its foul climate and the fact that no English ruler had ever scientifically tackled the problem of conquering the place. The latter undertaking remained unnecessary as long as Wales remained divided between sub-kings and princelings willing to pay homage to the English crown in order to be left alone. English kings before and after the Norman Conquest had found it enough to entrust the English shires along the Welsh border to tough fighting lords permitted to hold what they could take from the Welsh. None of these marcher lords was strong enough to tackle Wales by himself, and all previous royal expeditions against the Welsh had ended the same way. The Welsh would pull back into the heights of Snowdonia and wait, fed by the island granary of Anglesey, for the English to give up and go home.

The feudal wheeling and dealing behind Edward I's Welsh wars is deceptively complicated. They were the reply to over 20 years' successful exploitation of English internal strife by Llewelyn ap Gruffud, prince of Gwynedd and self-proclaimed 'Prince of Wales.' Edward knew perfectly well that the Welsh principalities were already neatly hedged by English marcher lordships and that the Welsh principalities formed a romantic idea rather than a united nation. The English king was quite prepared to recognize a native 'Prince of Wales' – provided that the said prince disgorged all the ill-gotten territorial gains acquired from the English over the past 20 years, did proper homage to the English crown for his lands and refrained from taking his 'independence' too seriously. Llewelyn's defiance

of Edward's claims was as intolerable as it was ill-judged, for Edward had already proved his formidable talents as a soldier in the civil wars before the death of his father and departure on Crusade.

Edward's campaign against Llewelyn in 1277 was a military gem. It was soundly prepared, perfectly timed and executed with a precision and economy of human life and material damage which still deserves applause. It was a blow against Llewelyn's fastness of Snowdonia. But there was no need for a direct assault. Edward had diagnosed Snowdonia's 'Achilles' heel': Anglesey. Once the Welsh in Snowdonia had been deprived of provisions from Anglesey, they must be defeated as surely as night follows day. To make certain of Anglesey Edward raised a picked force of knights, archers, crossbowmen, woodsmen and engineers to clear the way, and a well-organized supply train. He knew the maximum strength he would need, he took his time raising it, and the result was the best English army assembled since the Norman Conquest. By the end of August 1277 Edward had a maximum strength of 800 armored cavalry and 15,640 infantry. About half Edward's infantry was native Welsh – the best possible proof of the disunity of Wales and of the readiness of the people to serve English lords in return for a fair deal. The army was supported in the advance along the north Wales coast and during the amphibious bound to Anglesey by a fleet of 30 ships supplied by the Channel ports.

From his base at Chester Edward first advanced to command the Dee estuary, beginning a new castle at Flint (17 July 1277). He was in no hurry; the coming campaign was scheduled to coincide with the ripening of the crops on Anglesey. In August Edward made a 'progress' or royal visitation through Cheshire, with the queen and court in company, before moving on

to Rhuddlan, where a second castle was founded. The third and final move was an advance to Deganwy on the River Conway (29 August) and landing on Anglesey. By the middle of September Llewelyn, with all his intended supplies neatly harvested by the enemy, had no choice but to sue for peace.

This near-perfect use of military force to attain a political objective was not, and perhaps could never have been, mirrored by the political settlement of the 1277 campaign. In the ensuing Treaty of Conway (9 November 1277) the Conway became the new frontier between 'English north Wales' and Gwynedd; Llewelyn retained Anglesey and Snowdonia along with his title 'Prince of Wales' in return for recognition of Edward's lordship and authority over Wales. The south of the country and the marches reverted to English control, and new castles studded a containing arc of territory stretching from Aberystwyth southeast to Builth, and north through Montgomery to Dinas Bran on the upper Dee. From Dinas Bran the castle chain forked, one arm reaching down to the Dee estuary via Hope, Hawarden and Flint; the other arm controlling the Clwyd valley via Ruthin, Denbigh and Rhuddlan. A sense of being penned within a belt of alien strongholds, and a growing list of grievances and complaints against biased English crown officials, prompted the revolt of March 1282 and the second Welsh war.

From the start the rebels lacked effective leadership which was split between Llewelyn and his ambitious brother David. (It was David who opened the war with his surprise capture of Hawarden Castle on the night of 21 March 1282.) They also lacked an overall strategy save that of taking and demolishing as many castles as could be surprised, and ambushing English forces of sufficiently convenient size. Edward's planning, on the other hand, was as methodical

Right: Caernarvon castle; note how the Eagle Tower dominates the skyline. As much as anything this showpiece of castle architecture made a political statement about the English presence in Wales.

Below: Edward I's finest achievement in castle building: Caernarvon castle, Gwynedd.

as it had been in 1277. When he heard of the revolt in the last week of March, he ordered the marcher lords to hold the line with their own forces and called a muster of the English gentry at Worcester for 17 May. Building on this foundation, Edward then issued a formal summons of the feudal host at Rhuddlan for 2 August, the time of military service being the normal one of 40 days. He was planning a repeat performance of the 1277 campaign but this time also intended to use Anglesey as the base for a flank attack across a bridge of boats while the main English army advanced directly against the Welsh across the Conway.

Though Anglesey was taken in August, the campaign was delayed by the need to recover all the outposts east of the Clwyd lost to David since March, and Denbigh, the last of David's gains, was not recovered until October. By the end of the month David and Llewelyn had been pushed back into Snowdonia and the situation was rapidly resembling that of September 1277 – but events now took a dramatically new twist. John Pecham, Archbishop of Canterbury, insisted on traveling into Snowdonia to negotiate a peace settlement with the rebel princes. These negotiations had reached the mutual-statement-of-grievances stage when the commander of Angle-

sey, Sir Luke de Tany, suddenly broke the tenuous truce. Despite the king's strict orders that the Anglesey force was not to move until ordered, de Tany led an arrogantly small force of 150 knights across the bridge of boats to the mainland on 6 November. His motives will never be known. It may have been sheer impatience after weeks of inactivity or a deliberate attempt to torpedo the peace talks. Either way it was a fatal mistake, for de Tany's force was surprised and forced to retreat to the bridge by swarms of unarmored but fast-moving Welshmen, rushing in to close quarters, stabbing at the horses, and dragging the knights from their sad-

dles. In the final *mêlée* on the bridge, most of the survivors of the mainland ambush were hurled into the Strait and drowned, including de Tany. After this heartening success, the Welsh leaders broke off the surrender negotiations, apparently believing that Edward would now retire to winter quarters and resume the war in the spring.

Edward, however, had no such intention. He possessed that versatility characterizing all the 'great captains' of the Middle Ages: the will to wage war regardless of the normal summer-autumn campaigning season. Nothing would have suited the Welsh better than for the English to have retired to their castles and fortified towns for the winter, enabling the Welsh to dominate the intervening terrain. As it was, luck favored the English only five days after Edward announced his intention of fighting a winter campaign. Llewelyn had headed south to strike at the English forces around Builth. He had momentarily left his motley force of spearmen-warriors to confer with local chieftains when John Giffard, the Constable of Builth, marched confidently out to tackle the Welshmen. Llewelyn had left his men in a strong position on high ground near the River Yrfon, commanding the Orewin Bridge. But a Welsh 'friendly' showed Giffard a ford across which he pushed a force of cavalry which seized the bridge, allowing Giffard's main force to cross. Giffard then gave a perfect demonstration of how missile infantry and cavalry should be coordinated, using his knights to herd the Welshmen into a defensive spearmen 'hedgehog', then bringing up his archers. It was like the last act at Hastings with the wretched Welshmen, unable to move, sustaining ever-increasing losses from the archers until Giffard's knights were able to charge home

and complete the slaughter. Llewelyn meanwhile, hastening to the battlefield, ran into an English flanking force and was killed in the ensuing skirmish. It was a totally gratuitous piece of luck for Edward.

Edward's reaction to the welcome news of Llewelyn's death was to start sending his English levies home as soon as picked mercenaries from the English lands in Gascony could be brought over. He needed a disciplined and well-supplied force for his march of January 1283 through the heart of Snowdonia to take and hold Dolwyddelan Castle as a base for the hunting of David. He then withdrew to Rhuddlan until 13 March, when he advanced to the mouth of the Conway and spent the next three months supervising the foundation of a huge new castle. The Anglesey force had crossed to the mainland and advanced round the north west coast via Caernarvon, Criccieth and Harlech, all of which were marked down as the sites of new castles. Bere Castle, David's last refuge in the north, fell on 25 April and David himself, after two months as a harried fugitive, was betrayed to the English by his own people in June, taken to England and executed as a traitor.

This second campaign, liquidating as it did the two most prominent Welsh national leaders, was the decisive one. It was followed (March 1284) by Edward's 'Statute of Wales,' which blocked out the future of Wales as an English administrative unit, divided into new shires and girdled by strengthened castles at every key point. Those castles, and in particular the four guardians of Snowdonia – Conway, Caernarvon, Criccieth and Harlech, with Beaumaris in Anglesey added in 1295 – hamstrung the last two serious Welsh revolts of the century. These were launched by Rhys ap Meredudd in 1287-8 and

Madog ap Llewelyn in 1294-5. During the latter revolt English sea power was a crucial factor, being used to replenish Harlech and Criccieth before these castles could be relieved from the landward.

It was also in the course of Madog's revolt that the events of December 1282 repeated themselves. Madog and his spearmen were surprised at Maes Moydog (5 March 1295) by a force of 119 knights and 3000 foot under William Beauchamp, Earl of Warwick, advancing from Montgomery. At Maes Moydog Warwick proved that the tactics which had broken Llewelyn's force at the Orewin Bridge had been no fluke. The English commander used all arms in harmony, the knights forcing the Welsh into their hedgehog position, then the crossbowmen and archers pouring in a deadly fire before the decisive cavalry charge.

These prototype English successes with foot archers in Wales are of particular importance with regard to what should be regarded as the 'longbow myth.' There is a fiction that the English took the longbow fully developed from the Welsh: a terrible weapon capable, in the hands of an expert, of skewering an armored knight's leg to his horse, or penetrating solid oak doors. (The assumption presumably is that the Welsh were too stupid to see what a superb weapon they had in the longbow until the English showed them after taking it from them – not a convincing theory.) In the late thirteenth century the heavyweight longbow's development and perfection, by means of long and assiduous practice and considerable trial-and-error in battle, was still far from complete. Certainly the longer, stiffer bows favored by the Welsh offered foot archers a greater range and penetrating power than had been generally available. But the

Left: Conway castle, strategically sited at the mouth of the River Conway. It was built with impressive speed between 1283 and 1287.

Below right: The walled town of Conway is contemporary with the castle. The tidal waters of the river estuary ensure supply by sea in the event of a siege. The same consideration governed the siting of Caernarvon castle.

tactics used at the Orewin Bridge and Maes Moydog – attrition fire by foot archers clearing the way for the charge of the knights – had nothing new about them. Two obvious examples from over 200 years before are William's use of archers at Hastings in 1066 and Bohemond's use of crossbowmen against the Varangians at Durazzo in 1081. Thus the Welsh wars rediscovered the immense potential of correctly-used foot archers, rather than pioneering it as a new technique; and the process was taken another step forward by Edward I's Scottish wars.

The Scottish wars

Edward's embroilment with Scottish affairs and his subsequent attempt to conquer the country was a classic example of the 'tidying-up' process of feudalism at work. Precedent was the key, the precedent in this case being that for centuries kings of England had (with varying degrees of success) claimed suzerainty over the kingdom of Scotland. When the Scottish throne fell vacant in 1290 and the Scottish magnates invited Edward to arbitrate between the 13 Scottish claimants to the throne, he only agreed to do so on the precondition (10 May 1291) that he should be recognized as Scotland's legal overlord. Though their gentry and commons objected violently, the Scottish representatives reluctantly yielded the point because they knew that the only alternative was civil war.

What it came down to was a nice problem in the semantics of feudal law, a problem which Edward naturally tried to exploit to his own advantage. Of the two leading candidates, John de Balliol had the best claim under English law and Robert Bruce under Scottish law. Edward took the line that as Scottish law was inadequate to settle the succession it was up to the English law, which gave the king of England the right to

dispose of Scotland as though the country were a vacant manor. Balliol was duly crowned king of Scotland at Scone on 30 November 1292 and on 26 December did homage to Edward for the Scottish kingdom. If Edward had left it at that all might have been well. But he went on to demand not only that he had the right to hear appeals from Scottish courts, but that the king of Scotland must – as the king of England's loyal vassal – attend each hearing in person.

These background events were important because the Anglo-Scottish wars pressed by Edward I and his son evoked the recognizably modern phenomenon of patriotic resistance. The early Middle Ages had, of course, seen instances of patriotism at work in wars of national survival, such as the 'Byzantine Crusade' of the early seventh century and the rally of the Saxon English to Alfred of Wessex in the late ninth. Such examples, however, had been prompted by excellent royal leadership, and when this vital ingredient was lacking patriotic resistance had always lain dormant. But the late thirteenth century is the first clear-cut period in which it is possible to identify traces of nationalism and patriotism prompting resistance to the invader regardless of indifferent leadership. It was in 1291 that the Swiss 'forest cantons' of Schwyz, Uri and Unterwalden formed their historic mutual-defense league, and the consequent struggle of the Swiss to maintain their independence coincided with that of the Scots.

Edward attempted to manipulate Scotland by bending the feudal rules as far as they would go, but the Scots were a very different proposition to the Welsh. In Wales Edward always had a 'fifth column' working for him – at least half of the Welsh nobility supported him – and the built-in disunity of the country. With the Scots he had little advantage of this kind; only a handful of Scottish magnates supported him, and when it

came to the sticking-point the Scottish nation was ready to fight in rejection of the notion of English overlordship. Scotland, moreover, possessed a more 'Normanized' aristocracy than that of Wales, capable, given time and hard experience, of raising useful troops, and well able to force their unpopular king into signing an alliance with France against England (1295). As Philip IV of France had precisely the same ambitions toward the English-held lands in Gascony that Edward had toward Wales and Scotland, the treaty obliged Edward to cope with the Scots and French simultaneously. To Philip's satisfaction and Edward's chagrin, the French king was doing no more than imitate his English counterpart, as far as Gascony was concerned, by insisting on the letter of Edward's feudal obligations as a vassal of France.

The Scots' biggest initial failure, like that of the Welsh, was the lack of leadership and discipline in the face of the steamroller assault which Edward launched against them in the spring of 1296. Led by their seven earls – Mar, Atholl, Ross, Lennox, Strathearn, Menteith and Buchan – the Scots raided south over the border and attacked Carlisle. They managed to set a large area of the city on fire, but the defending citizens stoutly demonstrated the excellence of the new fortifications completed in Edward's reign. Most of the men concentrated on fighting fires while the women manned the parapets and pelted the attackers with stones and missiles. Disheartened by this resistance, the Scots turned for home at the very moment that Edward advanced on Berwick at the other end of the border.

Edward's formal summons for the surrender of Berwick (28 March) got him nothing but jeers and insults and he prepared for a two-fisted attack on the town with his ships attacking from the seaward while the main attack took place on land. The sailors, however, attacked prematurely and were beaten off with the loss of two ships before Edward led the army forward against Berwick's flimsy outer defenses. He seems to have used a trick which he learned during the civil wars in his father's reign: confusing the enemy during the advance by displaying the enemy's heraldic banners. The defenders of Berwick, fooled into thinking that this might after all be King John's relieving army, were taken completely by surprise as the English flooded through the defenses into the streets. As they did so a crossbow bolt hit the king's cousin, Richard of Cornwall, in the face and killed him. Already irritated by the insults and losses he had suffered before the attack, Edward fell into a fury and ordered that no quarter was to be given. The subsequent butchery, only halted by the urgings of the churchmen, remained one of the blackest marks on Edward's reign.

After a month spent at Berwick repairing the city and giving it proper fortifications, Edward resumed his advance along the coast, with the Earl of Surrey scattering a rabble of Scottish troops sent to save Dunbar by King John (27 April). Dunbar Castle itself fell the next day, with the surrender of three of the seven earls (Ross, Menteith and Atholl). The advance continued via Roxburgh (8 May), Jedburgh (22 May), Edinburgh (6 June), Stirling (14 June) and Perth (21 June). King John surrendered to Edward at Kincardine on 2 July and abdicated a week later. But Edward appointed no successor. Instead he treated Scotland as an appendix of

England with himself as king. After making a military progress as far north as the Moray Firth – the most exhaustive march of conquest Scotland had endured since the days of the Roman Septimius Severus 1000 years before – Edward returned to Berwick on 23 August. He finally returned to England on 17 September after holding a parliament at Berwick at which he received the submission and homage of Scotland's 2000 landowners, clerical and lay.

The following decade, from the abdication of John de Balliol to the coronation of Robert the Bruce in March 1306, saw Scotland emulate the achievement of the West Saxon kingdom against the Danes in the late 870s. First the resistance leader William Wallace, then Bruce as royal warleader, showed that given the right tactics and intelligent use of terrain, the 'amateurs' could get the better of the 'professionals.' Pitched battle with the Scots was what the English wanted; it was up to the Scots only to give the English their pitched battle on terms which suited the English least.

Wallace, one of the most intelligent as well as the most inspiring resistance leaders of all time, evolved the infantry formation known to the Scots as the *schiltron*. These were blocks of disciplined spearmen, miniature phalanxes wielding four-meter pikes to confound the English armored cavalry. At Stirling Brig (11 September 1297) Wallace pounced on the English army of occupation as it was struggling across a narrow bridge, after waiting for the English cavalry vanguard to cross and try to deploy in a swampy

meadow. While one *schiltron* took and held the bridge against the English main body, the helpless vanguard was massacred by the other *schiltron*. But the next year, at Falkirk (22 July), King Edward commanded the English army in person to prove that the *schiltron* had dangerous limitations. Declining to send his knights across the swampy ground behind which Wallace had drawn up his *schiltrons*, Edward launched flank attacks instead, drove off the outnumbered and inferior Scottish cavalry, and left the *schiltrons* isolated. He then applied the lessons of the Welsh wars and used massed archer fire to shoot the *schiltrons* to pieces.

Edward died on his last Scottish expedition in July 1307 in the knowledge that his Scottish enemies had a king of their own once more. Robert Bruce, grandson of John de Balliol's main rival in the 1291 succession dispute, bears favorable comparison with England's Alfred the Great for his tenacity and resilience amid frequent defeat and humiliation. His crushing victory over the English army at Bannockburn (24 June 1314) was just reward for exploiting one of the crassest pieces of generalship in all the Middle Ages. Unlike his father, King Edward II of England had not learned his trade in the field. His deployment at Bannockburn used all the least favorable ground and left the all-important English archers wide open to destruction by a Scottish cavalry charge. Having knocked the best card out of Edward's hand, Bruce advanced against the struggling English cavalry and annihilated it.

Left: William Wallace leading his Scottish infantry. Against the English cavalry the Scottish pikes, bills and halberds proved that mounted, armored nobility was not, after all, invulnerable to foot soldiers.

Below: Edward I's conquest of Wales, and the Anglo-Scottish wars.

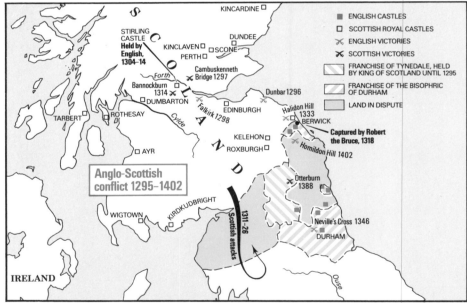

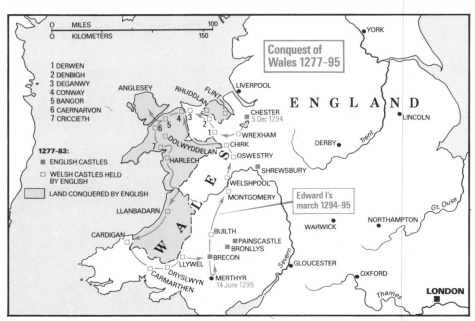

The lessons for the future

Bannockburn in 1314 was the latest in a series of battles which bear the greatest relevance to the coming English successes with the longbow. These battles, dating from the Welsh wars 30 years earlier, proved that infantry-based armies could, given shrewd generalship and choice of terrain, beat the weapon which had virtually reigned supreme for the entire medieval period – the armored lancer. As the English were to prove at the expense of the French, these early experiments lent themselves well to later imitation and improvement.

The accidental rediscovery of the virtues of the Macedonian phalanx in the closing years of the thirteenth century was a new demonstration of the long-established fact that well-handled infantry had an excellent chance of beating badly-handled armored cavalry. The Scottish *schiltron* was an emergency device, a tactic which could be quickly drilled into hastily-recruited patriot armies. It was as effective in defense as in attack – provided that the pikemen kept their heads and retained formation, and that the enemy made the right mistakes. And this, thanks to the inflated mystique of the mounted knights as the arbiter of the battlefield, the enemy proved gratifyingly ready to do on many separate occasions.

The re-emergence of the pike phalanx was by no means restricted to the British Isles. For the same reasons and at the same time as in Scotland, the phenomenon occurred on the Continental mainland. Across the Channel Edward's enemy, King Philip IV of France, was trying to achieve in Flanders what Edward had achieved in Wales and was attempting to achieve again in Scotland.

Five years after Stirling Brig, the massed nobility of France rode confidently out to destroy the upstart rebels of Flanders, who chose to meet the knights on foot – in pike formations. On the French side there was no pause for careful reconnaissance or study of the unusual deployment adopted by the Flemish citizen army at Courtrai (11 July 1302). From sheer arrogance, refusing even to consider the ridiculous idea that foot soldiers could stand up to them, the French knights rolled forward in dense masses against the leveled pikes, with each knight jealously struggling to get to the front and snatch the honor of striking first. They were an uncontrollable mob even before the leading knights' horses recoiled in terror from the pike-hedge and the first knights began to fall like flies. The flight of the survivors from the catastrophe of Courtrai dignified the proceedings as the 'Battle of the Spurs.' A second 'Battle of the Spurs' was to take place 211 years later. This also was a defeat for the knights, this time inflicted by heavy fire from mobile field guns.

Courtrai was the first major demonstration that the lofty inspirations of medieval chivalry had done terrible things to the role of the knight as an armored cavalryman, for whose employment every battle dictated a correct tactical time and place.

Though the lesson of Courtrai was delivered to the French by the new phenomenon of shock infantry, it was not yet unique. The lemming-like instinct of the French chivalry to be the first into action at all costs was to be punished with no less severity by the English missile infantry at Crécy, Poitiers, Agincourt and a host of lesser actions throughout the fourteenth and early fifteenth centuries.

Right and below: Caerlaverock castle in Dumfriesshire was ahead of its time in design when it was built in about 1280. Nevertheless, it fell to Edward I by siege in 1300.

The Anglo-French Struggle

Of all the misleading ideas which have become attached to the medieval period over recent centuries, that of the 'Hundred Years War' between England and France is high on the list. It is hard to find a better example of the urge to make history tidy by slicing it up into economy-sized units. In fact the fourteenth-century wars of England against France, ostensibly waged in pursuit of the conquest of France, were only the last act in a long drama on which the curtain had risen back in the eleventh century. Thus a more apt title would be the '*Four Hundred Years War*,' beginning with the Norman invasion of England in 1066 and ending with the English evacuation of Gascony in 1453. Even then a prologue and epilogue would be desirable, the prologue being the marriage of the English King Ethelred to Emma of Normandy in 1002 and the epilogue being the expulsion of the English from Calais in 1558. Far from being restricted to a single century, therefore, the Anglo-French struggle was one of the most enduring 'built-in' features of the Middle Ages. That overworked phrase 'crucible of war' is particularly relevant in this context, for out of their long wars England and France emerged as distinct nations.

The phases of the Anglo-French conflict

The contest is easier to understand as four distinct phases. The first phase, beginning with the Norman Conquest of England, made the feudal overlords of northern France kings of England as well. When Henry II, heir to the English throne and duke of Normandy, married Eleanor of Aquitaine in 1152, Aquitaine and Gascony were added to Poitou, Anjou, Maine and Normandy (the entire left-hand half of modern France) as lands held by the English from the French king. This phase ended in 1204 after the fall of Château Gaillard when Henry's son John lost Normandy, Maine and Anjou to Philip Augustus of France.

John's calamitous reign ended in civil war and the prospect of a second conquest of England from across the Channel, this time by invitation. In their struggle with John the rebel English barons called on Philip Augustus for help and Prince Louis crossed to England with an expeditionary force of knights and mercenaries. Though London and most of the southeast passed under Louis's control, Dover Castle was stoutly held for John's young son Henry and resistance fighters operating from the Weald Forest harried the French lines of communications. Led by the veteran knight, William the Marshal, who had served both Henry II and Richard before John, the English royalists drove the French out of Lincoln (20 May 1217). A final relief force dispatched by the reluctant French king was intercepted at sea, off Sandwich, on 24 August 1217. The English fleet worked round to windward of the French and then blinded the French sailors and knights with deadly streams of powdered quicklime, that cheap and easy alternative to the liquid incendiary 'Greek Fire' used by Moslems and Christians in the Mediterranean. Discouraged by these setbacks but mollified by English payments of substantial cash compensation, Louis abandoned his claims and withdrew from England.

After this dramatic interlude the second phase of the Anglo-French struggle, now centered on the Gascon lands south of the Loire which the English kings continued to hold, remained in low key until the reigns of Edward I of England (1272-1307) and Philip IV of France (1285-1314). It was in the time of these formidable monarchs that French ambitions toward Gascony, English ambitions toward Scotland and Scottish ambitions toward survival produced an international alignment which lasted for the next 300 years: France and Scotland against England (the 'auld alliance') and England and Flanders against France. This was the basic line-up for the Anglo-French wars of the fourteenth and fifteenth centuries, in which the English tried to succeed in France where the French had failed in England in 1217.

The third phase of the Anglo-French struggle – and the first two-thirds of what is usually meant by the 'Hundred Years War' – ended when Henry V died in 1422 having made himself master of all France north of the Loire and having won the succession to the French throne for his infant son. The fourth and last phase, with the last English victories speedily reversed by the great French revival inspired by Joan of Arc, ended in the 1450s with the English beaten out of Normandy for the second time, and this time losing their foothold in Gascony as well.

Here, severely compressed for the sake of simplicity, was the underlying 'grand strategy' behind the Anglo-French struggle. In terms of tactics and weaponry the third and fourth phases, with which this chapter is concerned, were fought out in one of the most exciting and

Left: Geoffrey Plantagenet, Duke of Anjou and Maine, from his tomb at Le Mans.

Above right: A fifteenth century mail-maker. Mail armor was probably first used by the Celts, and was well-known to the Romans. Over 30,000 individually riveted links were needed to make one mail shirt.

Right: Reconstructions of medieval arrow-heads. From left to right: a 'type 16' (general purpose); an armor-piercing bodkin; a bodkin to penetrate mail; a hunting broad-head (used against horses in war); and their predecessor, a Dark Ages arrow-head.

formative periods in the history of warfare. For this was the age in which the armored knight reached the peak of his development, receiving the best equipment he had ever had only to find his centuries of supremacy on the battlefield challenged by new breeds of specialized infantry.

Perhaps never – even in the age of the breach-loading rifle and machine gun – has the evolution of infantry accelerated so fast as it did in the fourteenth and fifteenth centuries. First shock formations of pikemen, then missile formations of archers, proved able to shatter the strongest arrays of armored chivalry. And as if all this were not enough the fourteenth and fifteenth centuries also saw the development and acceptance of the 'third arm': powder-and-shot artillery for siege and field use. From the end of the fifteenth century the new trinity of 'horse, foot and guns' reigned unchallenged until the birth of military aviation in World War I.

The improvements in late medieval armor

For the armored élite, the knights, a radical improvement in protection was already well advanced when the third phase of the Anglo-French struggle began. This was the transition from mail to plate, starting with the over-hasty development of the helmet from the simple conical pot of the eleventh century to massive, drum or barrel-shaped designs to give all-round armored protection to head and neck. This was over-hasty because it was not thought out. The flat tops of the twelfth and thirteenth-century barrel helms were natural targets for stunning blows by mace and axe. By the end of the thirteenth century one of the most important functions of armor – to deflect blows, not merely stop them – had been rediscovered; the domed or pointed helmet top was emerging again, leading to the lightweight pointed bascinet of the fourteenth century.

Against nearly every edged weapon mail was an excellent protective substance, its interlaced iron rings diffusing the line of impact of sword cuts and axe blows. It could also stop low-velocity missile weapons such as javelins, spears and arrows with broad-barbed heads. The biggest foe of mail were the high-velocity missiles such as crossbow bolts, composite bow arrows and longbow arrows with pointed 'bodkin' heads.

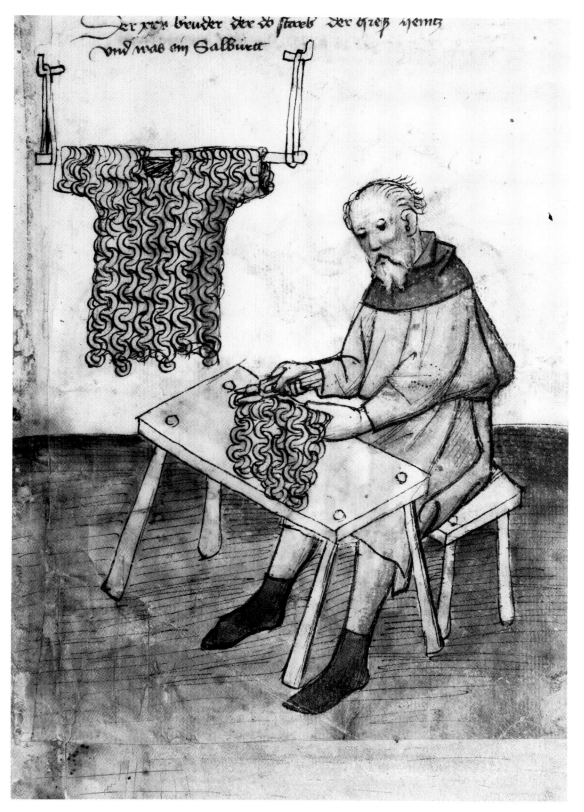

Such missiles had sufficient impact and penetrative effect to punch through mail rings, bursting the tiny rivets or butt-joints which closed the interlaced rings and driving the latter through the padded underclothing into the wearer's flesh.

When the victim was unable or too foolhardy to seek immediate medical treatment, the subsequent infection set up by rusty mail fragments and sweaty undergarments could prove fatal. The death of Richard I of England in 1189 was a case in point. The crossbow bolt which hit Richard in the shoulder would not have resulted in a death wound if the king had had it promptly seen to. It was peripheral damage, infection and gangrene which carried off the leading military genius of the Western world ten days after the wound was inflicted. Extracting the head of that bolt from amid a vicious tangle of fractured mail rings must have created a horrific wound which would have taken a long time to heal safely even under modern aseptic conditions.

The initial answer was to make mail rings smaller, and 'double mail,' as recommended by Piano Carpini against the Mongol arrows, really meant mail with rings of half the normal

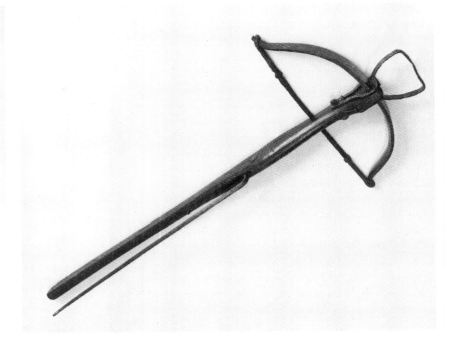

diameter. But this only tended to increase the dragging weight of mail and reduce the wearer's overall performance in a *mêlée*. It did nothing to solve other serious problems with mail armor. One such problem was the weakness of the junction-points where sections of a mail suit were linked by leather thongs. A well-aimed blow could slice loose a section of armor and create a gap open to a crippling thrust. Then there was the inevitability of massive bruising under a heavy blow caused by the 'give' of the mail, which could cripple the wearer at a shoulder, elbow or knee joint even if the mail fabric remained intact. Remember that a knight with a useless right arm, unable to couch his lance, draw his sword or swing a mace, was even less use on a medieval battlefield than a modern tank with a jammed gun.

So it was that from the early thirteenth century a sustained effort was made to *deflect* blows rather than *absorb* them using close-fitting convex plates at the most vulnerable points. Though it may seem a trivial comparison, contemporary illustrations make it clear that plate armor other than helmets began with pieces resembling a skate-boarder's protective elbow or knee pads: the *poleyn* for the knee and *couter* for the elbow, extended by blinker-like circular or pointed plates (*besagues*). Plate protection for the shoulder was known as the *spaudler*.

In the same period the shirt-like mail hauberk of the eleventh and twelfth centuries began to be supplemented by the coat-of-plates worn on top, plate protection sewn to a stout fabric surcoat. From the widespread early use of hardened leather (*cuir-bouilli*) came the names *curie* and *paires de cuiraces* to describe such coats, whence the modern derivative 'cuirass.' Before the coat-of-plates gave place to the breastplate proper in the second half of the fourteenth century, plate protection had spread from the shoulders, elbows and knees to the upper arm (*rerebrace*), forearm (*vambrace*), thigh (*cuisse*) and lower leg (*greave*). Jointed plate *gauntlets* had virtually replaced the clumsy, bag-like mail 'mittens' of the twelfth and thirteenth centuries, while similarly jointed plate *sabatons* enclosed the feet. Protecting the throat and lower face – and supporting the light bascinet helmet – was the curved plate known as the *bevor* or *beaver*. By the middle fifteenth century mail supplemented plate, not the other way round.

The advent of plate armor is, like so many aspects of the Middle Ages, the object of widespread modern misunderstanding. It is an utter myth that full plate armor converted a man into a futile, tottering juggernaut who had to be hoisted into his saddle by a crane, and who was quite helpless if pushed over on to his back. Twentieth-century experiments have indicated that a man wearing full plate armor could run, lie down, stand up and even turn a somersault if required (though this particular feat was not a normal part of medieval combat). Not only could an armored knight mount and dismount by himself, he could vault into the saddle, a

Above left and above: A view from above and underneath a Spanish crossbow of the early sixteenth century. The main difference between this and early medieval crossbows was that the horn and sinew 'composite' bowstave was replaced by a steel one, as here.

Left: This German mail hauberk (of alternate hammer-welded and riveted links) dates from the mid-fourteenth century. The helmet (a basinet) is furnished with a mail aventail.

Above right: The earliest hand-held firearms were ignited by a red-hot wire being thrust into the touch-hole, as shown in this fourteenth century manuscript illustration.

Right: A 14th century basinet with aventail, originally from the Armory of the Vogts of Matsch in Castle Churburg, South Tyrol (now in the Royal Armories). Unlike the earlier flat-topped 'barrel' helms, it was specifically designed to deflect blows rather than to absorb them.

much-admired feat then as now. When Shakespeare wrote, at the end of the sixteenth century:

I saw young Harry – with his beaver on,
His cuisses on his thighs, gallantly arm'd,
Rise from the ground like a feathered Mercury,
And vaulted with such ease into his seat,
As if an angel dropp'd down from the clouds,
To turn and wind a fiery Pegasus,
And witch the world with noble horsemanship

(Henry IV, Part I, IV:1.)

he was speaking literally, not figuratively. All these improvements in armor not only demanded new skills in metal-working craftsmanship but also created a new art form. The superb ceremonial suits of sixteenth and seventeenth-century plate armor, chased with intricate designs, and embellished with gold and silver, rank among the most beautiful artifacts of their age. But the improvement of armor was nothing more than the age-old attempt to enable fighting men to survive in an increasingly hostile environment. The obvious modern equivalent has been the development of armored cars, tanks and personnel carriers. Unlike the armored fighting vehicle of the twentieth century, however, the better-armored knight of the fourteenth and fifteenth centuries was not, as he stood, a more efficient fighting unit. He was still helpless when his horse refused – as cavalry horses have always done – to charge into resolute infantry formations in close order, hedged with leveled spears, pikes or bayonets. And he and his horse were intensely vulnerable to sustained high-velocity fire which dominated his line of advance.

The reason was that it was found possible to contrive a suit of deflecting armor capable of protecting a rider with reasonable success – but the same could not be done for his horse. Gallant attempts were made to drape horses with cumbersome padded and mail *bards* which led in due course to the contored plate *chanfron* covering the horse's face, the jointed *crinet* protecting the neck and the *peytral* across the chest. All such attempts, however, were beaten by the invariable natural law that increase in armor with no increase in power spells a decrease in mobility. And mobility was the horsed soldier's very *raison d'être*.

To sum up, the considerable improvement in armor of the later Middle Ages had definite limitations which demanded recognition and an appropriate modification of tactics – limitations which could be, and were, exploited with terrible results on the battlefield. But such recognition and modification never came. The newly-armored knight of the fourteenth and fifteenth centuries was, in historical overview, no more than a sophisticated development of the Palmyran – late Roman – Sassanid cataphract in that he was a super-heavy horsed soldier. But he did not think of himself as a *soldier* at all. He was a *gentleman*, whose main objective was not to hold ranks and follow the general's orders but to win personal glory by performing what his peers would consider to be 'noble deeds of arms.' This military snobbery was, of course, an offshoot of the knight's lofty role in the medieval social pyramid, and it gave a baneful twist to the age-old tendency of cavalrymen to consider themselves (literally) above the common infantry. In certain phases of the Anglo-French struggle, to the great advantage of the English, the worst effects of military snobbery among the French armored élite led to a fatal rejection of the hard realities of war.

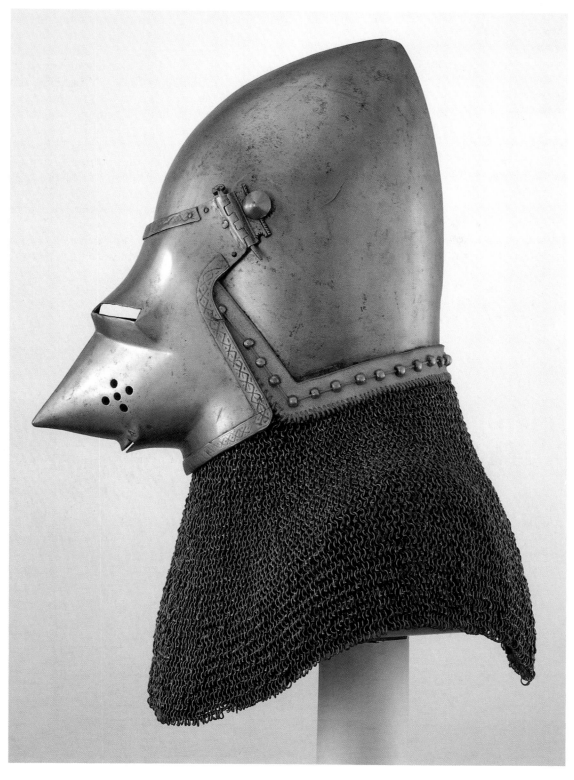

Left: Shooting at the butts – a drawing from the illuminated *Luttrell Psalter* of about 1340. Constant practice was necessary to maintain any skill with the longbow.

Jean Froissart, one of the most famous chroniclers of the 'Hundred Years War,' spent his life serving the English and recording the repeated shattering of their knightly delusions on the battlefield. But this never shook his firm and admiring belief that knights were the heirs of the 'Nine Worthies' and their deeds the essence of war:

...for the recorded deeds of brave and noble men will naturally stimulate and inspire young knights who are directing their lives towards achieving perfect honour, of which valour is the basic quality and the sure begetter ... For just as the Four Evangelists and the twelve Apostles are nearer to Our Lord than all others, so are valiant knights nearer to Honour and held in higher esteem than all other men ... From this we can perceive a division of society into various different groups: men of valour labouring in arms to advance themselves and increase their own glory; the common people who spend their time discussing the memorable deeds and fortunes of the valiant; and the clerks, who write down and record their rise to fame and the prowess of their youth.

Froissart wrote this in the 1370s, after his idealized order of knighthood had suffered an unbroken run of military disaster stretching back over the past seven decades. He was not a detached military historian but gifted clerk employed by royal and noble patrons; it is therefore hardly surprising that he did not go out of his way to offend his patrons by pointing out that those disasters proved that medieval chivalry had ludicrously debased the correct use of heavy cavalry. But so it was. At Courtrai (1302) and Bannockburn (1314) armies of pikemen had triumphed over atrociously-led armies of knights. It had always been suicide to launch unsupported cavalry against solid infantry. As the Norman Bohemond had demonstrated at Durazzo and Duke William at Hastings, the proper tactics were for cavalry to force the enemy infantry to hold formation, then shoot the enemy infantry to pieces with missile fire, and *then* – and only *then* – to send in the decisive cavalry charge. But by the fourteenth century such a subordination of cavalry to infantry was anathema to the gentlemanly, chivalrous school of war. Archers and crossbowmen had to be kept in their proper lowly station.

It was the English who first accepted – after the appalling lesson of Bannockburn – that the battlefield superiority of the armored knight had become a myth. They deserve credit for this because modern British history shows that the English later became adept at preparing for the next war with the tactics of the last. (The most recent terrible example of this weakness was Lord Kitchener's belief that the machine-gun was a grossly overrated weapon.) But on 19 July 1333, at Halidon Hill, the English army under the young king Edward III avenged Bannockburn with devastating arrow fire. The Scottish pikemen in the *schiltron* formations, supported by mounted knights were shot to pieces by small divisions of longbowmen supported by *dismounted* men-at-arms and knights. It was a blueprint of a new type of battle, the pattern for a new era of infantry superiority.

It also marked the end of the crossbow's long superiority as the ideal infantry weapon. The basic reason was rate of fire. A longbowman deployed for battle with a sheaf of 48 arrows, which he either kept slung from his belt or laid out at his feet for easy access (contemporary illustrations show both). Obviously, the slower he shot the longer his arrows would last – important in a hard-fought action, when ammuni-

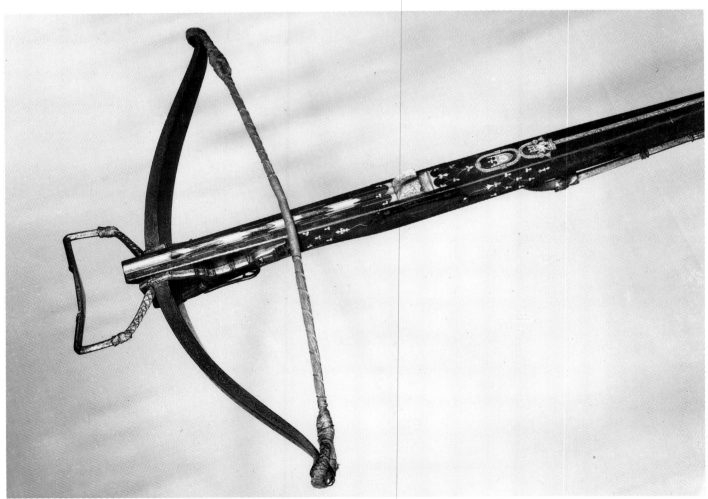

Left: A crossbow made for Louis XII of France. Crossbows took longer to shoot and were heavier to carry than longbows, but were easier to use and sometimes more powerful.

Right: In the first major sea battle since Sluys the combined French and Spanish fleet defeated the English at La Rochelle in 1372. The tactics of sea warfare, as seen here, had not changed at all.

tion supply from the baggage train was often interrupted – but the longbow was particularly well suited to volley fire. Even at the relatively slow rate of fire of six shafts per minute, a force of 5000 longbowmen could savage the head of an approaching enemy column with a torrent of 30,000 arrows in the first minute – a feat completely beyond the capability of the most expert crossbow force. A crossbowman could feel pleased if he managed to fire as many as two aimed shots per minute – and the accent was on *aimed* shots at individual targets. Nothing was to surpass the crossbow's excellence as a marksman's weapon, ideal for use from behind cover, until the emergence of the flintlock rifle in the eighteenth century. The longbow's forte, for all the English folklore stories about the cleaving of willow wands, was not marksmanship of this nature. It was, rather, the concentration of massed and rapid fire on a given point through which it was death for the enemy to advance – like repeatedly pounding a mallet into the head of a column of advancing ants.

Simple though it was in construction, and virtually immune to damage by wet weather once the string had been whipped off and stowed away, the longbow had one major disadvantage: the time required to become proficient in its use.

Such proficiency could only be reached by months of practice at the butts; and such practice was forcibly encouraged, on the eve of the French war, by the statute of Edward III (1337) banning all sports in England apart from archery – on pain of death. But the very fact that the longbow was a professional's weapon was a compensating advantage in that the longbow was the only weapon of its day which could not be snatched up on a battlefield and used at once by an enemy. The crossbow, on the other hand, could be used – and accurately – by any tyro with enough mother wit to work out how to cock the weapon. And wet weather was fatal to the crossbow's performance, slackening its fixed string and softening the glue which bonded its composite parts.

The victories of Edward III

Before the longbow got its first confrontation with the French armored chivalry on land there was another 'dress-rehearsal' of a battle, this time at sea. In the summer of 1340 the French fleet, powerfully reinforced by allied Spanish and Genoese contingents, massed in the port of Sluys to prevent Edward III from joining hands with his Flemish allies. As naval combat was still a mirror-image of hand-to-hand fighting on

land, the French and Spanish commanders chained the ships of their greatly superior fleet together in four lines, and confidently prepared to rely on their advantage in numbers. But Edward headed in to the attack with each ship manned alternatively with men-at-arms and archers – after waiting and maneuvering until he had the tide running with him and his archers had the morning sun at their backs. The French got the hand-to-hand fight for which they had prepared, but only after the garrison of each ship had been decimated by longbow archery to level the odds for the men-at-arms' assault. Sluys was a long and gory struggle, raging from ship to ship from early morning well into the afternoon – much longer than the main fleet action at Trafalgar in 1805. 'Sea fights,' observed Froissart distastefully, 'are always fiercer than fights on land, because retreat and flights are impossible.'

The resounding finale of the Crécy campaign (1346) tends to distract from the elegance of the campaign itself. As a strategist Edward III never believed in operating on a single front when he could improvise two or more. This was not military dilettantism but an interesting anticipation of what Montgomery, in World War II, was to call 'wet hen tactics': keeping a formidable enemy off balance and dashing to and fro by a series of jabbing offensives at different points, any of which could turn out to be the real thing. Having won command of the Channel at Sluys Edward's early attempts to operate from Flanders and Brittany came to nothing, but in June 1345 the Earl of Derby landed in Gascony with 500 men-at-arms and 2000 archers. This small force won a spectacular series of victories over the unprepared French in the Garonne and Dordogne valleys, drawing the attention of the French King Philip IV (1328-50) to the south. By the spring of 1346 a powerful army was massing at Toulouse under Philip's heir, the Duke of Normandy, and the English outpost at Aiguillon was besieged without hope of immediate relief.

Edward's invasion of France in July 1346 was therefore ripe with strategic possibilities. There had been no secret about his preparations, and Philip knew that an invasion was imminent. But he was forced to hold the bulk of his forces in the Paris region because the English could just as easily sail to Bordeaux and reinforce Gascony, or land in Brittany again, or strike at Normandy. Edward kept his options open to the last minute. He sailed on 11 July and had actually bypassed the Cherbourg peninsula reaching Guernsey before he decided on a destination for the expeditionary force. He now ordered a return to Cherbourg peninsula and an eastward march through Normandy, hopefully evading French attempts at interception, drawing off the French pressure on Aiguillon in the south, and more hopefully still effecting an eventual junction with Flemish forces invading France from the northeast. This improvised plan had a no less important financial motive. Edward needed a quick run of relatively easy successes and loot for all so that his campaign could reach the 'self-financing' point. Permanently short of funds for paying his own troops and subsidizing his allies, Edward was well aware that the English Parliament's purse strings would start to tighten very quickly unless the clergy and 'faithful commons' of England saw an early return for their outlay – with interest.

The latter part of Edward's plan was the first to be fulfilled, for the march through Normandy proved splendidly lucrative. It also incensed the French into raising the siege of Aiguillon, thus reprieving the English forces in Gascony. But King Philip's furious attempts to catch and crush Edward with the concentrated French army, first west of the Seine, then west of the Somme, came uncomfortably close to success. By brilliant feinting and counter marching Edward won a bridge across the Seine at Poissy, only to be

beaten to the Somme at Amiens by Philip's army. From 12 July, when he had landed at St Vaast la Hogue, to 21 August, when he reached the Somme only to find every bridge securely in French hands, Edward had marched his now-tiring army nearly 480 kilometers. He would have had no choice but fight west of the Somme had not a captured groom directed the trapped army to the tidal ford of Blanchetaque, which he swore was passable at low water.

The passage of Blanchetaque was a desperate business because a French force held the far bank, and Philip's army was now moving in for the kill down the left bank of the Somme. The rearguard had to hold off the bulk of the French army while the vanguard archers waded across the firm gravel causeway and won a bridgehead through which the English army passed in safety. To Philip's utter frustration pursuit was impossible because the tide was already rising by the

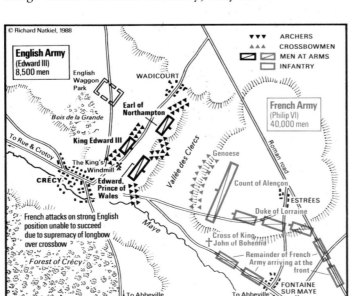

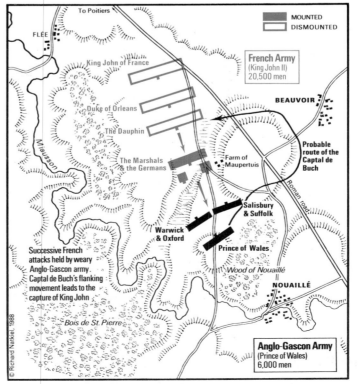

Above: Campaigns and battles of the Anglo-French Wars.

Far left: The Battle of Crécy (1346).

Left: The Battle of Poitiers (1356).

Right: A late fifteenth century armor for horse and man, in the German 'Gothic' style. Now in the Wallace Collection, London, it originally belonged to a member of the von Freyberg family, and was kept in their castle at Hohenaschau, Bavaria.

grans seignirs que chun vouloit
monstrer sa puissance. Si ngl
nul homme combien q'l fust
present a la tónee qui sceust
ne peust ymaginer ne recor
der la verite. Especialement
de la partie des francois tant
y eut poure arroy et petite
ordonnance en leurs grans
convoys qui estoient sans
nombre. Et ce que te scay
de leurs besoignes et ordon
nances et ce que ie deuise
ray et determineray y en ce

lant de lay scen et a pmis
le plus par moult vaillans
hommes dingleterre faietes
et dyxartz tant cheualiers
comme aultres qui moult
entenfiuemet auyerent
leur conuenant. Et aussi
par les gens de mess. rehan
de haynault qui furent
touiours delez le roy
phle de france. Cy ple de la
bataille de crecy entre le roy de
france et le roy dingleterre.

time the French vanguard closed up to the ford; the French had no choice but to turn in their tracks and recross the Somme farther upstream. And the respite thus gained gave Edward just enough time to find a suitable defensive position in which to fight the battle which he now knew was inevitable.

The Battle of Crécy

The position Edward chose was a low ridge commanding the ground up which the enemy must advance if he chose an impulsive frontal attack. Just behind the ridge ran the track connecting the villages of Crécy-en-Ponthieu and Wadicourt, making it easy for Edward to switch troops from one end of his flimsy-looking line to the other. The whole position had a wood behind it into which the army could retreat if things went very wrong out on the ridge; here Edward placed his wagon-park. But Edward

was on his own; time was not on his side, there was no friendly ally coming to his aid, and there was nothing to prevent the French from taking their time and encircling him. For all that, he radiated confidence as he deployed his army. Edward had about 13,000 men, over half of them archers, and approaching 3000 knights and men-at-arms.

The latter formed three 'battles' or divisions, with the king's lying back in the center to act as reserve. As Froissart describes it the ends of the battles were studded with wedge-shaped archer formations *en manière de herse* – like the points of a harrow – with each archer formation supported by Welsh spearmen. The men had time to dig pot-holes in front of their positions (as the Scots were wont to do, most notably at Bannockburn) and hammer in pointed stakes to deter cavalry from closing at the full charge. By late afternoon on 26 August 1346 the English

army, fed and rested, had its position as secure as it would ever be.

The ensuing destruction of the French army stands out as one of the most bizarre episodes in the history of warfare. There have been countless instances of confident armies dissolving into chaos after hours of sustained enemy pressure or because of a perfectly-timed enemy charge. But at Crécy the French army stumbled to destruction from the outset of the action, throwing away all cohesion before a single blow had been struck because they were convinced that they could not lose. There was no question of French morale crumbling because of an initial repulse. If anything, morale was the biggest problem the French had. They could not rally or even pause to consider a more sane plan of attack because knightly 'one-upmanship' compelled them to keep coming on like lemmings swarming over a cliff – or, to snatch at a more suggestive simile, like massed robots marching into a car-crusher. Not that any metaphor or simile will do. Froissart himself admitted that 'There is no one, even among those present on that day, who has been able to understand and relate to the whole truth of the matter. This was especially so on the French side, where such confusion reigned.'

What seems to have happened is that the French outriders sighted the English position at around 1530 hours. One of the four French knights who rode forward to reconnoiter, Le Moine de Bazeilles, advised King Philip to halt for the night. 'In the morning you will be able to give more thought to your battle-order and make a closer study of the enemy's position to see which is the best line of attack. You can be sure that they (the English) will still be there.' The king agreed and ordered a halt:

but those behind continued to advance, saying that they would not stop until they had caught up with the front ranks. And when the leaders saw the others coming they went on also. So pride and vanity took charge of events . . . Neither the King nor his Marshals could restrain them any longer, for there were too many great lords among them, all determined to show their power.

Before all trace of order vanished on the French side, Philip ordered his corps of about 6000 Genoese crossbowmen to advance and engage the English line. Their officers pointed out that after a 45 kilometer march from Abbeville carrying their heavy weapons 'they were not in a state to fight much of a battle just then.' Their readiness was not improved by a thunderstorm with drenching rain, but in the end the Genoese deployed and advanced. The sky had cleared after the storm and the late afternoon sun was shining straight into the crossbowmen's eyes; their damp weapons' range had been reduced, compelling an advance to within 'killing range' of the waiting longbowmen. As the Genoese staggered under the arrow-storm their destruction was completed by the leading French knights, who lumbered forward to slash the Genoese out of the way as a preliminary to their assault. This was unrelievedly chaotic and a triumph for the massed volleys of the longbow

Right: A detail from the *Froissart Chronicles* showing English archers at Crécy. A 120 to 160lb draw-weight war bow could send a lightweight 'flight' arrow over 400 yards.

which prevented any concentrated blow coming to bear on the English line. As Jean Le Bel has it:

The arrows of the English were directed with such marvellous skill at the horsemen that their mounts refused to advance a step; some leapt backwards stung to madness, some reared hideously, some turned their rear quarters towards the enemy, others merely let themselves fall to the ground, and their riders could do nothing about it. The English lords who were on foot advanced among them, striking them at their will, because they could not help themselves or their horses. The misfortunes of the French lasted until midnight, for it was nearly dark when the battle began, and the King of France and his company never came near the fighting . . .

The biggest menace to the English right-wing 'battle,' that of the 15-year-old Prince of Wales, was caused by the sheer weight of the mindless French advance. Froissart adds:

Yet some French knights and squires, and with them some Germans and Savoyards, succeeded in breaking through the Prince of Wales's archers and engaging the men-at-arms in hand-to-hand combat with swords. There was much brave and skilful fighting . . . At that point the Earls of Northampton and Arundel, commanding the second division on the left wing, sent support over to the Prince's division. It was high time, for otherwise it would have had its hands full. And because of the danger in which those responsible for the Prince found themselves, they sent a knight to King Edward, who had his position higher up on the mound of a windmill, to ask for help . . .

Edward's famous refusal to help his son – 'let the boy win his spurs' – was no mere knightly bravado. The French were estimated at 40,000 strong and the king, believing that Philip was bound to renew the action the next day, was

Left: This late fifteenth century German 'Gothic' equestrian armor is in the Tower of London.

Far right: Italian embossed and gilt 'parade' armor of 1590, by which date functional armor was becoming obsolete.

Below left: A fifteenth century shield (probably made as a tournament prize).

Below: Full plate armor of about 1450 (Royal Armories, Tower of London).

Right: A model of a mail-clad late thirteenth century knight; plate armor developed from this stage onward.

determined to keep his reserve intact. But as the light grew on the morning of the 27th, finding the elated English still holding their position, it became apparent that the cumulative suicide of the French chivalry had handed Edward a total victory. The ground below the English line is still known as the *Vallée aux Clercs* after the English clerks who listed the French dead: over 1500 knights (identified from their coats of arms) and 10,000 men-at-arms and common foot.

Crécy should have revolutionized the art of war, serving notice once and for all that massed armored knights were no match for superior fire power. The fact that it did nothing of the kind, and that the French continued to put their strength in their outmoded chivalry, should cause no surprise in a century which has seen the futile persistence with open-order attacks against entrenched machine guns in World War I and the no less futile persistence with anti-civilian bombing campaigns in World War II and Vietnam. And in truth the tactical superiority conferred by the longbow was no more than that: a tactical mastercard, not a strategic war-winner. After Crécy it took Edward III 11 months to starve Calais into surrender and this gain, useful though it was, did not win him France. The same applied to the two other classic longbow victories, Poitiers (19 September 1356) and Agincourt (25 October 1415). After Poitiers the war dragged on for another four years before the two sides agreed on a peace brought about by mutual exhaustion; after Agincourt it took Henry V five years just to conquer Normandy. For Edward III the most important aspect of the capture of King John II at Poitiers was not that

he now had the French crown literally in his grasp, it was the colossal ransom of 300,000 crowns demanded for the release of the French king, money desperately needed by a bankrupt country without the financial muscle to pay for the war.

Compared with Crécy the later longbow victories were undoubtedly more interesting as tactical exercises. At Poitiers the Prince of Wales (the 'Black Prince') gave his archers the best defenses enjoyed by the English in any of the three battles, including a trench line to extend the already formidable cover provided by thick hedges running across the army's front. After the archers and men-at-arms had broken the clumsy French frontal assaults the arrow-supply failed; but the Prince ordered his knights to horse and unleashed a general advance, crowned by a perfect cavalry flank attack against the French left center and rear led by the Captal de Buch. Agin-

court was a very different story. The unexpected resistance of Harfleur pushed the 1415 campaign into a miserably wet autumn, and in the desperate maneuvers during Henry V's attempted march from Normandy to Calais the weary English army, starved of supplies, was forced to march for its life. This time the French achieved a perfect interception, laying their entire army squarely across Henry's line of march. On 25 October Henry, knowing that his men only had one good fight in them, was faced with deep trouble when the French held their position and declined to attack. He only induced the French to launch their usual frontal assault by advancing himself to within bowshot of the French lines and precipitating the battle by opening fire – an extraordinary piece of audacity, but one assured of success once the first blind charge got under way. At Agincourt the French threw away an easy victory by allowing themselves to be goaded into attacking across muddy plowland which rapidly became a morass, slowing still further men who were already subtly fatigued after standing to arms for hours in full armor.

Joan of Arc and French victory

The humiliation of France during the last seven years of Henry V's reign was not so much military as political. A medieval kingdom did not run itself – it required effective and respected leadership on the part of its monarch. To set against Henry V, the French had the half-mad Valois Charles VI and his feeble son, who was reputed to be illegitimate and was a hopeless failure as a national leader. Nor could any of the cynical and unanimously unsuccessful leading

nobility provide such leadership. As is well known, however, the hour produced the man – or rather, the girl.

Joan of Arc was no more a military genius than she was a brilliant theologian, but there can be no doubt that she was one of the biggest military prodigies of the Middle Ages, if not of all time. She had no patience with the traditional knightly nonsense (as she saw it) but operated by making everyone feel uncomfortable with the *status quo* – starting with the English. If Joan could have heard Patton's dictum that wars are not won by dying for one's country but making the other so-and-so die for *his* country, she would have thoroughly approved. The only difference is that Joan would have begun by appealing to the other so-and-so (as she did to the English in 1429) to return in peace to his own country, because he was bound to lose and might well get killed if he stayed. Endowed with a blinding common sense which both her admirers and her enemies found unbearable, she both affirmed and demonstrated that previous French defeats had been very largely due to French mistakes. France had all the necessary military tools for winning victories and it was just a matter of using them correctly.

This was particularly true of her first feat – the raising of the English siege of Orléans in 1429. The fact that the siege was still dragging on after seven months was yet another demonstration of the biggest English military weakness in France: the lack of enough troops and equipment to win spectacular victories *and* reduce all key French strongpoints at will. At Orléans Joan not only pointed out what had to be done, she also proved

Left: The Battle of Agincourt. This English victory resulted from the French failure to learn the bitter lessons of Crécy 70 years before.

Right: Longbow archers particularly liked this type of light, brim-less, open-faced helmet.

Below: A powerful (sixteenth century) windlass crossbow from Limoges, France.

showed that she had the knack of convincing her volatile countrymen that the enemy did not stand a chance – a much rarer concomitant of French military success than the French would like to admit.

The consequent heartening string of French field victories won under Joan's brief leadership in 1429 – Jargeau, Meung, Beaugency, Patay – owed much to a new care in reconnaissance and ferocity in attack, leading to the English being caught in the open before they could form un-assailable defensive positions. The French chronicler Monstrelet records that at Patay (14 June 1429):

The French, who preferred to fight on open ground, nearly all dismounted from their horses and continued on foot, their vanguard impatient to attack the English, because they had lately found them to be ill prepared in defense. With a sudden bold onslaught they caught them before they could form up in any order, while Sir John Fastolf and the bastard of Thian, both knights, and their men, who had not dismounted took flight across the open country to save their lives.

Meanwhile those English who were fighting on foot were soon surrounded on all sides, since they had no time to make their customary defenses of sharp stakes in the ground. They were unable to inflict much damage on the French and were soon completely beaten. Some 1800 English were left dead on the field, and 100 more taken prisoner, among them Lords Scales, Talbot and Hungerford, Sir Thomas Remp-stone and several more.

Joan's capture at Compiègne on 24 May 1430 while trying to prevent Charles VII from hand-ing the town over to the Burgundians was the re-

that is *could* be done, step by step. The English siege lines were not complete and had been opened still more by the untimely departure of England's Burgundian allies; the first step must be to reinforce and replenish the garrison by advancing boldly through the gap. The English were able to command the vital river approaches to the city; the second step was to take the English strongpoints on the banks. The final step was the furious hand-to-hand assault on the English garrison in the stronghold of Les Tou-relles, assisted by an artillery bombardment (un-gentlemanly though such tactics might be con-sidered). And while all this was afoot Joan

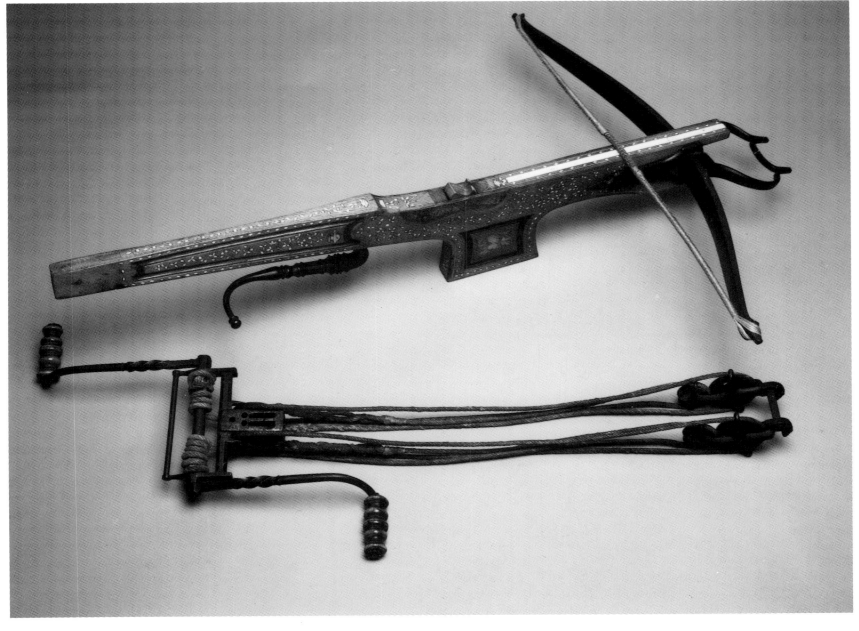

Above left: Detail from a late fifteenth century Swedish altarpiece, showing an earlier 'composite' crossbow stave of horn and sinew.

Above: This fifteenth century billman in the Royal Armories wears a 'brigandine', common armor for ordinary soldiers.

Left: A fifteenth century manuscript illustration of Agincourt; note the armor-piercing arrow penetrating a breastplate.

Right: This French fifteenth century manuscript illustrates the Battle of Najera (1367).

sult of one of those exploits which would still be lauded to the skies as brilliant if it had succeeded. As is was, at Compiègne Joan made the encouragingly human error of underestimating the speed of the enemy's reaction, and apparently overestimating the fighting spirit which she had instilled in her own side. The sortie she was leading with too small a force was beaten back, and she was covering the retreat of the rearguard when she was pulled from her horse by an archer. Instead of rallying and cutting her loose, her comrades continued their retreat into Compiègne.

The capture and execution of Joan gave the English their last illusory respite in the Anglo-French struggle but nothing could compensate for the fact Henry VI, their pious boy-king, had no interest in the war, despite being crowned King of France at the age of nine. Charles VII's successful detachment of the duchy of Burgundy from its alliance with England (1435) was the beginning of the end. While the acceleration toward civil war gathered speed in England, Charles VII proceeded with the far-reaching military reforms which had been overdue in France for over a century. And these reforms proved that the lessons which Joan of Arc had taught had not been wholly forgotten when she

was so abruptly removed from the scene in Rouen market place on 30 May 1431.

Joan had revealed three great secrets: that knights were most effective when they operated as versatile heavy cavalry, switching from mounted to dismounted action as circumstances required; that longbowmen were easy meat when attacked in the right manner; and that troops as well as fortifications were highly vulnerable to cannon. If Charles VII can hardly be said to have built the first modern standing army, he certainly achieved one of the earliest recognizable prototypes. In the direct tradition of Charlemagne, Belisarius and Alexander the Great, he created an élite or 'companion' cavalry based on six men to a *lance*, 200 *lances* to a company, 20 companies in all, each commanded by a captain appointed by the king. Auxiliary 'free archer' units, the *francs-arciers*, were formed at last on a territorial basis; and though they could not be given the same range and hitting-power as English longbowmen at least they were given superior mobility by putting them on horseback. Above all, through the industry of his artillery masters, the brothers Jean and Jasper Bureau, Charles established for France an ascendancy in artillery which she was destined to retain until the Napoleonic era and after.

The innovations of Charles VII's army

It was with this new army, built up during the uneasy truce of the 1440s, that Charles finished the job begun by Joan and expelled the English from Normandy and Gascony. The admiring Monstrelet, cataloging the soundness of Charles' preparations and army reforms, missed none of the salient points – the new discipline of the cavalry, the mobility of the missile troops and the excellence of the artillery, much of the latter highly mobile:

He equipped his fighting-men and archers with good, sound clothing and armour – the men-at-arms in cuirasses, greaves, light helmets called salades (the design chosen, 470 years later, as the pattern for the famous German 'coal-scuttle' steel helmets), silver-hilted swords, and a lance for their pages; each also had three horses, one for himself, one for his page and one for his servant, who was equipped with a salade, a brigandine or corselet, a jacket or hauburgeon, a battle-axe or a halberd. Each man-at-arms had two archers on horseback, also equipped with brigandines, greaves and salades mostly decorated with silver, though some had stout jackets and hauburgeons. All these soldiers were paid regularly each month . . .

The king had similarly made provision concerning

CHARLES · SEPTIESME · ET LE NO...

Left: Charles VII of France by Jean Fouquet.

Right: An interior view of a 'brigandine,' showing its construction.

Below: The 'Boxted Bombard,' a siege or artillery piece made in Sussex c1450.

artillery for his defence and for attacking towns and fortresses. Never in living memory had there been such an assemblage of large bombards, heavy cannon, veuglaires, serpentines, mortars, culverins and ribaudekins and these were amply provisioned with powder, protective coverings known as cats, a great number of carts to transport them, and everything necessary for the capture of towns and castles, and well provided with men to operate them all. They all received their pay daily, and were placed under the command of master Jean Bureau, treasurer of France, and Jasper Bureau, master of the artillery. These two men endured great dangers and hardships throughout the campaign, for they were very attentive to their duty . . .

Charles, in short, was willing to put military men even into the highest government posts to assist his final drives against the English in France; no other country in Europe could boast a gunnery expert as its treasurer.

The development of gunpowder-fired artillery took place in parallel with the emergence of shock and missile infantry, and the perfection of plate armor. The discovery of gunpowder as a propellant for missiles seems to have been made in the early thirteenth century and the first illustrations of recognizable cannon date from the 1320s, when cannon were used at the siege of Metz, and ordered by the *signoria* of Florence for the defense of the city. These proto-cannon,

known as *vasi* or *pots-de-fer*, consisted of bottle-shaped containers of gunpowder intended to fire barbed darts, which can hardly have been very successful because of the difficulty of making the narrow bore long enough and strong enough. The French are on record as being the first to use cannon in a naval bombardment during the attack against Southampton in 1338, using a *pot-de-fer* firing iron bolts. As the French fleet at this time relied heavily on Spanish and Genoese assistance, the weapon may well have been of Mediterranean provenance. But by 1340 wrought iron was being used to make simple tubes: the 'bombard,' named for the buzzing hum made by the projectile in flight.

Left: Joan of Arc at Château Chinon on 6 March 1428.

Right: Another illustration from the *Froissart Chronicles*; note the windlass crossbow in use in the foreground.

Below: A fifteenth century illumination from the *Life and Times of Henry V*, depicting a typical siege.

Below right: This early cannon in a manuscript by Walter de Milemetes (1326) is bottle-shaped and shoots arrows.

Some texts assert that Edward III had three bombards at Crécy, and indeed a 25-centimeter diameter cast iron shot of the right period was unearthed on the site of the battle in 1850. Edward's army lacked a siege train during the Crécy campaign and he is unlikely to have had more than three guns, each carried on a wagon; but if there were bombards at Crécy it is hard to see them contributing more than a few flashes, bangs and smoke-clouds at the very onset of the action. Fourteenth-century cannons were far too cumbersome to be of any real use in the field, but by the end of the century their place in the siege train was assured. It was usual to 'back-up' siege guns with old-style spring and counterweight siege artillery because of the distressing frequency with which the cannon blew up. The role of siege cannon – 'cracys' and 'great gunnys' – in Henry V's bombardment of Harfleur in August-September 1415 is well documented. The biggest guns were three-and-a-half meters long with a bore of over 60 centimeters; they fired mill-stones, huge tumbling missiles that carved great chunks out of masonry and sprayed lethal fragments when they broke up on impact. Henry's gunner poured tar over the gun-stones to set alight woodwork in the defenses and provide a 'tracer' effect at night. Certainly the French had an unspecified number of bombards in the field at Agincourt, and if any discipline had prevailed in the French host they might have had the chance to maul the frail English line as it marched forward to within bowshot of the French. But the impatient forward surge of the mounted knights seems to have blocked the French gunners' line, preventing them from firing as much as a single round.

Thirty-five years later, after Charles VII and his experts had transformed the French army, it

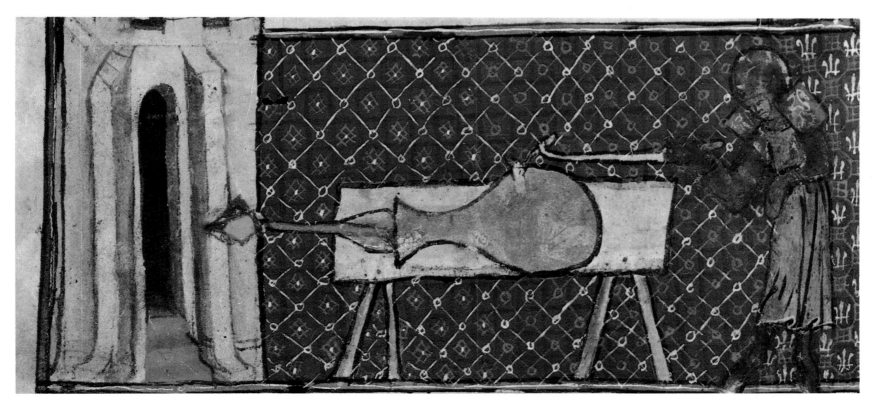

Left: The bombard Mons Meg, made *c*1450. King James II of Scotland used it in 1454 to subdue Threave castle held by the rebel Earl of Douglas.

Right: The storming of Nantes from an early sixteenth century German woodcut, showing artillery being used to breach the walls for an assault.

was a very different story. On 15 April 1450 the fate of Normandy was decided in battle at Formigny (a place of bitter memories to all Americans who survived the D-Day landings on Omaha Beach in 1944). The English commander, Sir Thomas Kyriell, deployed his force of about 4500 men on high ground in classic style and waited for the French to come on – but the French refused to oblige. While the division commanded by the Comte de Clermont skirmished in front of the English and kept them pinned down, another detachment worked round to the English flanks with two light culverins and opened a destructive fire on the archers. Kyriell ordered a charge which succeeded in 'taking out' the culverins, but this was what the French had been waiting for. Their armored infantry charged in and cut the archers to pieces. When the English prepared to hold Cherbourg the city was reduced by 'such a heavy battering from cannons and bombards that the like had never been seen before':

There were even bombards situated on the sea shore between high and low tide, which were weighted with boulders; although they were under water when the tide came in, they were covered with greased skins so that the sea did no harm to their powder, and as soon as the tide went out the cannoneers removed the coverings and continued firing into the town, to the

Left: An early wheeled cannon of about 1450 being deployed against a castle wall. Note the primitive (but effective) barrel elevating gear. Such siege guns eventually developed into more mobile field artillery pieces.

great astonishment of the English, who had never seen anything like it. Four bombards and one cannon burst while firing at the town, and great deeds of bravery were performed on sea and land, but more to the detriment of the English than in their cause.

(Monstrelet)

When Cherbourg surrendered on 12 August 1450 it had taken Charles VII a year and six days to complete the conquest of Normandy. Two years later he did even better, clearing the English out of the Garonne and taking Bordeaux in three and a half months. With the exception of the Calais enclave, France was free of the English at last. It had taken just 24 years for the French to apply the bitter lessons of over a century of military humiliation.

The end of England's dreams of power in France

There was nothing revolutionary or even new about the rediscovery, in the early fourteenth century, that well-handled shock or missile infantry could 'see off' heavy cavalry, no matter how numerous or well armored the latter might be. Nor was there anything surprising about the time it took for the knightly élite to realize that gallant frontal charges, particularly against prepared missile infantry, spelled virtual suicide.

The English longbow, with its unbeatable fire power, proved a master-weapon when used from well-chosen positions; but its most resounding successes were the result of fundamental tactical errors on the part of the enemy. Moreover, even the greatest longbow victories

had little strategic 'under-pinning.' Armies of archers were of little use against castles and fortified towns; the English only managed to tackle these piecemeal, in isolated campaigns. Given the lack of finance, siege weaponry and sustained political will to devise a methodical plan of conquest, the English ambition of holding France was never more than a dream.

Though the extraordinary career of Joan of Arc provided the initial inspiration for national recovery, the decisive French triumphs of 1429-53 were the well-earned reward for sound military reforms based on past experience. Above all they were the result of the acceptance that gunpowder artillery, for use in the field as well as in siege warfare, must now form an essential element in any modern army.

Germany and Italy

By the middle thirteenth century the fiercely disparate kingdoms and principalities of Germany, together with their Polish and Hungarian neighbors to the east, were fast recovering from the traumatic shock caused by the Mongol irruption of 1241-2. As pointed out earlier, the entire pattern of medieval warfare in the Christian West would have been forced into a very different configuration if the Mongols had succeeded in conquering central Europe. As it was, the very speed with which the Mongol threat had been presented and immediately withdrawn, with the Mongol tide of conquest receding from the eastern confines of Germany, meant that although the entire feudal military system and armory of the West had been proved totally inadequate, there was no subsequent compulsion to evolve or contrive anything better.

The German Emperor at the time of the Mongol invasion was the last great Hohenstaufen, Frederick II (1212-50), the last of the great medieval emperors who managed to extend and maintain effective rule on both sides of the Alps in the style of Otto the Great and Charlemagne. After Frederick II's death came the period of chaos known as the 'Great Interregnum' until 1273 when Rudolf of Hapsburg emerged as the next effective, purely 'German' emperor. Though the prestige of the old imperial title never ceased to be sought avidly by rival claimants and dynasties down the succeeding centuries, Germany lapsed into a fragmented, kaleidoscopic jumble of lay and clerical states and free cities which survived in essence until Napoleon arrived on the scene. Part of his attempt to create a new pattern of German states, all of whom would be firmly under France's thumb, included the final abolition of the title of 'Holy Roman Emperor' in 1806.

From the military viewpoint three themes naturally stand out from Germany's tortuous medieval history: the extraordinary career of the Teutonic Knights and the Crusader state they founded in the eastern Baltic lands; the Hapsburg defeat of Slav Bohemia at the Marchfeld in 1278; and the revolt of the Swiss and the rapid rise to supremacy of their magnificent infantry.

The last Crusader states

Though the Empire had never been backward in supplying Crusader contingents, the Crusading Order of the Teutonic Knights was formed comparatively late in the day. It evolved from a hospital organized at Acre in 1190 during the Third Crusade, funded by Bremen and Lübeck merchants to care for German pilgrims during the siege of Acre. Eight years later, after a number of German knights had naturally gravitated together, the Order received its official papal confirmation as the 'Teutonic Knights of the Hospital of St Mary of Jerusalem,' also known as the 'Knights of the Cross' and the 'German order' (*Deutscherorden*). From start to finish, as its name implied, it was recruited exclusively from the German knightly cast and ruled by a *Hochmeister* or Grand Master.

Though the headquarters of the Order remained at Acre from 1191 until the loss of the city 100 years later, the Teutonic Knights had to cope with intense rivalry on the part of the far more influential Templars and Hospitallers. The Templars were particularly resentful as the Teutonic Knights followed their rule, and seemed to ape the distinctive black-and-white heraldry favored by the Templars. Contingents of Teutonic Knights loyally served in most of the thirteenth-century Crusader battles in the Holy Land, but their unique career outside the Levant, as the champions of eastern Christendom, really began under the Grand Master Hermann von Salza (1210-39). Accepting that his still impoverished and insignificant order would have little chance to flourish in what was left of Christian Syria and Palestine, von Salza sought for other theaters of war in which it could legitimately fulfill its vow to fight the infidel.

After a disastrous debut in Christian Armenia in which the Order was all but wiped out (1210), it was invited to Hungary by King Andrew II to defend the kingdom against the heathen, fast-riding Cumans of the Black Sea coast. The Teutonic Knights' 14 years in Hungary (1211-25) were strongly reminiscent of the old Roman Empire's troubles with the *federati*. The mailed Knights of the Order kept the Cumans safely in check, but the sizable estates which Andrew was obliged to grant them soon grew too extensive for comfort and in 1225 Andrew expelled the Order by force. For his new patron Hermann von Salza turned to his close friend – the Emperor Frederick II. By the 'Golden Bull of Rimini' of 1226, Frederick reorganized the Order on Sicilian lines. To avoid the possibility of the Order degenerating into a mere *corps d'élite* to further Frederick's costly adventures in

Left: A battle between German and Italian knights from a fourteenth century manuscript.

Above right: A reconstruction of the Grand Master and a Knight of the Teutonic Order as they might have appeared in the thirteenth century.

Right: A romantic nineteenth century reconstruction of a battle between Knights of the Teutonic Order and their Lithuanian and Polish enemies.

Italy, von Salza promptly accepted a new offer elsewhere. This time the appellant was Conrad, Duke of Masovia in Poland, who needed help against the heathen Prussians (*Prusiaskai*) on his northern borders. Within four years of their arrival in 1230, Conrad granted the Knights the wild border province of Kulmerland, in the great bend of the lower Vistula, with the promise of all the land they might conquer from the Prussians. Four years later von Salza played his masterstroke, dedicating all the Prussian conquests made by Order to the Pope who, according to custom, returned them to the Order as a fief of the Church. Now the Knights of the Order were obliged to recognize the authority of no other lord but their own Grand Master, the Pope's tenant-in-chief. The last and most enduring of the Crusader states had come into being.

The Teutonic Knights had been preceded into the eastern Baltic by a lesser German Order of Knighthood, the 'Knights of Christ in Livonia' or 'Brotherhood of the Sword,' which operated from the German missionary base of Riga (founded 1201). Von Salza's excellent groundwork, however, meant that the Teutonic Knights retained pre-eminence over both the Livonian Knights and a lesser Polish Order, the Knights of Dobrzyn. The latter were affiliated into the Teutonic Knights in 1228 and the Brotherhood of the Sword in 1237, though the Livonian branch of the Order continued to call itself a Brotherhood of the Sword. From 1237, therefore, the Teutonic Knights operated on two fronts, in Prussia and in Livonia. Their iron rule in Prussia was anchored, like the Crusader states of Latin Syria, on castles and fortified bases which rapidly grew into major centers of Baltic and east German trade. Thorn was founded by the Knights in 1231, Kulm in 1232, Marienwerder in 1233 and Elbing in 1237. Memel followed in 1252 and Königsberg two years later.

Though their lands lay well to the north of the Mongol line of invasion, the Teutonic Knights contributed a contingent to the motley German-Polish army shattered by Kaidu Khan at Liegnitz. This disaster had absolutely no effect on the Order's eastward drive against the Russian principality of Novgorod, which produced one of the most spectacular early defeats of armored chivalry, the 'Ice Slaughter' of 1242, at the expense of the Livonian branch of the Order.

Unfortunately for the Teutonic Knights, the Novgorodians had an inspiring leader in the form of Alexander 'Nevsky,' who owed his nickname to his defeat, two years earlier, of an invading Swedish force on the River Neva. The Teutonic Knights also seem to have been taken by surprise – or to have discounted – the fact that the Novgorodians had developed a marked proficiency in fighting on horseback, with lancers and javelin-throwing warriors clad in mail and lamellar skirt armor suggestive of Norman knights of the early eleventh century. When the Teutonic Knights advanced on the city of Pskov across the ice of frozen Lake Peipus, Alexander chose to meet them out on the ice. He formed the Russian militiamen into a line behind which he held back a strong concentration of cavalry. The Teutonic Knights advanced in a ponderous wedge formation, apparently aiming for a quick victory by breaking clean through the Russian line without bothering to hold any forces in reserve. But the Knights' horses inevitably flinched at the hedge of spears resolutely presented to them, the line held, and Alexander and his horsemen came crashing in on the Knights' flank with an irresistible charge. As the Knights broke and

fled for the western shore, many were drowned as the ice gave way beneath them. Though it is hardly suggested by Eisenstein's film, many Russians met the same fate.

The disaster to the Livonian Knights on Lake Peipus was echoed in the same year by the first of many Prussian revolts, put down with great severity with Bohemian and Hapsburg aid. This

was a just and prompt recompense for the assistance which the Teutonic Knights had offered against the Mongols, but it was also clearly to the advantage of the German rulers to have a strong allied bastion holding down the Baltic lands. Now fed by a constant stream of German colonists to the lands it had conquered, the Order came to rely far too heavily on this ready supply of external help in times of crisis. Instead of becoming the core of a self-sufficient defense force, it ossified.

The pretence that the Teutonic Knights were a temporarily transplanted organ of the Mediterranean Crusading movement was briefly sustained when Acre fell in 1291 and the Grand Master of the Order moved to Venice. In 1308, however, the headquarters of the Order was transferred permanently to Marienburg on the lower Vistula. The 'State of the German order' was not a virtually autonomous military dictatorship, growing increasingly rich since its grant of a licence to trade (in theory at least, not for profit) by Pope Urban IV in 1263. But it was also becoming a blatant anachronism; the Grand Master's move to Marienburg took place in the very year that the officers and knights of the Templars underwent horrific torture in France, as part of the deliberate destruction of that order (ratified by the Council of Vienne in 1312). And from 1326 the Teutonic Knights came into repeated conflict with the Polish kingdom over the latter's claim for access to the Baltic via the Order's lands west of the lower Vistula – a claim soon upheld by the Pope. In their first war with Poland (1326-33) the Teutonic Knights emerged triumphant thanks to help – for the last time – from Bohemia, Brandenburg, Hungary and Austria, and the Order went on to seize the Danish colonies of Estonia (1346). The rule of the Teutonic Knights now stretched from Pomerania to the Gulf of Finland, but it was not to endure for any length of time.

Above left: Another romantic engraving of Teutonic Knights giving thanks for a God-given victory.

Above: Not all armor was blued or polished bright; some, like this German sallet *c*1500, was painted.

Above right: A Polish helmet (*c*1560) showing Eastern influence.

Far left: Detail of a late thirteenth century reliquary; note the 'barrel' helm and coat of plates.

Left: Another detail of the same reliquary; this figure wears a 'kettle hat' and mail shirt.

Right: Swiss mercenaries of about 1530 by Holbein. This was the *landsknecht* style of fighting.

The fate of the Order was sealed with the union of Poland and the huge duchy of Lithuania under the Jagiello dynasty in 1385, by which time the Order had definitely outlived its role as a bastion for the defense of Eastern Europe which had to be upheld. Ever-mounting Polish and Lithuanian pressure found the Teutonic Knights on their own, unsupported by the Empire, and holding down an increasingly restive population. On 15 July 1410, the Knights were swamped at Tannenburg by a massive Polish-Lithuanian army, and the break-up of the Order's lands began with the transfer to Poland of the central province of Samogitia, between the Düna and Niemen rivers. By 1525, when the last Grand Master, Albrecht of Hohenzollern, finally secularized the Order, the Poles had taken Prussia west of the Vistula – no less than the fateful 'Polish Corridor,' destined to play so baneful a role between the twentieth-century world wars. The original conquest of 'East' Prussia survived as an isolated enclave, a detached fief held by the Hohenzollerns from the Polish crown, until it was reunited with Hohenzollern Brandenburg with the partition of Poland in 1772.

The once-great name of the Teutonic Knights, however, lived on in the form of an honorary brotherhood until 1809; later, in 1840, the Hapsburgs revived the title to fulfill the original function of 650 years before as an ambulance service in time of war.

The Battle of the Marchfeld (1278)

In southern Germany by far the most unusual encounter of the thirteenth century, and the one with the most far-reaching results, was the Battle of the Marchfeld (26 August 1278). This defeat of the powerful King Ottokar II of Bohemia by the Hapsburg Emperor Rudolf I ended the prospect of the future Austrian heartland passing under the control of a Slav, rather than a German ruling line. Ottokar had made good his claim to the imperial fiefs of Austria, Styria, Carinthia and Carniola after the line of the Austrian Babenbergs had ended in 1246. He had hoped to be elected emperor in 1273 and refused allegiance to the successful candidate, Rudolf of Hapsburg. Not content with ousting Ottokar from the Austrian duchies in 1276 and extorting Ottokar's homage for Bohemia, Rudolf marched to destroy him in the summer of 1278.

The ensuing battle was unusual on two counts. The encounter was fought exclusively between armies of cavalry (surprising enough for any age) and the winning side, Rudolf's, owed much of its victory to the virtues so recently displayed by the Mongols: horsed archers. These were Cuman auxiliaries from the Black Sea coast – once the enemies of the Teutonic Knights – now in the pay of Hungary, whose king sent a strong contingent to help Rudolf in his struggle with Ottokar. For the last

Left: Armor designed at the end of the fifteenth century was a combination of beauty and function (an almost modern ideal); drawing by Albrecht Dürer.

time, heirs to a tradition dating back to Stilicho and his Huns, Asiatic horsed archers appeared on a western battlefield – in the angle between the Danube and the March, just east of Vienna – working in harmony with armored heavy cavalry. For it was the Hungarians and their Cuman allies who won the day, with the Cumans sweeping round Ottokar's right flank, showering it with arrows as a preliminary to the decisive Hungarian charge. Ottokar himself, commanding on the other wing, had repulsed the imperial attack, but his Bohemians and Moravians panicked and fled when they saw what had happened to their comrades. Ottokar was killed as the Hungarians and Cumans took up the pursuit of his fleeing army, hundreds of whom were drowned as they tried to swim the March. With the power of Bohemia broken, Rudolf was left in peace to invest his sons with the Austrian duchies, establishing Hapsburg power on the upper Danube until 1918.

In 1291, however, Hapsburg pride was affronted by the revolt of the Swiss 'Forest Cantons' of Uri, Schwyz and Unterwalden, which joined forces in rejecting Hapsburg rule. The

Above and right: A German or Swiss halberd of about 1480, and another (Austrian or Swiss) some 30 years earlier. These descendants of agricultural implements enabled the foot soldier to strike back against the previously invulnerable horseman.

Swiss did exactly what the rebel Scots and rebel Flemish burghers were doing at the same date in that they adopted the most likely weapons they had in common and devised basic tactics with which to confound the armored knights which they knew would be sent against them. The weapons in question were initially the long-shafted poleaxe or halberd, and soon afterward the long pike. These weapons served as the mainstay of a citizen army which would have to survive the charge of armored cavalry.

The success of the Swiss 'citizen army'

With the territory of their homeland as their natural ally, the Swiss relied on guile as much as on weaponry and tactics in their first actions with the punitive forces they faced – but, fortunately for them, this confrontation did not happen at once. The original Swiss confederation seemed a trivial affair and it merely sought token recognition from the emperors Adolf (1292-8) and Albrecht (1298-1308), who had their hands full at the time with France and Bohemia. Thus the Swiss earned time to evolve a basic drill, and by the reign of Henry VII (1308-13) they were sufficiently well trained to send 300 of their citizen-soldiers to join the emperor's expedition to Italy. But the next emperor, Louis IV, was a Wittelsbach whom the Hapsburgs challenged with their own claimant, Frederick; the empire suffered another prolonged civil war; the Swiss stuck to their policy of supporting the emperor – and Duke Leopold of Austria led a punitive expedition to crush these presumptuous peasants. Twenty-four years had passed since the 'Forest Cantons' had formed their confederation, and the crisis for which they had long prepared was on them at last.

At Mortgarten (15 November 1315) the glorious military career of the Swiss infantry opened with a perfect ambush which any indignant knight of the old school could be excused for considering a thoroughgoing insult to his talents. The Swiss caught Leopold's force of knights and spearmen in a defile flanked on one side by Lake Ägeri. They blocked the path of the Austrian knights in the van with rocks and tree trunks, then charged in among the halted knights with halberds and maces. Swordplay was totally inadequate against such tactics and the only way out for the surviving knights was a bloody stampede through their own infantry, adding to the numbers hurled from the track into the lake. The gratified Emperor Louis rewarded

Right: From the *Berner Chronicles* (1483). Against the superior mobility of cavalry, infantry could shelter behind a wagon laager fortified with artillery and hand-guns. Note the chests of round shot and ready-made cartridges of gunpowder for the cannon.

155

the Swiss with a charter confirming their confederation and three years later a still-chastened Leopold made peace with them.

When Lucerne joined the confederation in 1332 the forest men received an injection of aid from the lowland compatriots and their favored weapon – the pike. Very soon the Swiss national army consisted of massed formations of *light* pikemen, wearing very little armor and capable of movement at great speeds. This restored the true offensive role of the pike phalanx, the resurrection of which in the late thirteenth century had concentrated on the problem of defense against knights. And it was a course of evolution which flourished mightily, because in their formative years the Swiss never came up against missile troops.

One of the great unanswerable questions prompted by the wars of the fourteenth and fifteenth centuries is 'what would have happened if the French had hired the Swiss army to fight the English longbowmen?' It is very hard to see a decisive advantage on either side. Certainly the mobility of the Swiss pikemen would have exposed the longbowmen to unpredictable and highly dangerous attacks, launched from new positions and pressed with a speed impossible to formations of armored knights, whether mounted or dismounted.

As with the English longbowmen, the fourteenth century was, for the Swiss, the age of great victories: Laupen (1339), Sempach (1386) and Naufels (1388). All were battles won over outmatched and out-dated feudal armies unable to find an answer to the pike phalanxes, even when the knights fought dismounted with shortened lances.

By the late fourteenth century nearly a quarter of the Swiss army consisted of light troops armed

Left: The armorers' workshop of the Emperor Maximilian I (*c*1515).

Below: Verrocchio's equestrian monument to Colleoni in Venice.

Far left: An Italian (Milanese) breastplate of about 1500, showing its more rounded contours in contrast to the German fluted and pointed style.

Left: Infantry using crude early hand-guns side-by-side with crossbows in a drawing taken from a woodcut of 1499.

with missile weapons – crossbows at first but, from the 1380s, handguns or arquebuses. Firearms designed for use by infantry had appeared at a very early stage and consisted basically of a miniature cannon barrel mounted at the end of a pole. The first use of these ancestors of the musket by the Swiss was during the 1386 Sempach campaign, when they took Neuregensberg from the Austrians. Throughout the fifteenth century the Swiss continued to use their light missile infantry to save the pike phalanxes from premature commitment, skirmishing and generally 'setting up' the enemy for the decisive charge of the pikemen. The Swiss infantry reached a peak of excellence not matched by other armies until the early sixteenth century and by the last quarter of the fifteen century they were beginning to hire themselves out as mercenaries, serving in most European wars of the period.

The splendid career of the Swiss infantry only serves to highlight the military backwardness of

Germany in the later Middle Ages, where the old feudal nature of armies survived the longest. Much the same applied to Italy, where there was also little or no military evolution on the Swiss, English or French models. The tendency of continued reliance on the armored knight was not helped by the fact that southern Germany and Italy, as Europe's major ironworking centers, were also the centers of armor development and manufacture. As the Swiss had proved to the world, military excellence could far easier be attained from a starting-point of military nakedness. Nuremburg, Innsbruck, Augsberg and Landshut were the most famous German armor-producing centers; Milan and Pisa led the field in Italy. It was from these centers that the final refinements of plate-armor development were taken to their peak of excellence in the early sixteenth century.

The 'free companies' of Italy

The predominant characteristic of warfare in

Italy during the fourteenth and fifteenth centuries was the hiring of professional 'free companies' of mercenaries, of which there was an abundant overspill from the Anglo-French struggle after the English had signed the Peace of Brétigny with chastened France in 1360, the fruits of Crécy and Poitiers.

The innocuous modern term 'freelance' has its origin in these 'companies of free lances' who sought their fortune amid the endless wars of the Italian city-states. The most famous of them all was the 'White Company' of Sir John Hawkwood, whose origins and career show how far the most expert practitioners of medieval warfare had come from the knightly romantic ideal of the twelfth and thirteenth centuries. Hawkwood was no Roland or Lancelot; if he had served with the French, he would never have been allowed to ride with the front-rank knights. He was the son of an Essex tanner, a former tailor's apprentice, knighted by the Black Prince for sterling service in the French wars. For 30

Left: Jacques de Molay, Grand Master of the Templars, being burnt alive for heresy. His chief accusers (Philip IV of France and Pope Clement V) died within a year of him as he foretold.

Right: Thomas Neville, Bastard of Fauconberg, and his Kentish army lay siege to Yorkist London during the Wars of the Roses.

years Hawkwood's hard core of 1000 armored men-at-arms, assisted on foot by about 2000 (at peak strength) archers and crossbowmen, were the bane of northern and central Italy. They fought for the Visconti of Milan; they fought for the Papacy; they fought for Pisa, and finally for the Republic of Florence. Hawkwood became Florence's foremost general and ended his days in Florentine service, being honored by a splendid equestrian monument in the Duomo. Hawkwood's White Company was able to command record wages and protection money; 25,000 florins a month was the rate paid during the Company's brief spell in the service of Pisa. His record *coup* was a joint payment of 220,000 gold florins put up by five Italian cities. This was the price of being left alone by the White Company for the space of five years – Danegeld come again, in a new professional guise.

Like the foreign free companies, Italy's 'home-grown' free companies of *condottieri* fought on a strict cash basis, not for land or loot. Their activities throughout the fourteenth century helped maintain a decidedly unreal style of warfare; there was no point, for instance in causing genuine damage to the property of a state which might well be a future employer. This warfare for wages and protection money enabled the participants to purchase the latest improvements in armor, and as battles tended to consist of collisions between armies of well-armored men-at-arms, casualties were often absurdly low. When the hirelings of Florence and Milan clashed at Molinella in 1427, half a day's furious clangor resulted in only 300 men being killed out of a total 20,000 combatants.

It was this abstract, chess-like aspect of 'warfare Italian style,' lasting as it did until the French invasion of 1494, that encouraged Macchiavelli to draw up his handbook on princely *realpolitik – The Prince –* in which particular attention was paid to the importance of mercenary forces as an extension of princely politics.

The encouragement of war by proxy

The sudden withdrawal of the Mongol menace in the mid-thirteenth century meant that Germany's military feudalism, so far from being goaded into new paths, ended by lagging behind and outlasting that of the kingdoms of Western Europe. As with the Scots and Flemings, it was the Swiss who forcibly demonstrated the power of drilled shock infantry to confound knightly armies of the old school.

Italy remained, as she had since the beginning of the Middle Ages, a theater of war rather than a school for new developments in war. Germany and Italy shared the paradox of being outstripped by their more advanced military neighbors, while at the same time producing the most perfect 'hardware' in the form of plate armor. But another paradox, particular to Italy, was the continued encouragement of 'war by proxy,' featuring hireling armies in an era when new weaponry and tactics were confirming the utter obsolence of the old-style mercenaries.

The Hussite Wars: the shape of things to come

Apart from the splendid career of the Swiss infantry phalanxes, the early fifteenth century produced one other notable phenomenon which demonstrated the obsolescence of knightly warfare in later medieval Germany. This was the use of cannon and handguns in the unique *wagenburg* of the Hussite Wars (1420-33), forerunner of the deadly 'wars of religion' of the sixteenth and seventeenth centuries, which produced what is commonly regarded today as the formative early stage in the quest of an armored fighting vehicle.

Many threads came together to produce the Hussite Wars. This conflict formed part of the shameful epilogue to the story of the Crusades when, having failed to oust the Moslems from the Holy Land, the Church's obsession with stamping out heresies proceeded to set Christian against Christian. Here was a theme dating back to the very dawn of the Middle Ages, when Orthodox Roman Christians had clashed ferociously with the Arian Christian barbarians whose aid had been enlisted for the preservation of the Empire. Since those tumultuous decades war after war, fought with special cruelty, had underlined the perversion of Christianity from a unifying doctrine of peace and love to a savage medium of rivalry and hate. There had been the scandal of the Fourth Crusade in which the champions of Latin Christendom had turned greedily on the Orthodox Greeks of the Byzantine Empire and conquered it for themselves. Hard on the heels of the Fourth Crusade had come the 'Albigensian Crusade' of 1208-13, when the Papacy had considered it far more important to exterminate the Albigensian 'heretics' of Provence than to send reinforcements to the struggling Crusader states in the Holy Land. But the followers of the Czech religious reformer John Hus, betrayed and burned at the stake at Constance (October 1415), were inspired by more than a fierce determination to defend their religious principles by force of arms. This was a war of Czech national resistance to imperial German rule, following the earlier struggles for independence by the Scots, Flemings and Swiss, and overlapping with the subsequent rally of the French against English overlordship. The Hussite Wars, in short, featured that most corrosive blend of motives for military conflict: religion and patriotism.

The unorthodox tactics of Jan Žižka

After the burning of their leader the Hussites (inevitably) remained divided among themselves on many religious details, but they were unanimous – from noble to peasant – in standing firm against further imperial attempts to eradicate the Hussite creed from Bohemia. When King Wenceslas IV obeyed the Emperor Sigismund (1410-37) and appointed an anti-Hussite town council in Prague, a Hussite mob hurled the offending councillors from the Town Hall windows on 30 July 1419. Wenceslas died in a fit of rage on hearing the news and his cousin and heir – Emperor Sigismund – not only refused to accept the Hussites' 'Four Articles' but proclaimed a crusade against them. Determined to resist, the Hussite Czechs refused to recognize Sigismund as their king and set about forming an army at the Hussite town of Tabor in southern Bohemia. And for once God was not on the side of the big battalions, for the man chosen to lead the Hussites turned out to be a military genius.

The Hussite war leader was Jan Žižka, a tough experienced 60-year-old fighter, blind in one eye, who nevertheless saw at once that it would be suicide for his people to try to imitate the structure of the imperial forces. As the Hussites were lacking numbers, training and experience in orthodox tactics, they had to wage unorthodox war on their own terms. But where in similar circumstances the Swiss had chosen to pit massed shock infantry against the armored knights of Austria, Žižka boldly chose to enlist fire power – and not the obsolescent fire power of crossbow or longbow, but the modern fire power of handguns and light cannon.

For the medium via which this fire power was to be brought to bear on the enemy Žižka chose the laager or defensive park of wagons, an item dating back to the Gothic wars of the later Roman Empire. Žižka trained the Hussites to

Left and below left: The face and reverse side of a contemporary medallion depicting John Huss, and his being burnt as a heretic.

Above right: Design for a 'wagon castle,' perhaps the earliest form of armored fighting vehicle, from *Das Mittelateriche Hausbuch* (late fifteenth century).

Right: The *wagenburg* of the Hussite Wars from the same manuscript.

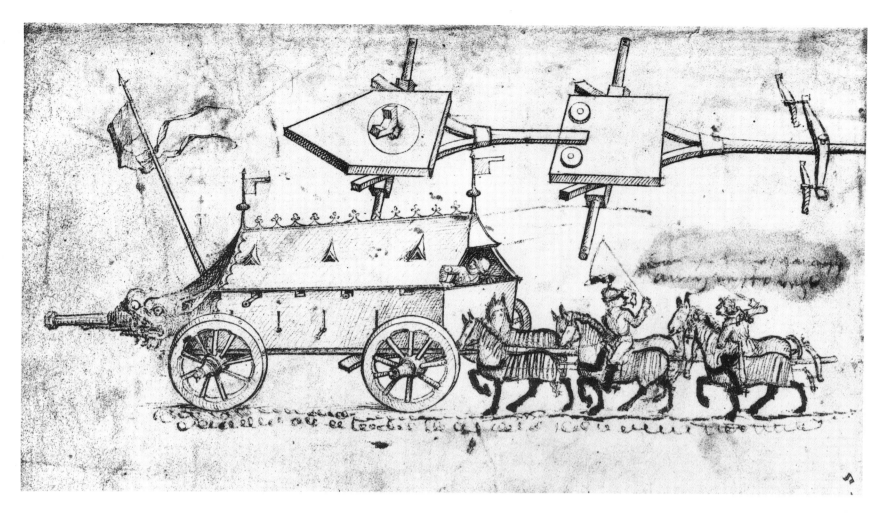

travel with guns mounted in groups of four or more heavy wagons, which at the word of command could be wheeled together and linked at the ends by reinforced wooden boards. The re-

sult was the *wagenburg* or 'wagon stronghold.' bristling at all angles with gun barrels and capable of shattering all conventional attacks upon it. The Hussites were trained in the no less im-

portant art of disconnecting the *wagenburg* into its component wagons, hitching up and moving off at speed. Here was a blend of mobility and hitting power which even the Mongol horsed

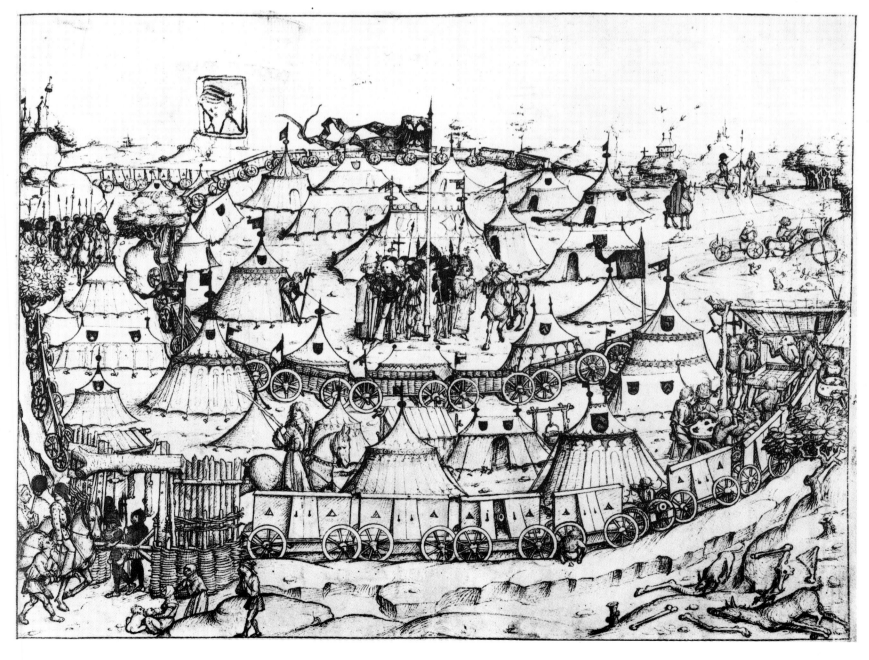

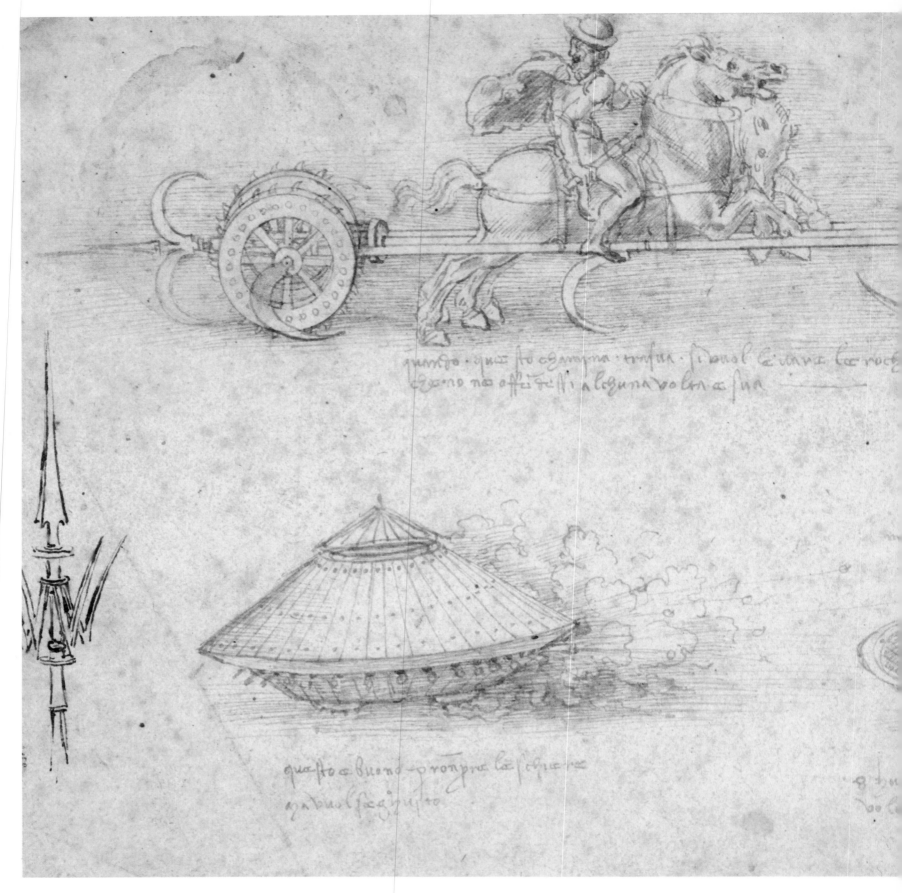

archers in their heyday would have found a disconcerting prospect. To the opposition which Žižka, from his years of military experience, knew that his people were bound to encounter, the *wagenburg* was a revolutionary and utterly impossible concept, as frightening an apparition as the first tanks on the Somme in 1916.

The *wagenburg* units of a Hussite army were backed up by strong artillery train, including heavy bombards firing 45-kilogram projectiles, the heaviest pieces ever enlisted for field service in that era. The essence of Žižka's system was centuries ahead of its time: the biggest possible concentration of gunners to the right spot at the right moment – or, as the inimitable Nathan Bedford Forrest was to put it in the American Civil War, moving 'fustest with the mostest.' But the Hussite order of march devised by Žižka was an even bigger prodigy, and would not be seen again until the formation of the first mechanized

and armored divisions in the twentieth century. As it was vital for all arms to fight together, it was therefore equally vital for all arms to move together. This was done in five parallel columns with cavalry and field artillery in the center column, sandwiched between two outer columns of wagons with their infantry.

It is no exaggeration to say that the first appearance of these troops in 1420 caused as big an impact as the debut of Guderian's *panzer* divisions in Poland in September 1939. After the first shattering defeat of Sigismund's feudal host in 1420, the emperor's reaction was – as Žižka had anticipated – to raise still bigger traditional armies for a repeated crusade in 1421-2. In the one-sided action at Deutschbrod, the second Crusading army went the way of the first.

By the time of Žižka's death in 1424 the Hussites were carrying the war out of Bohemia into the neighboring German principalities, always

with success. Under the leadership of Žižka's gifted successor, the Taborite priest Prokop 'The Bald,' the Hussites went from strength to strength. Prokop's victory at Aussig in 1426 firmly established for the Hussites a reputation of invincibility, and at Tachov in the following year the imperial levies took to their heels and fled from the field before a single blow had been struck. The same thing happened at Taus in 1431. By this time, riding at will through Germany in bitter parody of the traditional medieval *chevauchée* of armored knights, the Hussites had proved that they could raid as far as the Baltic if they so wished. When the Papal legate Cardinal Cesarini witnessed the rout at Taus, the Church was finally prepared to negotiate a compromise.

True to its origins – the bitterness of religious dissension – the Hussite story ended in civil war which did nothing but assist a more subtle reim-

Above: Leonardo da Vinci's designs for war vehicles; note in particular the lower sketch, which can only be described as a prototype armored car.

Right: An engraving of 1575 showing mortars on 'portable' carriages; transported by wagons to the site of a siege, these were in effect the same form of bombard used in the late fourteenth century for battering fortifications.

position of imperial power. Yet, fleeting though it was, Žižka's formula for victory had achieved a revolution in war, the disappearance of which is less surprising when the failure of the French to emulate the English longbowmen or the Austrians to emulate the Swiss pikemen is brought to mind.

Early designs for armored vehicles

Though the Hussite *wagenburg* vanished as a tactical reality as the fifteenth century wore on, this did not mean that the concept of the armored fighting vehicle died with it. In the 1470s and 1480s various weird and wonderful designs for artillery-carrying vehicles were sketched, the most famous of them by the Italians Roberto Valturio and Leonardo da Vinci. Valturio's *De Re Militari* included drawings which showed a grasp of one of the principles established with the *wagenburg*: all-round fire power, which Valturio envisaged as feasible by means of a capstan and turntable carrying small cannon like the spokes of a wheel. Valturio also toyed with sketches of cannon suitable for mounting in vehicles, equipped with elevating gear and shields to protect the gunners. The most famous of these pipe dreams is the sketch made by Leonardo of a futuristic armored car. It shows a circular vehicle covered in with a conical top and bristling all round with guns. This sketch seems to have been made to substantiate Leonardo's outrageous claim to Lodovico Sforza around 1481:

Also I can make armored cars, safe and unassailable, which will enter the serried ranks of the enemy with their artillery, and there is no company of men-at-arms so great that they will not break it. And behind these the infantry will be able to follow quite unharmed and without opposition . . .

But Leonardo's vision of the tank as it actually developed over 400 years later was considerably more impressive than the design he actually produced, which featured a touching faith in human muscle power. Leonardo's conical 'tank,' had it ever seen the light of day, would have depended for its motive power on eight human pistons laboring at a hand-turned crankshaft. A more practical design was that of Nikolaus Glocken-

thon for an Austrian 'war chariot' which comprised a two-wheeled cart carrying a daunting-looking array of cannon (presumably breech-loaders), pushed into action by teams of armored men-at-arms, with the gunner protected by a sloping shield bearing a striking resemblance to the glacis-plate of a modern battle tank.

Though these over-optimistic designs of the fifteenth and early sixteenth centuries were inevitably foiled by the power problem – which even the advent of the steam engine in the eighteenth century was not to overcome – they were nevertheless firm proof that even in the new and unfamiliar field of mobile artillery the evolutionary urge was already at work. For the secret of that urge was the eternal quest of the fighting man for better artificial aids to survival in the supremely hostile environment of the battlefield. The Middles Ages had made cannon a reality, first to batter walls, then troops. This meant that troops would need whatever protection from artillery fire that could be devised, while the demands of the battlefield would require more and more maneuverability for the artillery. Sooner or later, the resolution of these conflicting requirements was going to produce the self-propelled armored fighting vehicle.

The *Wagenburg* – 'instant fortress'

Devised in a crisis to defeat the traditional pattern of feudal warfare, the Hussite *wagenburg* was the most effective reply to the centuries-old domination of the armored knight produced in the fifteenth century. Jan Žižka's revolutionary formula produced an effective if crude solution: the convoy of guns which moved to the most suitable point, then sat down and converted itself into an 'instant fortress' capable of simultaneously defending itself and dealing out destruction. But that was only a beginning. By the end of the century, military theorists already knew that the next step must be a vehicle with similar fire power which would not need to be halted and converted into a fighting posture. As the sixteenth century began, the thread of military ingenuity, leading down the following centuries to the birth of the armored car and tank, had already received its first cautious extension.

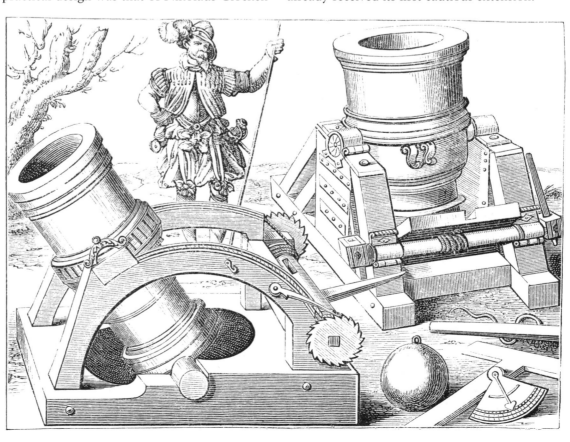

The Turks and Constantinople

While the fourteenth and fifteen centuries were replete with resounding military events and developments in central and Western Europe, another phenomenon of equal magnitude was taking shape in the Levant. This was the steady rise of the Ottoman Turks to supremacy in the eastern Mediterranean and southeast Europe, crushing the last fragments of the Byzantine Empire and finally, in 1453, encompassing the fall of Constantinople.

Though the latter event sent a shock through the civilized world comparable only to the fall of Rome to the Goths over 1000 years before, one of the biggest surprises from the twentieth-century viewpoint is that the 'second Rome' survived as long as it did. For, as explained earlier, the Byzantine Empire lost its military self-sufficiency long before, with the destruction of its army at Manzikert in 1071 and the subsequent loss of its Anatolian recruiting grounds to the Seljuk Turks. After Manzikert, indeed, the patent weaknesses of the Empire finally tempted the Latin West into making a bid to overthrow it with the notorious 'Fourth Crusade' of 1202-4. The story of how the Byzantine Empire not only survived this mortal stroke but struggled on for another two centuries is one of the most remarkable sagas in medieval history.

The heart of the Empire, the imperial city of Constantinople with its mighty fortifications, was kept beating by sea power – Byzantine or allied. In its darkest days, when Goths, Bulgars or Avars had plundered as far as the city walls, the Empire had been repeatedly saved by sea. For Constantinople was not only the best fortified city in the world, it also had the best mercantile anchorage and naval base in the world. Geography dictated that as long as the Byzantines retained enough sea power to keep the Bosphorus and Golden Horn clear of enemy warships and troop transports, and as long as regular reinforcements and provisions kept coming by sea, Constantinople would be able to hold out even if the entire territory of the Empire was overrun.

The weakening of the Byzantine Empire

In 1203-4, however, Constantinople – for the first time in its long history – was treacherously assaulted by a well-equipped naval expeditionary force which had been assembled to fight as the Empire's nominal ally. But the fact that the incredible had happened and that Christian sea power had been turned against the city did not affect the fundamental hostility between the Greek and Latin worlds. When the now-modest imperial Byzantine territories on the European shore were parceled out as Latin feudal lordships, nothing was going to make the Greek population welcome in their new future with open arms – particularly as the old Empire had not been totally destroyed, but was carrying on as best it could in the Byzantine territory on the Asian shore.

For this reprieve the Greeks, ironically enough, had only their Latin blood-enemies to thank. One of the most important achievements of the Latin Crusade had been the reconquest, with the help of the Latin Crusaders, of Nicaea and the north west corner of Anatolia; and it was in this enclave across the straits, the 'Empire of

Nicaea,' that the Byzantine imperial tradition was maintained after 1204. Intent as they were on looting Constantinople and seizing the imperial territories in Europe, the vultures of the Fourth Crusade left the Empire of Nicaea to its own devices. Throughout the brief span of the 'Latin Empire' of Constantinople (1204-61) geography took over again. The Latin emperors now depended on the Venetian and Genoan fleets for their retention of Constantinople; and Byzantine strategy, bent on recovering Constantinople and the lost provinces, consisted of depriving the Latin emperors in the city of their maritime lifeline.

The Nicaean Empire was small in extent but it enjoyed one priceless asset because it controlled the straits. Its goodwill was essential for mercantile trading success in the Black Sea, and as the biggest mercantile states in the western Mediterranean (Venice and Genoa) were the two props of the Latin Empire, this parallel fact of geography was enlisted by the Nicaean Empire as a crucial strategic weapon. On 10 July 1261 the Nicaean Emperor Michael Palaeologus signed the Treaty of Nymphaeum with the

Genoese Republic, recklessly giving away enormous trading concessions to ensure the future friendly neutrality of the Genoese fleet. All that remained was to wait until the Venetian fleet happened to be away from Constantinople, and on 25 July the Nicaean general Alexius Strategopoulos led a well-judged amphibious pounce across the straits. The Greek population of Constantinople rose in support, the hated Latins fled in whatever ships they could commandeer and the Byzantine imperial tradition was triumphantly resumed in Constantinople.

Nothing, however, could repair the damage which the Latin conquest had inflicted. The restored Byzantine Empire was a 'thing of threads and patches': Nicaea and an enclave around Trebizond on the eastern Black Sea coast; the city of Constantinople and its immediate surroundings; the coastal strip of Thrace; southern Macedonia with Thessalonika; and the islands of Imbros, Lesbos, Samothrace and Rhodes. The Latins retained their imperial fiefs in Greece which consisted of the principality of Achaea and the duchy of Athens. Most of the Aegean islands remained in the grip of Venice, organized as a duchy. Nevertheless, Michael Palaeologus set himself to recover the lost imperial grounds in Europe. In the immediate aftermath of the 1261 *coup* he made a promising beginning, snatching a foothold around Mistra in the Morea (or 'Lamorie', as it was known in the Latin West) and making it the capital of a Byzantine principality. In the following year, Michael put sustained pressure of the Greek ruler of Epirus, which had survived the Latin conquest, and suc-

Left: A Turkish 'turban' helmet; the mail aventail, like that on a European basinet, served to protect the neck.

164

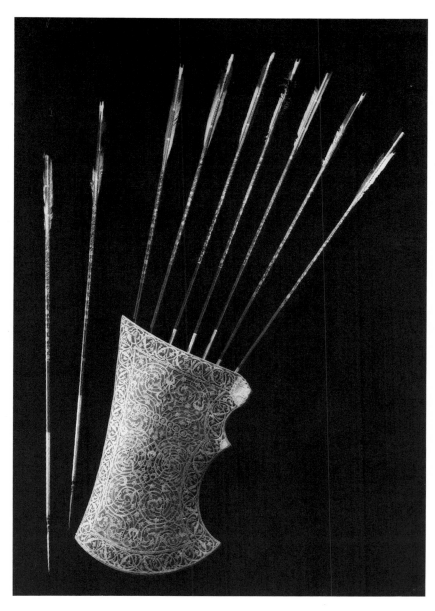

Right: Early sixteenth century Turkish arrows and a quiver in the Kunsthistorisches Museum, Vienna. Their forms had not changed for centuries.

Right: A Turkish helmet in Persian (traditional) style, dating from the late fifteenth century.

ceeded in restoring Epirus to direct imperial rule. But these early successes were jeopardized by the spirited resistance of the Latin overlords in Athens and the Peloponnese, and by the refusal of Western rulers to accept that the Latin Empire could not be restored.

The trouble began in 1266 when Charles of Anjou, not content with becoming the new king of Sicily, set his sights on restoring the Latin Empire with himself as emperor. By marrying his son to the heiress of the ruling Villehardouins, Charles established his authority in Achaea and in 1267 assumed the claim of the last Latin emperor, Baldwin II. While Emperor Michael prudently strengthened his maritime lifeline by permitting the Genoese to establish themselves at Galata, Charles took the island of Corfu as an offshore base for the reconquest of Epirus. Durazzo fell in 1272, and the ominous pattern of conquest as attempted by Robert Guiscard and Bohemond 200 years before seemed to be taking shape once more. Desperate to strengthen his hand still further, Michael took the extra-ordinary step of accepting the Roman creed and the primacy of the pope (1274). This 'reunion with Rome' cut out papal encouragement of Latin attacks on the Byzantine Empire, but it was bitterly resented by the Greek clergy and people on whom its political brilliance was lost. Limited campaigns with the slender forces which could be raised in Nicaea and spread from the other pockets of Byzantine rule enabled Michael to hold the Angevins of Sicily at bay during the last ten years of his reign.

When he died in 1282 Michael Palaeologus had restored a precarious caricature of the Byzantine Empire. Though his achievement deserves admiration as a political rather than a military *tour de force*, the Empire was weak everywhere, strong nowhere, and still totally dependent on the goodwill of such allies as could be procured by ruthless diplomacy pre-pared to hold no principle sacred. The reunion with Rome, by its implications the only real gua-rantor of constant assistance from Italy and the maritime republics – and that only when the in-terests of the maritime republics did not happen to clash with those of the Roman papacy – was the first of Michael's policies to be abandoned by his feeble successors. They were now confronted by the same dilemma with which the Empire had been hard put to cope in its last years of power before Manzikert – simultaneous pressure in the Balkans and in Asia Minor. In the Balkans they were faced with the rapidly expanding kingdom of the Serbs; in Asia Minor by the new menace of the Ottoman Turks.

The Ottoman Turks enter Asia Minor

The branch of the Turkish race which had brought the Empire to the verge of total dis-solution in the eleventh century had been the Sel-juk Turks, whose 'Kingdom of Rum' had been crippled and its extent constricted by the armies of the First Crusade. The downfall of the Seljuks in Anatolia had been completed by the Mongols, who had briefly held Anatolia in suzerainty; but from about 1260 onward the Turkish popula-tion of Asia Minor began to receive new in-jections of Turkish trekkers from the east. Once arrived in the territorial *cul-de-sac* of Asia Minor these newcomers set about a career of banditry, bearing down particularly hard on the flimsy borders of Byzantine Nicaea. To the newly-re-stored Byzantine Empire, however, these Turkish raiders were no more than a pest com-pared with the formidable Latins in Achaea and Athens, the Angevins of Sicily and the Serbs in Epirus. The restored Empire's obsession with re-covering its lost European territories led the suc-cessors of Michael to resume the old imperial Roman ploy of setting a thief to catch a thief by enlisting the aid of Turkish bands against the Empire's enemies in the Balkans.

Left: The martyrdom of St Sebastian by the Pollaiuolo brothers (National Gallery, London) showing Eastern style re-curved bows in use alongside European crossbows.

Right: Nineteenth century Turkish Janissaries; note the bow-case, which had basically not changed shape since the fourteenth century. In the East, archery maintained its importance even after the introduction of firearms.

It was in the reigns of the co-emperors Andronicus II (1282-1328) and Michael IX (1295-1320) that one group of Turkish raiders began to take on a worrying eminence around Dorylaeum in Bithynia, absorbing other clans and rising to the status of a recognizable principality. These Turks were led by a warrior chief by the name of Osman, after whom they called themselves the *Osmanli* or 'Ottomans.' And his policy of strict but fair dealing with all and sundry who were prepared to recognize him as their ruler won him growing support from the citizenry of central Anatolia.

In 1303 the emperors unwittingly heaped coals of fire on their own heads by hiring Spanish mercenaries, unemployed after a term of Sicilian service, to cope with Osman in Asia Minor. These mercenaries, Roger de Flor's 'Catalan Grand Company,' excelled even the unscrupulous career of Hawkwood's White Company in Italy later in the century. In 1304 they saved Philadelphia from Osman but almost immediately returned to Europe to avenge themselves on the Empire for arrears in pay. This they did with a vengeance, terrorizing Macedonia and Thrace for the next six years, and ending up as the new Latin ruling dynasty of Athens. But the depredations of the Catalan mercenaries, made worse by an ensuing civil war between the Emperor Andronicus and his grandson, permitted the advance of Osman's Turks to continue in Asia Minor. It was at the invitation of the Catalan Grand Company that the first Turkish warband crossed to Europe in 1308. Having reached the Aegean coast the Turks showed great aptitude at embarking on piratical raids on sea as well as on land; and it was to combat them that the Crusading Order of the Knights Hospitallers occupied Rhodes in 1309.

Nothing, however, eroded the persistence of Osman, who continued to expand the Turkish principality in western Asia Minor. In 1308 he took Ephesus before turning north and pressing toward the Sea of Marmara, finally laying siege to the Byzantine town of Bursa (1317-26). The fact that the Byzantines, after nine years' effort, failed to hold this important outpost – which lay barely 95 kilometers across the Marmara from Constantinople itself – was the clearest possible proof of the bankruptcy of imperial sea power. At this stage the Turks still lacked the siegecraft with which to take fortified cities and were forced to rely on starvation to reduce Bursa, which finally fell on 6 April 1326. Though he had

167

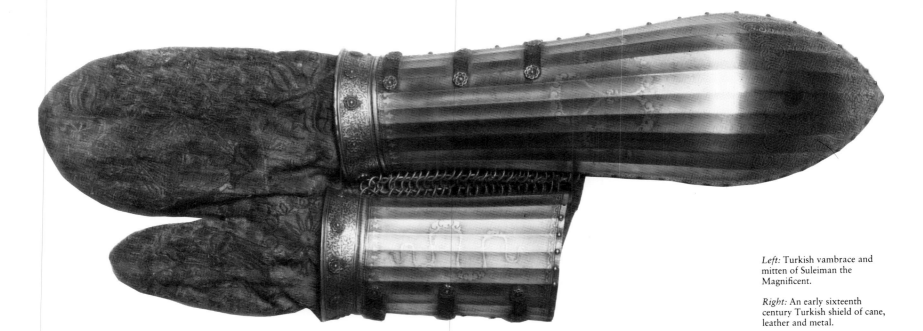

Left: Turkish vambrace and mitten of Suleiman the Magnificent.

Right: An early sixteenth century Turkish shield of cane, leather and metal.

not lived to see the day, the capture of Bursa may be counted as Osman's finest achievement.

His son Orkhan now showed that the Ottoman Turks, far from being a mere confederation of bandits, were a tenacious and enquiring race with one of the most amazing gifts for learning and developing ever known. In this the Ottomans far outstripped their predecessors, the Seljuks. After receiving the surrender of Bursa Orkhan took the title of Sultan and gave his

followers the title of *Ghazis* – warriors of the faith. He then addressed himself to the double task of administering his Christian and Moslem domains as a coherent whole, and converting his warrior bands into a trained army. The result was a practical compound of channeled banditry, military feudalism and regular maintenance. The wilder elements – light horse and foot – were irregular skirmishing forces who enlisted for loot. A new feudal class, the 'Tima-

riots,' held lands and supplied troops for military service. The 'Sipahis' were picked warriors, paid for each campaign. But the *corps d'élite* of the new Turkish army was the standing regiment known as the 'Janissaries' (from *Yenicheri*, 'new troops'). Youth of the sultan's Christian subjects, they were then strictly reared in the Moslem faith as warriors. Their main weapon was the composite bow, giving the Turkish army an unbeatable infantry fire power.

Left: An ornate damascened steel Mamluk shield of about 1500.

Right: A richly decorated battle-axe of traditional form once carried by a member of the bodyguard of the Sultan of Egypt and Syria (late fifteenth century).

With these troops Orkhan proceeded steadily with the clearance of the last Byzantine footholds in western Asia Minor. After beating the last effective Byzantine field army at Pelekanon in June 1329, Orkhan went on to take Nicaea in March 1331 and Nicomedia in 1337. The inevitable crossing of the straits took place in 1345, when the Emperor John Cantacuzene called in Turkish aid to assist his claim to the throne. This was in the middle of another futile civil war which profited nobody but the Turks to the east and the Serbs to the west, both Turks and Serbs being enlisted by the Byzantine antagonists. The Venetians, true to type, took advantage of the confusion by appropriating Smyrna in 1345. John Cantacuzene eventually became sole emperor in 1347, but not before the Serbs had taken the whole of Macedonia and rendered Cantacuzene almost totally dependent on Turkish aid.

A new era began in 1353 when Cantacuzene summoned the Turks to his aid against the rampaging Serbs of King Stephen Dushan. Orkhan duly defeated Dushan but, instead of recrossing the straits established his forces on European soil, taking and holding the Gallipoli peninsula. Dushan's death in the following year left the field clear for the Turks to overrun Thrace, and under the energetic leadership of Orkhan's successor Murad (c 1361-89) they became the leading power in the Balkans. In 1365 Murad took the Thracian capital of Adrianople.

The miserable story of Murad's Byzantine contemporaries shows the impressive resources still open to the imperial rulers of Constantinople and their lamentable failure to exploit those resources as Michael Palaeologus had done only a century before. In 1369 the Emperor John V, who had dethroned and supplanted John Cantacuzene in 1345, voyaged west to the

papal court at Avignon and agreed to another union of the Greek and Roman churches in return for substantial military aid against the Turks. Not only was this mission fruitless, but in

1376 John V was dethroned by his son Andronicus IV who *had* succeeded in enlisting Latin aid – a Genoese fleet to help him oust his father from power. Andronicus lasted for three years before

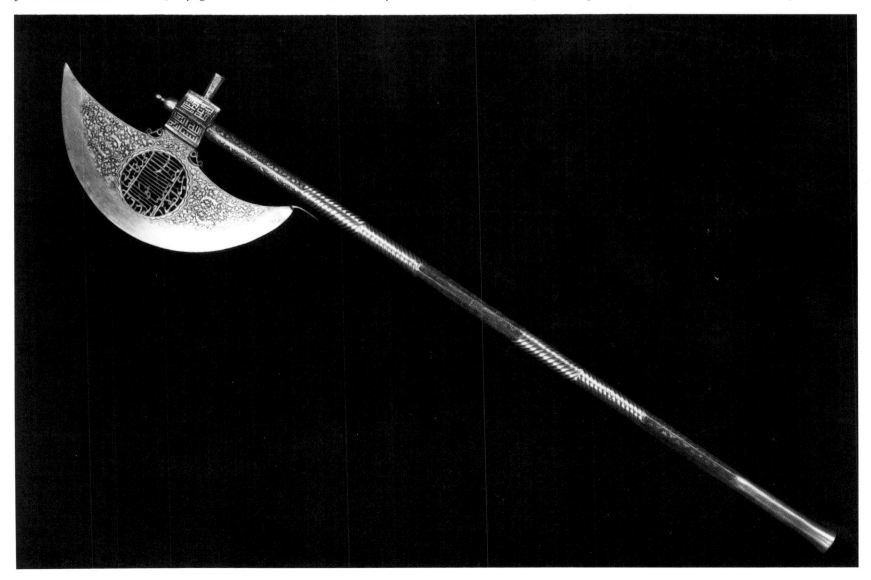

John, who had fled to Murad, recovered his throne with the help of the Turks. Meanwhile the Venetians, apprehensive as ever that their Genoese rivals would achieve a monopoly of interest in the Aegean, were once again on the look out for the next opportunity for gain. In 1386 they recaptured Corfu (which remained part of the Venetian Republic until its overthrow in 1797), and in 1388 purchased Argos and Nauplia as colonies. But in the following year Murad I accomplished the total isolation of Constantinople by shattering the confederated Serb armies in the Battle of Kossovo (15 June 1389), one of the most decisive events in later medieval history, which reduced the Balkans to Turkish rule for nearly 600 years. The fact that a Serb managed to assassinate Murad on the battlefield was small consolation for the completeness of the defeat.

Murad's successor, chosen sultan on the Kossovo battlefield, was Bayazid I (1389-1402). Bayazid's first problem was a civil war of his own, against the rebel emirates of Anatolia which he reduced (1390-2) with the Byzantine

Left: A late fourteenth century Italian sword captured by the Saracen Turks.

Far left: A typical armor of the Saracen Turks, the riveted mail hauberk reinforced with small metal plates.

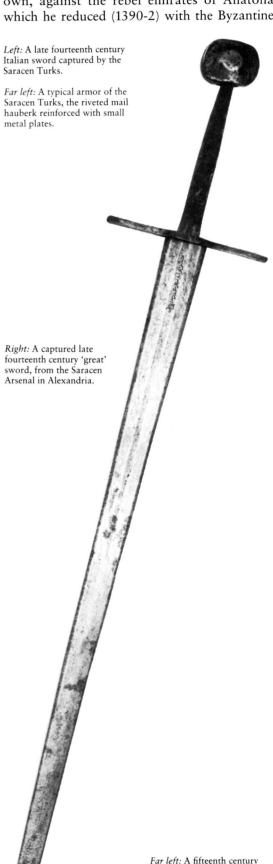

Right: A captured late fourteenth century 'great' sword, from the Saracen Arsenal in Alexandria.

Far left: A fifteenth century armored river boat furnished with cannon, for use against the Turks on the River Danube. The Saracen armies reached Vienna in the sixteenth century, but could advance no further into Central Europe.

Right: A typical Mameluk armor of mail and plate.

Emperor Manuel II following in the sultan's train as an Ottoman vassal. It goes without saying that Manuel failed to exploit the supreme opportunity presented by the spectacular career of Timur and the second Mongol conquest in eastern Anatolia. Bayazid, to his own undoing, was slow to realize the threat posed by Timur. Instead (1395) he made the first serious attempt to take Constantinople, imposing a blockade which dragged on for the next seven years. The siege prompted the last genuine Western crusade, led by King Sigismund of Hungary and launched down the Danube. The result was yet another demonstration of the obsolescence of European chivalry. The crusading host fell in with the Turkish army south of Nicopolis on 25 September 1396. The knights insisted on a frontal charge which was shattered by the archery of the Janissaries. Constantinople was eventually saved by Timur's destruction of the Turkish army and capture of Bayazid in the Battle of Angora (Ankara) on 28 July 1402. This, the last great Mongol victory in pitched battle, gives some answer to the speculation as to whether or not first-class foot archers were capable of beating the Mongol horsed archers.

Timur's death in 1402 saved the Ottoman Empire from almost certain destruction, but many years of civil war ensued before the next strong sultan emerged in the person of Murad II (1421-51). In the ensuing period the Venetians established the upper hand in the Aegean and fought their first sea battle with the Turks, destroying a Turkish fleet off Gallipoli (1416) – prelude to a century and a half of similar conflict at sea. The other notable event of these years was the transfer of the Turkish capital from Asia to Adrianople. But when Mohammed II became sultan in 1451 he was determined to reduce a long-standing anomaly: the continued existence of Constantinople as the capital of a vanished empire.

One of the greatest ironies in the long history of the Byzantine Empire was the excellence of the leadership it received under its last emperor, Constantine XI (1448-53). Left in the lurch by his Venetian and Genoese allies, Constantine closed the Golden Horn with an iron chain and inspired the citizenry to resist the most formidable assault the city had ever known. Though the massive walls were breached at last by the huge siege guns built for Mohammed by the Hungarian renegade Urban, the defenders valiantly sealed the breaches and fought on. The end came on 29 May when Mohammed, having dragged a flotilla of 70 small ships overland to the Golden Horn, launched an irresistible attack on the Germanos Gate. As the Turks flooded into the city Constantine was killed, his body only being identified by his boots of imperial purple. The imperial city, after being given up to loot for three days, later became the Turkish capital of Istanbul.

The inevitable fall of Constantinople

Even after the crippling territorial losses suffered between Manzikert and the Fourth Crusade, the Byzantine Empire's unique territorial advantages would have enabled it to survive – given a suitable adjustment of imperial strategy. But once the Ottoman Turks – thanks mainly to the very inadequacy of Byzantine strategy – had established themselves on either shore of the straits, the superior talents and energies of the Turks made the fall of Constantinople only a matter of time.

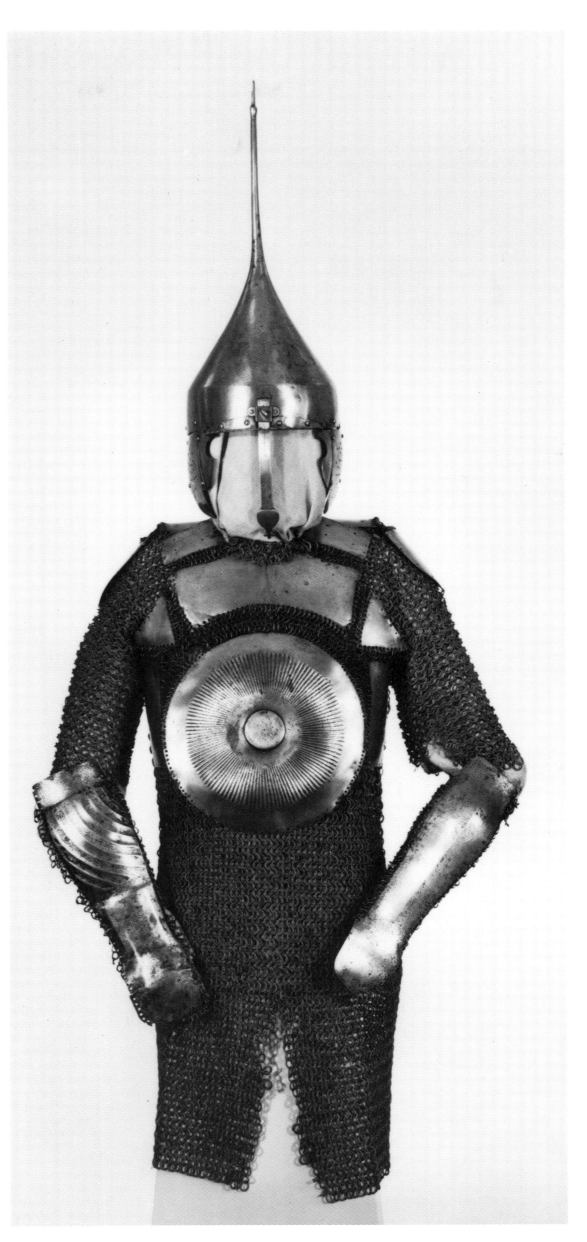

The Wars of the Renaissance

As observed in the Introduction, defining historical periods is an unavoidable but invidious method of looking at history, and the period known as 'the Renaissance,' generally accepted as the years of transition from the 'later Middle Ages' to the 'early modern period,' is no exception. Very loosely speaking, the Renaissance spanned the second half of the fifteenth century and the first half of the sixteenth. Its most praiseworthy memorials were the fruits of a glorious outburst of art and learning comparable with the glories of Greece in the fifth century BC – hence the notion of a 'rebirth' (*rinascita*) of the cultural achievements of the ancient world. Setting aside the fact that there had been such cultural 'rebirths' throughout the medieval period, in one respect at least this interpretation of the Renaissance has a depressing validity. Almost exactly like the golden age of Greece – Athens in the time of Pericles – the Renaissance was the backdrop to an unusually protracted and vicious series of wars.

Naval warfare in the Renaissance

As with all transitional processes, the Renaissance wars were a baffling mixture of the old and the new. They were prompted and motivated by medieval experience and the workings of medieval history; and they were fought with weaponry and tactics sometimes totally outdated, usually obsolescent, and often revolutionary.

The changes in naval warfare were a case in point. That ancient warship type, the oared galley, survived for centuries after the Renaissance because of its virtues. Nothing, before the advent of steam power, could beat the galley for speed and maneuverability in light winds and calm weather, when heavy sailing ships were virtually helpless. Now armed with forward-pointing guns, the galley could lie off the quarter of a becalmed sailing ship, and batter its victim with shot. But the galley still retained a reinforced underwater prow extension for the old-style ramming attack with which the Greeks had fought the Persians, the Romans had fought the Carthaginians, the Byzantines had fought the Arabs, and with which, throughout the late fifteenth and the sixteenth centuries, the Venetians and their allies continued to fight the Turks.

Yet the galley could never develop as the ideal warship. Only stoutly-built ships could operate safely in the high seas and treacherous tidal waters encountered outside the Straits of Gibraltar. The sail warship of the Middle Ages, supplanting the Viking longship design in the twelfth and thirteenth centuries, had gone into battle packed with troops. The objective was to close and board enemy ships under cover of crossbow fire and archery. But by the end of the fifteenth century naval powers were beginning to experiment with guns mounted in broadside, firing through ports cut in the ship's side. The ability thus granted for a warship to stand off and batter an opponent added a totally new dimension to naval warfare. Closing and boarding would remain the ultimate ideal of naval combat – but only after maximum destruction had been wrought by the broadside gun batteries, smashing at the enemy's upperworks and cutting down the 'garrison' of troops in the enemy ship.

From the moment that England's new King Henry VIII came to the throne in 1509 at the age of 18, crammed with a better education than any English heir-apparent before him, he took an immense interest in pushing forward these new ideas in warship design. One of Henry's revo-

Right: 'Noah's Ark' as an example of medieval shipbuilding, from the *Nuremberg Chronicle* (1493). Fifteenth century ships were ungainly and awkward to handle.

Below, far left: This woodcut (1496) shows the Turkish fleet attacking Rhodes in 1480; note the Mediterranean galleys and (top) a galleass.

Below left: The Turks, having landed on Rhodes, attack from land and sea.

Below: Over 100 years of ship design resulted in a more streamlined hull and a rigging plan that permitted both speed and increased maneuverability.

lutionary 'great ships,' the *Mary Rose*, was in 1982 raised from the bottom of the Solent where she sank in 1545. Enough is already known about *Mary Rose* to demonstrate that when first completed in the late summer of 1511 she represented a major leap forward in warship design. But *Mary Rose* did not rely on her formidable batteries of cast bronze and built-up guns. Her stores included 250 yew longbows, six gross of bowstrings, 300 sheaves of arrows, and 300 pikes and bills – exactly the same basic weaponry with which Edward III's fleet had fought at Sluys 200 years before.

Here, then, was a Renaissance prince – a dynamic young ruler hailed by his contemporaries as an ideal product of the new era – who was clearly imbued with the will to break free from the traditional waging of war. He could not be blamed for having to accept the limitations of contemporary weaponry which compelled a blend of the old and the new – from being forced, as it were, to keep one foot in the Middle Ages. But what of Henry's attitude to the strategy and tactics of land warfare? Nothing more hopelessly reactionary could be imagined. Henry had the option of choosing a new national strategy, most temptingly challenging the Spanish and Portuguese monopoly of the ocean routes to the Indies which had been opened up over the past 20 years. But instead of urging his country forward into new paths, Henry planned to drag her back into the past by re-opening the Anglo-French struggle and surpassing the achievements of Edward III and Henry V.

Left: The English and Spanish Fleets Engaged, a near contemporary English painting showing the defeat of the Spanish Armada in 1588.

Below: The excavation of the *Mary Rose* (which sank in action against the French in 1545) has revealed many hitherto unknown facts about sixteenth century warships. Beside cannon, their armament included longbows (as seen here).

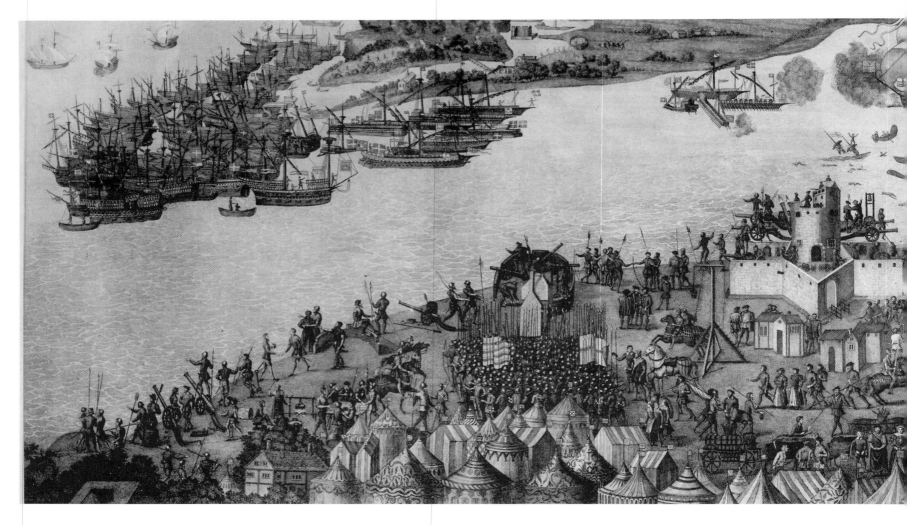

iron   wood

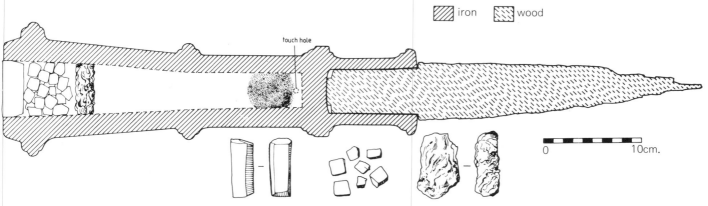

touch hole

tampion   sample of cast-iron shot   wad

0   10cm.

Above: The Cowdray Engraving of the Solent battle in 1545.

Left: Diagram showing horizontal cross-section through one of the *Mary Rose* guns, showing the tampion, shot, wad and powder. The broken hatching indicates wooden pieces; the continuous lines, iron.

Below left: A bronze sterncastle gun from the *Mary Rose* on a replica carriage.

Right: Some of the many Tudor arrows recovered from the *Mary Rose* wreck. They were stored in bundles of 24 and kept apart by leather spacers.

Far right: These carved wooden linstocks held a piece of smoldering slow-match to ignite and fire the cannon.

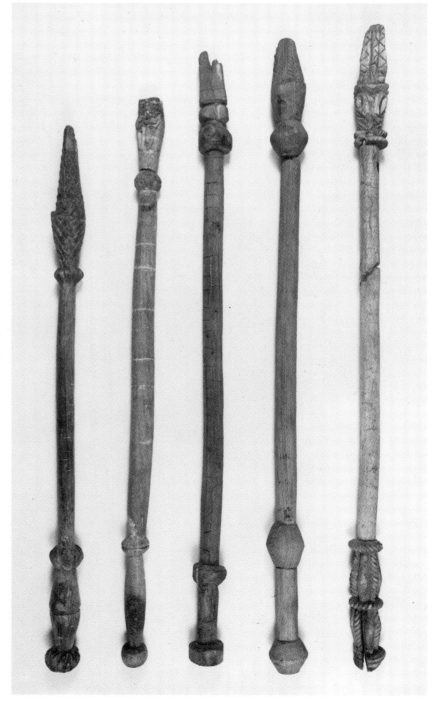

The Italian wars

The hopeless obsolescence of this policy lay in the hard fact that England and France were no longer the two most powerful monarchies of Western Europe. By the opening of the sixteenth century England had in fact become an onlooker in a contest between France, Spain, the Hapsburg emperors and the Papacy to settle which of the great powers was going to emerge as arbiter of Italy, that eternal battleground of the Middle Ages. Henry VIII's cynical but brilliantly successful father Henry VII (1485-1509) had set himself to profit by proxy from this international poker game, refusing to join the contestants round the table and take a hand himself. By reversing his father's policy, Henry VIII proved himself an adolescent in international power politics, in which the name of the game was the reliability of each power's allies and the professional viability of its mercenary troops.

The Italian wars had begun with a secret deal between Florence and Naples in 1492 to plunder Milan, upon which Ludovico Sforza of Milan had turned the clock back 700 years, repeated the strategy of Pope Stephen II when menaced by the Lombards, and called in the French. King Charles VIII of France invaded Italy, hammered Florence into submission and marched south to make good his claim to the Kingdom of Naples, entering Naples in February 1495. But this unexpected overturning of the Italian apple-cart prompted the formation of the 'Holy League' against France, comprising Milan, Venice, the Emperor Maximilian, Pope Alexander VI and the powerful King Ferdinand of Aragon, who only three years before had completed the reconquest of Moslem-held Andalusia and had at his disposal one of the most powerful armies in Europe. Ferdinand sent his general Gonzalvo de Cordoba with an expeditionary force which threw the French out of Naples, and four years of uneasy peace ensued.

The struggle was reopened in February 1499, this time at the instigation of Venice which

Left: The Emperor Maximilian I by Albrecht Dürer.

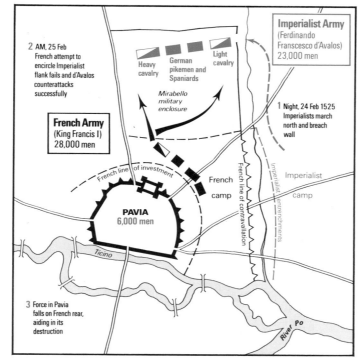

Below: The Hapsburg victory over France at Pavia.

Right: The Battle of Pavia (1525).

Below right: A medallion of 1495 depicting Gonzalvo de Cordoba.

Bottom right: The Emperor Maximilian on a medallion of 1509.

agreed to support Louis XII of France against Milan in return for the town of Cremona. A second French invasion in August 1499 chased Ludovico Sforza out of Milan, but in the following year Sforza returned with an army of the mercenary *landsknechte* raised in imitation of the Swiss mercenaries employed by the French. After initial successes Sforza was hopelessly let down by the instability of his surrogate army; he was captured and ended his days eight years later in a French prison. Sforza's defeat left the French as masters of the Lombardy basin.

Confronted with this *fait accompli*, France and Spain concluded the Treaty of Granada (11 November 1500) agreeing on joint military action to partition the Kingdom of Naples. In June-July 1501 Louis took Capua, the Spanish fleet took Naples but the victors almost immediately fell out over the division of the spoils. In the ensuing war a new factor was revealed: the excellence of the Spanish infantry which ended the myth of Swiss invincibility at Cerignola (28

April 1503) and the Garigliano (28 December 1503). The most notable factor was the Spanish use of that new powder firearm, the arquebus. The French surrender at Gaeta on 1 January 1504 completed the Spanish conquest of Naples but left the French still supreme in the north of Italy.

The war of the League of Cambrai (December 1508-June 1513) set new records in surprise changes of alliance and the betrayal of partners in crime. This time the initial intended victim was Venice, whose extensive mainland possessions the Emperor Maximilian hoped to acquire with the help of France, Spain and the Papacy under the redoubtable fighting Pope Julius II. After a French victory over the Venetians at Agnadello (14 May 1509) Verona, Padua and

Vicenza were duly handed over to Maximilian, while the papal forces seized the former Venetian holdings of Ravenna and Rimini. In the south the Spaniards added to the tally of plunder by taking Brindisi and Otranto; but in July 1509 the Venetians rallied. Brilliantly exploiting the inevitable distrust of German imperial ambitions south of the Alps, they not only recaptured and held Padua but in the following year also induced Pope Julius to desert the League and join them. Ferdinand of Spain meanwhile, more than content with his gains, became an instant neutral in the affair.

Henry VIII tries to conquer France

The war was transformed by the defeats of the papal forces which, so far from expelling the French from Italy, lost Bologna in May 1511. Desperate efforts by Pope Julius revived the Holy League, joined by Spain; and it was at this point that Henry VIII chose to plunge England into the struggle. His bid to open a 'second front' in northern France, hopefully in the style of Henry V, was endorsed by the Emperor Maximilian and the Spanish king.

That the English had become hopeless tyros in the art of international power politics was demonstrated by the events of 1512-13. Henry and Ferdinand agreed on a joint campaign against France, with the English shipping out an expeditionary force to reconquer Gascony while a Spanish army came north over the Pyrenees into Navarre. The result was humiliation for the English, whose wretchedly-equipped force

Left: Gonzalvo de Cordoba expelling the French from Spanish Naples.

under the Earl of Dorset broke up in sickness and mutiny, and re-embarked for home. Ferdinand, once he had made certain of Navarre, prepared for another spell of neutrality. But in the following year English prestige was restored in the north. For in the year 1513 Emperor Maximilian, deferring most satisfactorily to his young

English ally, agreed to serve under Henry, contributing *landsknechte* and artillery for an advance out of the Calais beachhead into northern France. On 16 August 1513 Henry and Maximilian were besieging the insignificant town of Thérouanne when a force of French knights, advancing to the relief of the town, indicated

The Ship HARRY GRACE a DIEU from an Original Drawing preserved in the PEPYSIAN Library in Magdalen College Cambridge.   N.º 991.

Vol. VI. Pl. XXII. p. 208.

Tunnage.....1000.

MEN
Soldiers...........349
Mariners........301 } 700
Gunners...........50

Basire Sc.

Left: The 1000-ton *Henri Grace à Dieu* (contemporary with the 700-ton *Mary Rose*) was built for Henry VIII.

Right: Part of a fresco by Holbein depicting Henry VII and his second son, Henry VIII. His elder son, Prince Arthur, died before he could become king.

181

that the chivalry of France was still capable of the inadequacies so fatefully displayed at Agincourt 100 years before. The French knights rode straight across the front of the allied host, being quite ignorant of the latter's true position – hardly the best way to set about raising a siege – and were driven off when the allied artillery opened fire on them. English knights sprang to the saddle and gave chase. The ensuing confused pursuit across the plain of Guingates, glamorized as the 'Battle of the Spurs' from the speed of the French retreat, gave Henry his first crumb of credit as the would-be hammer of the French. After Thérouanne surrendered a week later, Henry marched on to Tournai, where the garrison capitulated on 23 September after being pounded by artillery for eight days.

By far the biggest English success of the war, however, did not take place in France at all. It came about as the result of that legacy of the original Anglo-French struggle: the 'auld alliance' between Scotland and France. King James IV of Scotland crossed the border with the most powerful Scots army which had ever been seen in England, 20,000 men, backed with artillery. Two centuries after Bannockburn, the Scottish *schiltron* was given its last, disastrous encounter with the longbow at Flodden Field (9 September 1513). But although the Earl of Surrey's archers inflicted savage punishment on the Scottish right-flank divisions, the real victors at Flodden were the English infantry armed with bills and halberds who met the charge of the *schiltrons* head-on, and held it. The tactic of using these chopping weapons to lop off the long pikes of the *schiltrons* had never been learned in the medieval Scottish wars, however; it was a continental tactic, painfully developed during the Swiss pikemen's years of supremacy.

The most spectacular product of anti-phalanx tactics, prompted by hard experience with the Swiss pikemen, was developed by the German *landsknechte*: the huge double-edged sword. This seems to have been swung horizontally,

Above: The Embarkation of Henry VIII for Calais (1520). Note the coastal gun forts.

Left: A 'sword of war,' early sixteenth century.

Below: Henry VIII and Maximilian I meet at the Battle of the Spurs (1513).

Right: A Yeoman Gaoler in traditional Tudor dress at the Tower of London.

scythe-fashion, against the legs of the front-rank enemy pikemen as well as diagonally to cleave the hedge of pikes. The *landsknechte* who opted for this extremely high-risk form of combat, fighting at the 'sharp end' of armies confronted with pike phalanxes, earned double pay – hence the name also given to their monstrous swords, *doppelsöldner*.

The ever-changing pattern of coalitions and alliances in the Italian wars were a mercenary's paradise and in these years the *landsknechte's* flamboyance reached its peak. It was more obviously reflected in the outlandish technicolor costumes of vivid colors favored by the *landsknechte*: slashed and striped hose and doublets, outsize hats with outsize feathers, the choice of vertical stripes for one leg and horizontal stripes for the other and so forth. This gaudy display of military 'costume sense' was something quite new, and was not to be matched until the gorgeous uniforms of the Napoleonic era. In each case the motivation and underlying psychology was the same. It was a colorful boast that the wearer was a professional and proud of it, implying also that he was not worried about any enemy living long enough to spoil such a splendid turnout. As these troops were in no sense rich knights or great lords proudly arrayed in the colorful heraldry which their birth entitled them to display, it was obvious that a new age of warfare had arrived.

Colorful uniforms and the resultant *esprit de corps* also featured in the standing regiments raised in this period, of which the most well-known (to the tourists of the modern world) are surely those of the English 'Beefeaters' and Yeomen of the Guard. Their main anti-pike weapon was the chopping halberd.

When Pope Julius II died in 1513, his ten-year attempt to bring about the expulsion of the foreigners from Italy lay in ruins. Italy was still at the mercy of the Empire, Spain, France and the waning power of the Papacy. But the field was dramatically reduced in 1519, when the Hapsburg King Charles I of Spain became the Emperor Charles V. The resultant alignment of the military excellence of Spain with the mercenary hiring power of the Empire at the expense of France and the Papacy could not be long delayed. Pope Adrian VI's valiant attempt to postpone the evil hour by proposing a joint crusade against the Turks was ignored.

Above left: A *Schweizerkrieger* (Swiss mercenary) in *landsknecht* dress by Niklaus Manuel (1529).

Left: Two pike *schiltrons* clash in this German woodcut (*c*1520).

Right: A *landsknecht* 'puffed and slashed' armor (*c*1520).

Far right: A 'jack' of plates in the Tower of London; probably the commonest form of armor in the fifteenth and sixteenth centuries, but now the rarest survival.

Below: An English bill-head in the Tower of London.

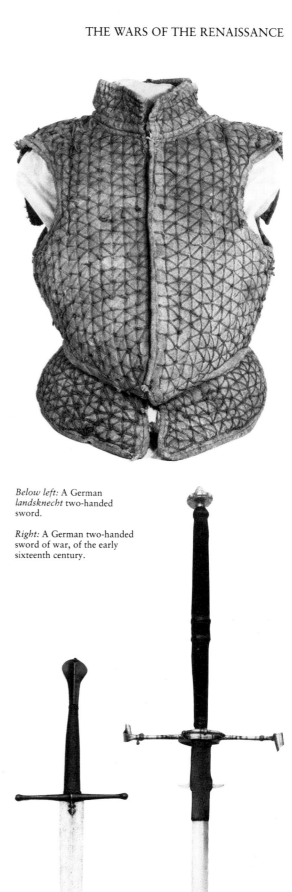

Below left: A German *landsknecht* two-handed sword.

Right: A German two-handed sword of war, of the early sixteenth century.

The upshot was the shattering of the French and client Swiss army in the Battle of Pavia – 24 February 1525 – in which the French knights and Swiss pikemen were torn apart by the fire power of the Spanish arquebusiers. Pavia has justly been called the first battle of the modern era, fought as it was with weaponry which would hardly have been credible even 25 years before. Its eventual sequel, the notorious sack of Rome for the benefit of the imperial mercenaries (6 May 1527) was itself only the prelude to 50 years of conflict between Hapsburg and Valois – conflict in which the superiority of the new warfare was confirmed and extended.

Hand firearms and artillery – a new era begins

Superficially the Italian wars of the Renaissance were little different to a typically medieval occurrence – a disunited country serving as the area for the resolution of conflict between the dominant military powers. The real difference lay not in strategy but in weaponry and tactics, for the wars led in the 1520s to the first successful challenge of shock infantry – the pike phalanx – by professional missile infantry armed with hand firearms as well as artillery. It was the latter combination which confirmed that a new era in warfare had begun.

The New Warfare

In a sense it is easier to list those elements of medieval warfare which survived, rather than those which vanished for ever as the sixteenth century wore on.

The *eques, clibanarius, ritter, chevalier, knight* – the armored lancer certainly survived the Middle Ages, though his metamorphosis from a lofty gentleman into a mere heavy cavalry trooper of humble birth would take a century or more. The armored lancer had ridden triumphantly out of the collapsing Roman Empire and right through the Middle Ages as the irreplaceable unit of shock cavalry – the 'charging Frank who could smash a hole through the walls of Babylon.' With the combined weights of rider and horse concentrated into the point of his couched lance, nothing could replace the lancer until the development of the armored fighting vehicle.

Even the most plebeian heavy cavalryman of later centuries would inevitably cut a bigger dash than his comrade in the despised infantry. But it would be the cavalry officer who retained most of the age of chivalry, so misplaced as this had been on the battlefield. On the eve of World War I a cavalry officer would be heard to say – when asked the purpose of cavalry in the modern world – that cavalry existed 'to give tone to what would otherwise be a vulgar brawl.' Not one of the armored aristocrats who had ridden to destruction at Crécy or Agincourt could have put it better himself.

Another survivor was the shock infantry, the pikemen. Massed in square with leveled pikes, these troops would continue to repulse cavalry and bowl over less substantial enemies for another century or more. Then the seventeenth century adoption of the ring bayonet, enabling a musket to double as a short pike, would cause the role of the pikemen to merge with that of the musketeer, the missile infantryman, whose clumsy firearm had nevertheless already ensured the demise of the crossbow and longbow.

That latecomer of the fourteenth and fifteenth centuries, the gunner with his massive artillery pieces on their awkward mountings, was destined to go from strength to strength, as the art of casting and boring true gun barrels continued to advance. But there would be a price to pay in that the original, instinctive experiments with detachable firing-chambers and the advantages of breechloading would soon give place to muzzle-loading designs, in order to ensure a gastight chamber for the exploding charge. The breechloading cannon would not reappear until the nineteenth century.

Since the end of the fourteenth century powder artillery had made towering castle walls a ludicrous anachronism as well as a progressively easy target – but the development of artillery would certainly not mean the obsolescence of fixed defenses carefully sited to dominate the surrounding terrain. Fortifications would become more squat, presenting less of a vertical target; their surroundings would be geometrically scarped to make it as hard as possible for siege guns to pound them at ideal range; but the basic role of the castle would not change.

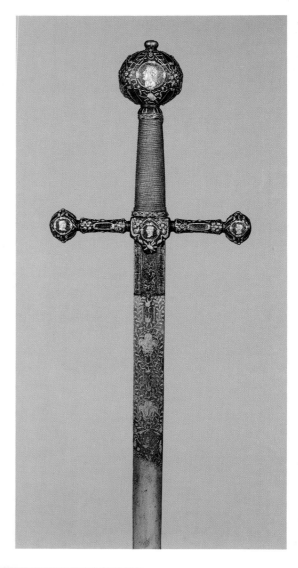

Above: A ceremonial dress sword (*c*1610) of Charles I's brother Henry; like modern swords of ceremony, its form is the medieval 'cross hilt.'

Left: This 40-ton bombard was cast in Russia in 1586; over 17-feet long, it is the largest of its type in the world.

Right: Traditional vertical castle architecture such as this (the Norman keep at Dover castle) was finally made redundant by the devastating power of artillery.

Many courtesies of medieval warfare that seem ludicrously out of place amid the horrors of war would also endure for centuries – the formal summons to surrender which, if responded to in good time, would allow the yielding garrison the courtesy of marching out with weapons in hand before the ignominy of surrender became real. And above all the symbolism of the sword, emblem of medieval knightly honor – the sword that would be proffered as a token of surrender even by the representative of a nation pulverized by the first atomic bombs.

Far left: A triple-barreled breach-loading cannon made for Henry VIII in about 1533. Henry had a 'modern' monarch's fascination for the power and innovative possibilities of artillery.

Left: This Flemish cast bronze cannon dated 1535 shows how deadly weapons of war could also be works of art.

Right: An Ottoman Turkish multi-barreled bronze cannon cast in about 1715; the basic principles and form of siege artillery had not materially changed during the past 2000 years, and would not change again for another 150.

Below: Henry VIII's low profile fortifications at Deal castle in Kent would not have looked out of place on a World War I battlefield; this was the castle-builder's inevitable response to the power of artillery.

189

Index

Acknowledgments

The author and publishers would like to thank Martin Bristow for designing the book, David Edge for providing the captions, Sam Elder for proof-reading and Ron Watson for compiling the index. The following agencies provided photographic material:

Ann Munchow/Weidenfeld Library: page 49.
Archbishop of Canterbury and the Trustees of Lambeth Palace Library: page 142(below).
Archiv Gerstenberg: pages 54(below), 55(both), 146(top), 152(top).
Ashmolean Museum, Oxford: pages 64(center), 67(left).
Bibliothèque Boulogne-sur-Mer/Weidenfeld Library: page 94(below).
Bibliothèque Nationale, Paris: pages 37(below), 89(top), 92(below), 93, 136,/E.T. Archive:143,/Weidenfeld Library: 43, 52, 82(top), 87(top), 90(top left), 98(below), 99(below), 101, 102(top).
Bodleian Library, Oxford: pages 42(below) [Ms.Ouseley Add.176.fol.63v], 87(below) [Ms.Bodley 264.fol.51v], 103(top) [Ms.Ouseley 381.fol.61r],/Weidenfeld Library: 62(below) [Ms.Bodley 614.fol.32].
British Library: pages 41, 56(top), 83(top), 84(below), 86,/Bridgeman Art Library: 158.
Burgerbibliothek, Bern/E.T.Archive: page 155,/Weidenfeld Library: 80(top).
C.M. Dixon: pages 6(below), 7, 9, 10(below), 11, 14, 15(both), 18(both), 34, 35, 42(top), 59(below), 66(below), 69(below), 71(all 3), 78(top), 79(top), 90(top right and both below), 115, 142(top right), 186(below), 187.
Cathedral Treasury, Monza/Hirmer Photo Archiv: page 26,/Weidenfeld Library: page 53(top).
Central Library of Ghent/Weidenfeld Library: page 159.
Cleveland Museum of Art/Weidenfeld Library (Dudley P. Allen Fund): page 149.
Courtesy of the Trustees of the British Museum: pages 1, 19(below), 58, 74-75(center), 138(below left),/E.T.Archive: 161,/Weidenfeld Library: 46, 68(top left), 94, 103(below), 105, 107(below), 114, 146(below).
Crown Copyright Reserved/Department of the Environment: page 64(below),/Weidenfeld Library: 183.
Detroit Institute of Arts, Founders Society Purchase (Edsel B. Ford Fund): page 107(top).
Edinburgh University Library: pages 47[Or.Ms.161,Al-Biruni's *Chronicle of Ancient Nations* (AD 1307-8) detail from folio 93V], 106[Or.Ms.20,Rashid al-Din's *Jami al-Tawaikh* (Tabriz c AD 1314) fol.125V].
E.T. Archive/Private Collections: pages 51, 143.
Germanisches National Museum, Nuremberg: page 184(below).
The Governing Body of Christ Church College, Oxford: page 147(below).
Graphisches Sammlung Albertina: page 134(top).
Harvard University Art Museums: Arthur M. Sackler Bequest-Estate of Abby Aldrich Rockefeller: 109, The Arnold H. Knapp Bequest Fund by Exchange: 179(top).
Hulton Deutsch Collection: pages 77(both), 97(below), 112(below), 113(both), 116, 189(below).
Istanbul Arkeoloji Muzelerini: page 22.
Jean Williamson: page 30(top).
John Eagle: pages 27, 28(both), 29, 129(below).
Mansell Collection: pages 30(below), 45, 48, 54(top), 80(below), 92(top), 96(all 3), 100, 140, 144, 147(top), 151(below), 167, 172(both), 180(below),/Alinari: 12(top), 25, 31,/Anderson: 12(below), 16 (below), 38, 157.

Mary Rose **Trust:** pages 175, 176(all 3), 177(both).
MAS, Barcelona: page 84(top),/Weidenfeld Library: 2, 97(top).
Metropolitan Museum of Art, New York, Harris Brisbane Dick Fund: page 44,/The Cloisters Collection: 78(below).
Mick Sharp: pages 23, 110(both), 111(both), 112(top), 118(both), 119, 120, 121(both), 122(both), 123, 124, 125.
Musée du Louvre/Photo: Service Photographique de la Réunion des Musées Nationaux: page 20(below).
National Gallery, London: page 166.
National Maritime Museum, London: page 174-175.
National Museum, Denmark: pages 66(top), 68(below).
National Portrait Gallery, London/Weidenfeld Library: page 181.
Offentlichen Kunstsammlung, Kupperstichkabinett, Basle: pages 153(below), 184(top).
Peter Clayton: page 20(above).
Peter Newark's Historical Pictures: pages 19(top), 24(below), 33(top), 74-75(top and below), 83(below), 85(both), 88(top and below left), 98(top), 102(below), 104, 117, 126, 132(top), 137, 148(below), 150, 151(top), 163, 170(below left), 182(center), 188(top).
Pierpoint Morgan Library, New York: page 67(right), 70(both),/Weidenfeld Library: 95.
Riksantikvarieambetet, State Historical Museum, Stockholm: pages 8(top), 59(top), 61(both), 63(both), 64(top left and right), 65.
Royal Collection, Reproduced by Gracious Permission of Her Majesty the Queen/Weidenfeld Library: page 182(top and below).
Courtesy of the Board of Trustees of the Royal Armories, HM Tower of London: pages 17(top 2), 130(both), 131(below), 138(top and below right), 139(below), 142(top right), 145(both), 152(below left and right), 154(below left and right), 156(top), 164, 165(below), 170(top left, top right and right), 171, 178-79, 185(top right), 187(both).
Royal Commission on the Ancient Monuments, Scotland: page 148(top).
Courtesy of the Trustees of the Science Museum, London/Weidenfeld Library: page 173(below).
Simon Archery Foundation, Manchester Museum: pages 17(bottom 4),141(below).
Simon Fenelon: page 127(both).
Stadtbibliothek, Nuremberg: page 129(below).
Stiftbibliothek, St.Gallen, Switzerland: page 50.
Swiss National Museum, Zurich: page 91.
Tunisian National Tourist Office: page 32.
University of Gottingen/E.T.Archive: page 131(top).
University Museum of National Antiquities, Oslo, Norway: pages 6(top), 8(below), 53(below), 56(both), 57(both), 60, 62(top), 69(top).
Courtesy of the Trustees of the Victoria and Albert Museum: pages 108,/Weidenfeld Library: 99(top), 173(top).
Vienna, Kunsthistorische Museum: pages 33(below), 37(top), 82(below), 165(top), 168(both), 169(both),/Weidenfeld Library: 51(below).
Permission of the Trustees of the Wallace Collection, London: pages 130(top left and right), 135, 139(top), 141(top), 153(top left and right), 156(both left), 160(both), 179(both), 180(top), 185(top left, below left and right),186(top).
Weidenfeld Library: pages 67(below), 72, 73(both), 76(both), 81, 88(below right), 89(below), 117.